Functional Materials
A Chemist's Perspective

Functional Materials
A Chemist's Perspective

K Vijayamohanan Pillai
Scientist, Physical & Materials Chemistry Division,
National Chemical Laboratory, Pune,
Acting Director, Central Electrochemical Research Institute,
Karaikudi, Tamil Nadu

Meera Parthasarathy
Assistant Professor, School of Chemical & Biotechnology,
SASTRA University, Thanjavur, Tamil Nadu

Editor-in-Chief: Baldev Raj

IIM Metallurgy Materials Engineering

Series in Metallurgy and Materials Science

Universities Press

UNIVERSITIES PRESS (INDIA) PRIVATE LIMITED

Registered Office
3-6-747/1/A & 3-6-754/1, Himayatnagar, Hyderabad 500 029 (A.P.), India
info@universitiespress.com; www.universitiespress.com

Distributed by
Orient Blackswan Private Limited

Registered Office
3-6-752 Himayatnagar, Hyderabad 500 029 (A.P.), India

Other Offices
Bangalore / Bhopal / Bhubaneshwar / Chennai
Ernakulam / Guwahati / Hyderabad / Jaipur / Kolkata
Lucknow / Mumbai / New Delhi / Noida / Patna

First published in India by
Universities Press (India) Private Limited 2012

ISBN 978 81 7371 768 0

Typeset in MinionPro 11/14.2 *by*
OSDATA, Hyderabad 500 029

Printed in India by
Indcom Press
Chennai

Published by
Universities Press (India) Private Limited
3-6-747/1/A & 3-6-754/1, Himayatnagar, Hyderabad 500 029 (A.P.) India

Foreword

Functional materials are important because of their exciting potential applications. Many of these materials form part of indispensable devices, which could be as diverse as cell phones, laptops and retinal and cochlear implants. Their essential functions arise from the astounding combination of intelligence, flexibility, stimuli-sensitive response, sensitivity, selectivity, etc. An understanding of the structure–function relationship in biological systems helps us design better functional materials.

This book lucidly explains various aspects of functional materials, beginning from fundamental definitions to specific applications and methods of introducing functions, emerging synthetic tools and many attendant challenges. The authors admirably unravel the subject's multi-disciplinary breadth and convey their smart understanding of the new innovative trends in the design, synthesis and manufacture of new materials. They elegantly combine various aspects of molecular design, material preparation, organization, characterization and applications with many fascinating, real-life examples.

I have admired many of these outstanding advances in functional materials and also thought carefully about 'built-in obsolescence' in the area of advanced materials. The work of my own research group on intelligent gels and soft matter at National Chemical Laboratory has given me a rare opportunity to experience the exquisite beauty and challenge of designing functional materials. I can see the same pattern unfold here in all the chapters dealing with wonderful forms of soft, ultra-hard and hybrid forms of materials.

At first sight, this book appears to be a collective elaboration of different types of functional materials such as intelligent materials, bio-inspired materials, nanocomposites, etc. However, one cannot miss the obvious connection—something very special that only chemists and chemical engineers can sense—of an invisible fabric of functional materials seamlessly linked by a story or an anecdote.

Functional materials are not merely a collection of atoms and molecules, as the word functional represents; the meaning of the adjective goes deep into utility, in terms of amazing applications—much beyond semantics.

The elementary aspects of materials are described in this book in a student-friendly manner to elicit the curiosity of the young mind. I have great pleasure in recommending this book to students and teachers of materials science and engineering.

R A Mashelkar
National Research Professor,
CSIR Bhatnagar Fellow &
President, Global Research Alliance
National Chemical Laboratory,
Pune, India

Preface

The idea of writing a book of this kind occurred in one of our classes at IISER, Pune. What began as a course outline in response to some naïve questions from undergraduate students soon developed into an idea for a book for a course offered to PhD students at NCL, Pune. Thus, the credit for the initiative must go to the students and to their probing and, often, innocuously simple questions. We have enjoyed teaching and writing most of the chapters of this book, and hope to pass on the pleasure to other teachers and students.

The book opens with a virtual tour of the basic themes of functional materials, explicitly mirroring our philosophy, which sets it apart from similar titles in Materials Science and Engineering. **Chapter 2** presents possible schemes of classification based on chemical identity, function and applications, while **Chapter 3** provides valuable insights on the basic thermodynamic framework of molecular self-assembly, along with experimental techniques and related synthetic strategies for relevant applications. In **Chapter 4**, the importance of bio-inspired materials is explained with interesting examples. **Chapters 5, 6 and 7** discuss the different classes of functional materials that are tailor-made for application in electronic devices and energy generation, while **Chapter 8** unravels the fascinating structural aspects of designing nanocomposites, using carbon nanotubes and polymers as examples. **Chapter 9**, the last chapter, highlights the technological relevance of developing functional materials, and provides a glimpse of the existing material challenges, along with interesting predictions related to the next generation of functional materials.

The chapters on *Functional Materials for Sustainable Energy* and *Materials for Polymer Electronics* are not exhaustive; the primary objective of these chapters is to showcase some of the astounding technological advances in these rapidly expanding themes. The selection of topics is based on current interests. We have tried to simplify (sometimes even to exaggerate) several concepts so that students get a feel for the excitement of designing functional materials, where chemistry plays a key role. In that vein, the chapters are sequenced to provide a holistic view of recent advances as well as limitations, keeping future developments in mind.

We have been encouraged by the support and inspiration of men of eminence such as Prof. C N R Rao, Dr R A Mashelkar and Prof. Sameer Brahmachari. The discussions with Dr Swaminathan Sivaram (CSIR-NCL) and Prof. A K Shukla (IISc, Bangalore) relating to functional materials, particularly about polymer and energy-related applications, contributed much to the quality of this book. Special thanks are due to PhD students Beena, Dhanraj Shinde, Joyashish Debgupta and R Kannan, who fine-tuned the presentation.

Vijayamohanan K Pillai
Meera Parthasarathy

Dedicated to the fond memory of

Mrs A Vijayalekshmi Amma (Vijayamohanan's mother)

and

Mr R Parthasarathy (Meera's father)

Acknowledgements

We thank Harikrishnan (Vijayamohanan's elder son), who breathed a whiff of fresh air into the project by clearing ambiguities that had crept into the manuscript. It is also a pleasure to acknowledge the encouragement received from Dr Sourav Pal (Director, CSIR-NCL), Dr Anilkumar, Dr P A Joy, Dr Sreekumar, Dr Asish Lele, Dr Ullhas Kharul, Dr V Yegnaraman (former Director, CSIR-CECRI) and Dr T Prem Kumar. We also thank Javanthi Singaram and her team, especially Madhavi Sethupathi, for the unstinted help received during various stages of manuscript preparation. The many helpful suggestions of Dr Baldev Raj, Dr U Kamatchi Mudali and Prof. G Amarendra are gratefully acknowledged.

We would like to thank the Vice-Chancellor, SASTRA University, for academic support, and the CeNTAB team of SASTRA University for their enormous encouragement and inspiration. We are indebted to Prof. Goverdhan Mehta, who has always been a fountain of help and advice.

We thank Manju (Vijayamohanan's wife) and Jayakrishnan (Vijayamohanan's younger son), who were robbed of months of family time that rightfully belonged to them during the preparation of this book. We are indebted to them for their patience and understanding. We also thank Mr Kumaran and Mr Sivaraman from the CSIR-CECRI office for their generous help.

We would like to thank Ambujam (Meera's mother) and Sriram (Meera's brother), for their incomparable love, patience and support. We finally thank all our common friends at NCL, CECRI and SASTRA for their help and suggestions.

Vijayamohanan K Pillai
Meera Parthasarathy

About the Series

The study of metallurgy and materials science is vital for developing advanced materials for diverse applications. In the last decade, the progress in this field has been rapid and extensive, giving us a new array of materials, with a wide range of applications, and a variety of possibilities for processing and characterizing the materials. In order to make this growing volume of knowledge available, an initiative to publish a series of books in Metallurgy and Materials Science was taken during the Diamond Jubilee year of the Indian Institute of Metals (IIM) in the year 2006. As part of the series we have already brought out seven books, and five of them have been copublished by CRC Press, USA, for distribution overseas. This is the eighth book in the series.

The IIM is a premier professional body representing an eminent and dynamic group of metallurgists and materials scientists from R&D institutions, academia and industry in India. It is a registered professional institute with the primary objective of promoting and advancing the study and practice of the science and technology of metals, alloys and novel materials.The institute is actively engaged in promoting academia–research and institute–industry interactions.

Universities Press, an associate of Orient Blackswan, with its long tradition of publication of quality books in engineering and sciences, has come forward to undertake the publication of this series, thus synergising the professional expertise of IIM with the publishing experience of Universities Press towards effective knowledge dissemination. This book series shall include different categories of publications: textbooks to satisfy the requirements of undergraduates and beginners in the field, monographs on select topics by experts in the field, and proceedings of select international conferences organized by IIM after mandatory peer review. To increase the readership and to ensure wide dissemination, some of the books in the series will be copublished with international publishers.

The international character of the authors and editors has helped the books command a global readership. An eminent panel of international and national experts acts as the advisory body in overseeing the selection of topics, important areas to be covered, and the selection of contributing authors. These publications are expected to serve as a source of knowledge to a wide spectrum of students, engineers, researchers and industrialists in the field of metallurgy and materials science. I look forward to receiving your valuable response to the present book as well as the other books in the series.

Baldev Raj
Editor-in-Chief

SERIES IN METALLURGY AND MATERIALS SCIENCE

Contents

List of Colour Plates

Fig. 1.1 (*Chap. 1, p.* 4) The Lycurgus Cup is made of ruby glass containing gold and silver nanoparticles. It appears green in reflected light and red when light is shone into the cup and transmitted through the glass. It was designed in Rome in the 4th century AD—truly classical evidence for the existence of functional materials in the pre-historic ages. Recent chemical analysis showed that the glass contains 80 ppm of Au nanoparticles and 300 ppm of Ag nanoparticles of 70 nm each, which is extensively used by proponents of nanotechnology to illustrate the size dependent optical properties of nanoparticles. The scene on the cup depicts the attack of Lycurgus, a violent king of the Thracians (800 BC), by the Greek God Dionysos and his maenad Ambrosia, who transformed herself into a vine, punishing him for his evil behaviour. [Reproduced from http://commons.wikimedia.org/wiki/File:Lycurgus_cup_british_museum.JPG and http://commons.wikimedia.org/wiki/File:Brit_Mus_13sept10_brooches_etc_046.jpg under the terms of the GNU Free Documentation License]

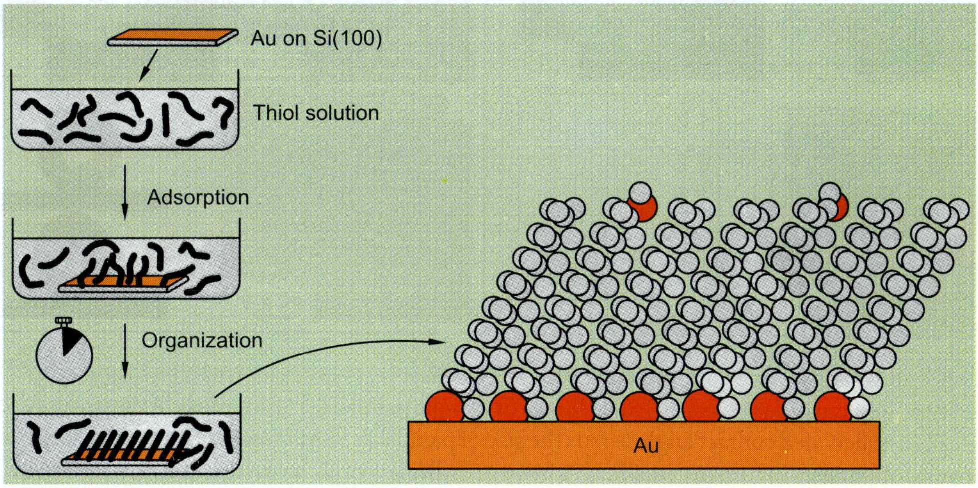

Fig. 3.5 *(Chapter 3, pg. 36)* Solution-route synthesis of alkanethiol self-assembled monolayers on a smooth gold surface [Courtesy: Prof. Bo Liedberg, Linkoping University, Sweden]

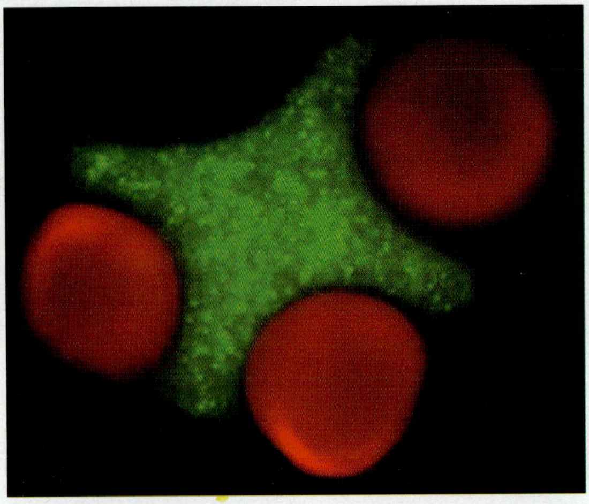

Fig. 3.13 *(Chap. 3, p. 44)* Living Legos: Polymer building blocks studded with cells, self-assembled into structures whose complexity mimics that of human tissues. The cross-shaped gel contains cells stained green; rod-shaped gels which are about 200 microns across contain cells stained red [Reproduced with permission from the National Academy of Sciences, USA: Du Y, Lo E, Ali S and Khademhosseini A, Directed assembly of cell-laden microgels for fabrication of 3D tissue constructs, *Proc. Natl. Acad. Sci.*, 105(28): 9522, 2008]

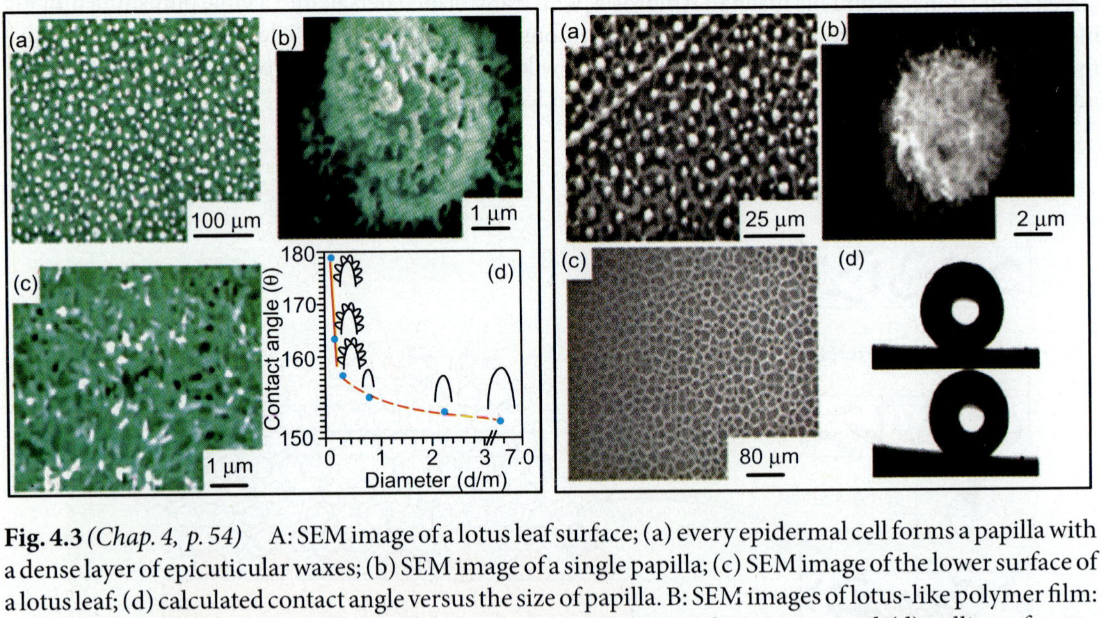

Fig. 4.3 *(Chap. 4, p. 54)* A: SEM image of a lotus leaf surface; (a) every epidermal cell forms a papilla with a dense layer of epicuticular waxes; (b) SEM image of a single papilla; (c) SEM image of the lower surface of a lotus leaf; (d) calculated contact angle versus the size of papilla. B: SEM images of lotus-like polymer film: (a) network of papilla; (b) single papilla; (c) large area honeycomb structure and (d) rolling of water droplet on the surface of the lotus leaf–inspired polymer film [Reprinted with permission from John Wiley & Sons: Feng L. Li S, Li H, Zhang L, Zhai J, Song Y, Liu B, Jiang L and Zhu D, Super-hydrophobic surfaces: From natural to artificial, *Adv. Mater.*, 14(24): 1857, 2002]

Fig. 4.4 *(Chap. 4, p. 55)* A water strider walking on water [Reproduced from http://en.wikipedia.org/wiki/File:Water_strider_-_strider_surface_tension.jpg under the terms of the GNU Free Documentation Licence]

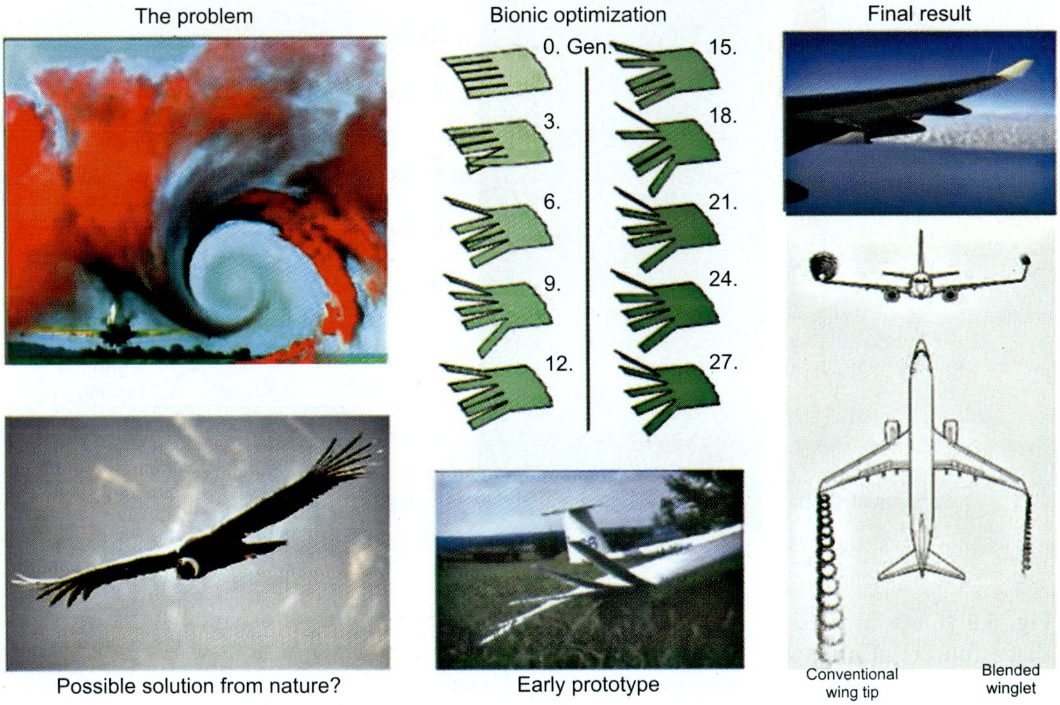

Fig. 4.9 *(Chap. 4, p. 63)* Bionic approach to minimize energy loss due to vortex generation at the wing tips of airplanes [[Reprinted with permission from Neurohr R and Dracomirescu C, Bionics in Engineering—Defining new Goals in Engineering Education at "Politehnica". International Conference on Engineering Education (ICEE-2007), September 3–7, 2007, Coimbra, Portugal.]

Plate 4

Fig. 5.3 *(Chap. 5, p. 75)* A water drop resting on lotus surface, its cross-sectional images by AFM and TEM (top) and demonstration/application of superhydrophobic surfaces

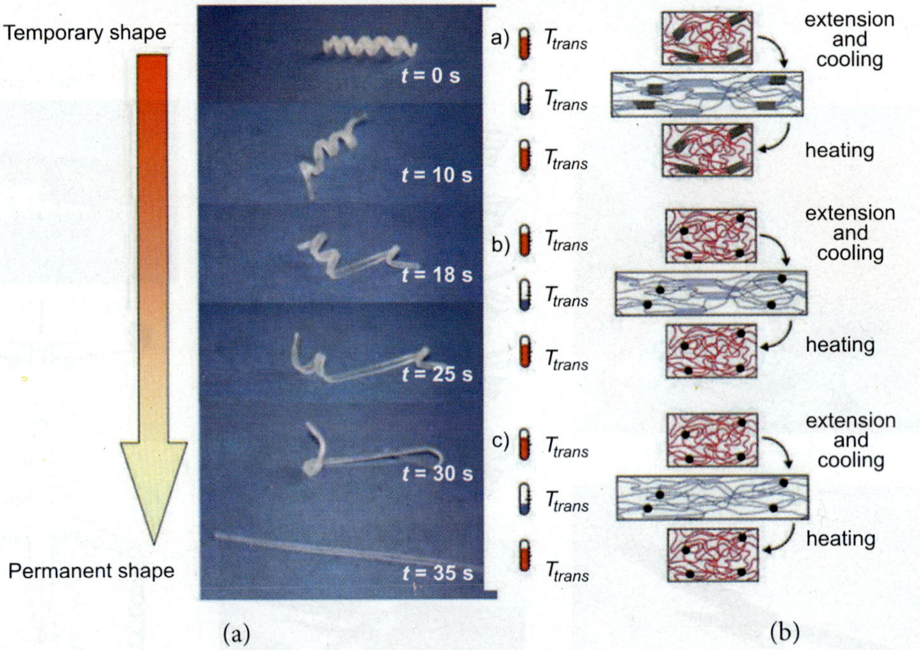

Fig. 5.5 *(Chap. 5, p. 83)* (a) Transition from the temporary shape to (spiral) to the permanent shape (linear) of a network polymer synthesized from a poly (ε-caprolactone) dimethacrylate and butylacrylate. The switching temperature of the polymer is 45°C. (b) Schematic representation of the molecular mechanism of thermally induced shape memory effect in a) Block copolymer with $T_{trans} = T_m$; b) covalently cross linked polymer with $T_{trans} = T_m$; c) a polymer network with $T_{trans} = T_g$. T_{trans} is the temperature above which the chains are flexible, Tm is the melting point of the polymerand T_g is the glass transition temperature at which the polymer transforms to a rubbery/viscous state. *[Reprinted withpermission from John Wiley & Sons]*

Fig. 6.1 *(Chap. 6, p. 94)* Photograph of a swarm of fireflies [Source: http://en.wikipedia.org/wiki/File:Leuchtk %C3%A4ref_-_Firefly.jpg; reproduced under the terms of the GNU free documentation licence]

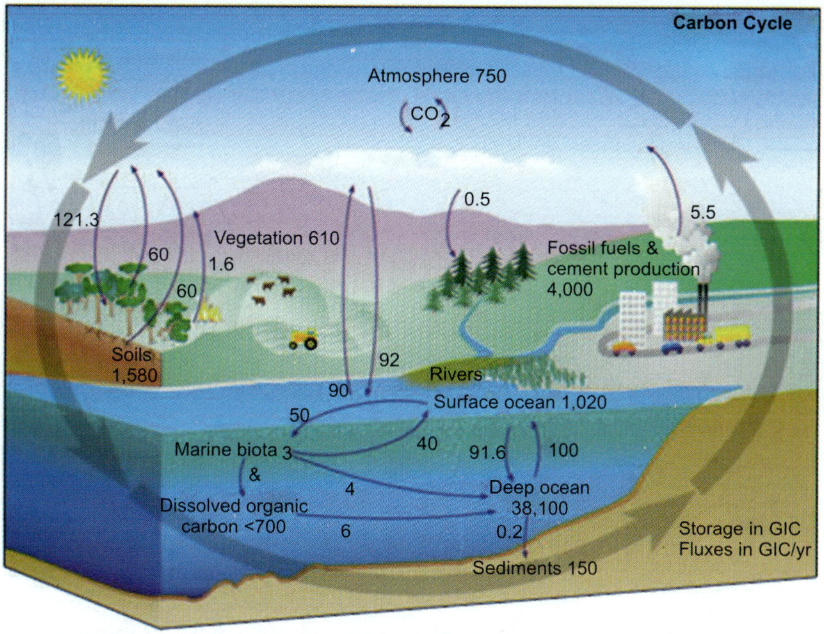

Fig. 6.3 *(Chap. 6, p. 98)* Storage and yearly changes of carbon content (expressed in gigatons of carbon) in the atmosphere, hydrosphere and geosphere [Adapted from http://en.wikipedia.org/wiki/File:Carbon_cycle-cute_diagram.svg under the terms of the GNU Free Documentation Licence]

Plate 6

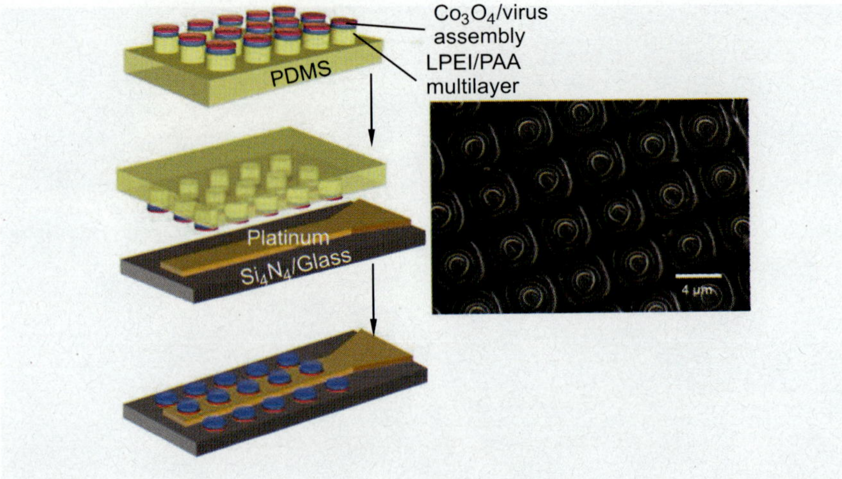

Fig. 6.10 *(Chap. 6, p. 110)* Cobalt oxide (CO_3O_4) nanowires assembled on a polyelectrolyte film using spiral M13 viruses are stamped on platinum microband electrodes to form a virus battery [Reproduced with permission from National Academy of Sciences, USA: Nama K T, Wartenaa R, Yoob P J, Liaua FW, Leea Y J, Chianga Y-M, Hammond P T and Belcher A M, Stamped microbattery electrodes based on self-assembled M13 viruses, *PNAS*, 105(45): 17227, 2008]

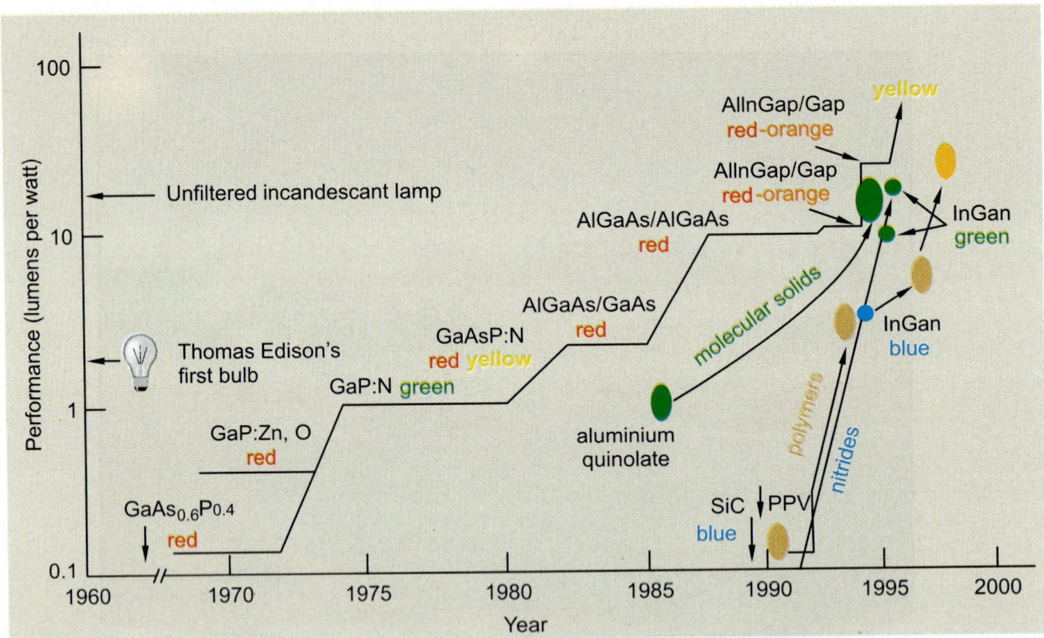

Fig. 7.8 *(Chap. 7, p. 135)* A comparison of the 'luminous efficiency' of inorganic and organic light emitting diodes. The semiconducting material in organic LEDs can either be a polymer or a sublimed film of small molecules [Adapted with permission from Institute Physics Publishing: Friend R, Burroughes J and Shimoda T, Polymer diodes, *Physics World*, June 1999]

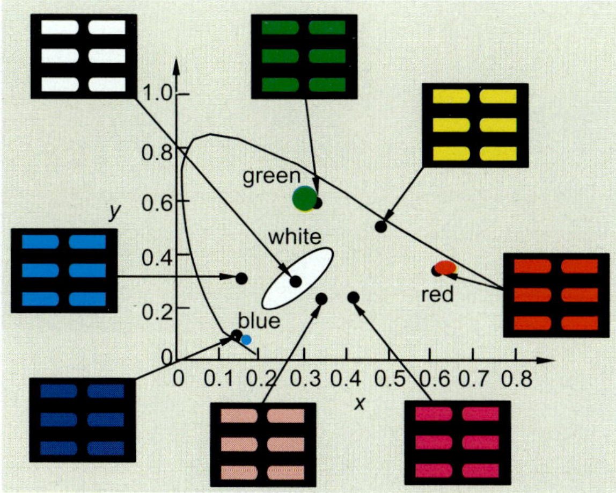

Fig. 7.12 *(Chap. 7, p. 141)* Polymers based on poly(fluorene) emit light over a wide range of colours [Adapted with permission from Institute of Physics Publishing: Friend R, Burroughes J and Shimoda T, Polymer diodes, *Physics World*, June 1999]

Fig. 8.3 *(Chap. 8, p. 152)* An iridescent abalone shell with all the colours of the ocean [Reproduced from http//en.wikipedia.org/wiki/File:AbaloneInside.jpg under the terms of the GNU free documentation license]

Fig. 8.4 *(Chap. 8, p. 155)* A Mayan painting from Mexico made of an organic–inorganic nanocomposite belonging to 800 BC [Reproduced from from http://en.wikipedia.org/wiki/File:Juangerson.jpg under the terms of the GNU free documentation license]

Plate 8

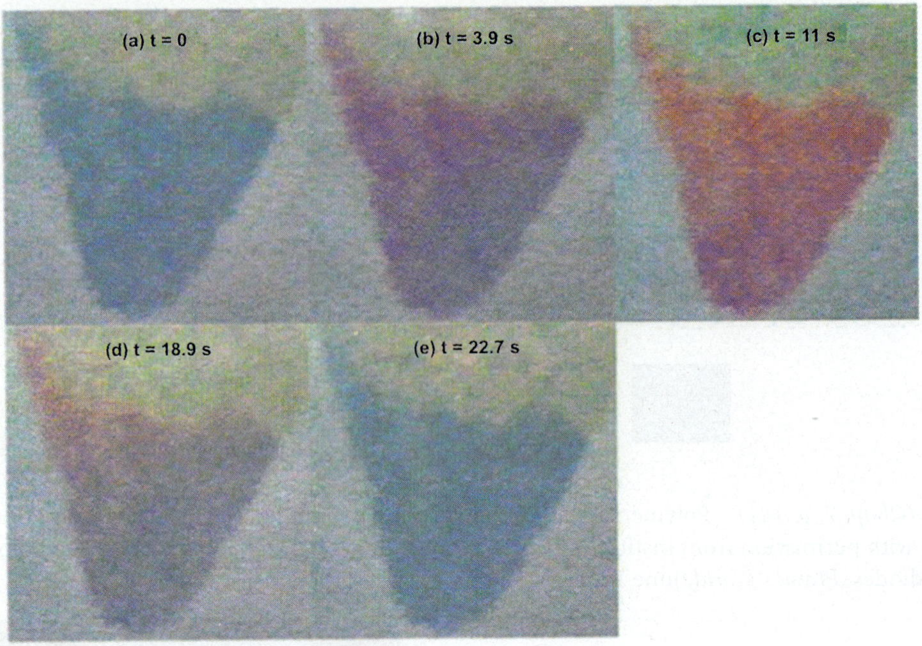

Fig. 8.6 Rapidly reversible thermochromic behaviour of PDA–silica nanocomposite films soaked on filter paper and heated using a heat gun [Reprinted with permission from the American Chemical Society: Yang Y, Lu Y, Lu M, Huang J, Haddad R, Xomeritakis G, Liu N, Malanoski A P, Sturmayr D, Fan H, Sasaki D Y, Assink R A, Shelnutt J A, van Swol F, Lopez G P, Burns A R and Brinker C J, Functional nanocomposites prepared by self-assembly and polymerization of diacetylene surfactants and silicic acid, *J. Am. Chem. Soc.,* 125(5): 1277, 2003]

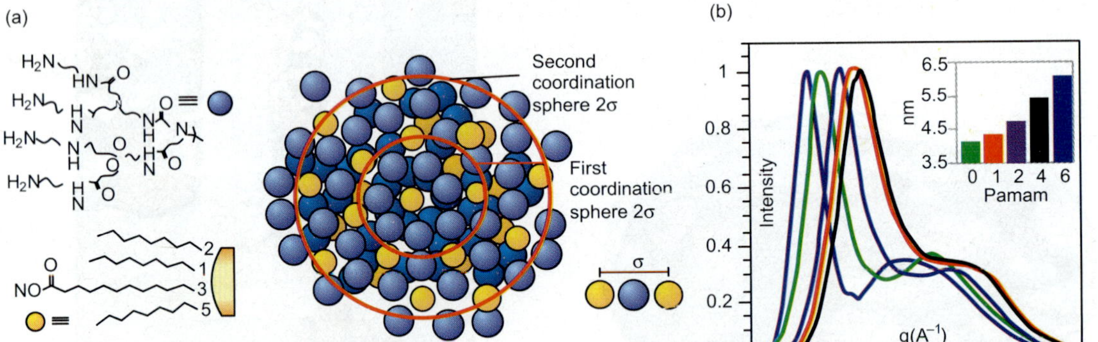

Fig. 8.7 Assembly of nanoparticles using poly (amido amine) (PAMAM) dendrimers and control of inter-particle spacing using dendrimer molecules with increasing levels of branching [Reprinted with permission from the American Chemical Society: Frankamp B L, Boal A K and Rotello V M, Controlled interparticle spacing through self-assembly of Au nanoparticles and poly (amidoamine) dendrimers, 124(51): 15146, 2002]

1

Functional Materials
A Virtual Tour

The world of functional materials is introduced briefly in this chapter. The significance of the topic is brought out with the help of relevant examples from nature. Both the historic as well as modern perspectives are highlighted. The different means of engineering the functions of various materials is illustrated with recent trends in research and development in this field. Finally, the reader is introduced to the importance of theoretical modelling and simulation aspects of functional materials.

LEARNING OBJECTIVES

- To define the term functional materials and understand its significance
- To distinguish functional materials from other structural and engineering materials
- To illustrate, with examples, many functional materials abundant in nature and to find the differences between them and those being developed in laboratories
- To understand the concept of dematerialization
- To highlight the importance of functional materials being developed for futuristic applications

1.1 MATERIALS SCIENCE AND ENGINEERING—THE CONVENTIONAL OUTLOOK

Human life cannot exist without materials. We are made of materials and are surrounded by materials like metals, alloys, rubber, ceramics, plastics, artificial and synthetic fibres, etc. These substances play a vital role in a country's economy (and prosperity). We cannot imagine a world without automobiles, aeroplanes, computers, medical implants, mobile phones and many other gadgets and instruments that are invaluable in a variety of fields ranging from healthcare to electronics. Materials science and engineering deal with the preparation, characterization and applications of materials, enabling the production of components and systems to improve the effectiveness and quality of human life.

Conventionally, materials have been very important for progress and development; prehistorically, the different eras of human existence have been classified as Bronze-age, Stone-age, Copper-age, Iron-age and Ceramic-age, based on the material used predominantly during that period. In contrast, many advanced materials have been developed in the last few centuries based on the criteria of knowledge content per gram of material. Some of these advanced materials are obviously functional. However, the vast majority of the structural and engineering materials that are grouped under the conventional umbrella of materials science is not considered in this text despite their valuable applications [1, 2]. Thus materials with important functions like concrete, ultrahard alloys, conventional ceramics, commodity polymers, etc., are not being considered unless they have been artificially maneuvered to introduce enhanced functions. For example, concrete and polypropylene are not considered per se, although we might discuss them when concrete has been endowed with intelligence to warn us about imminent crack initiation in buildings and bridges, or when polypropylene has been surface-functionalized to make it display different colours depending on environmental changes [3].

Excellent textbooks are available for the synthetic, structural and engineering aspects of materials, where the primary emphasis is on crystallography, band structure, structure–function relationship, electronic, optical, magnetic, thermal and mechanical behaviour [1–5]. Conventional materials like metals, polymers, ceramics and composites, as well as their applications or end-use–based subsets like electronic, magnetic, optical and biological, have been described well in many of these books, along with processing and manufacturing issues linked with life cycle performance. The importance of nanotechnology in these domains of applications has been realized recently, as demonstrated by excellent textbooks [6–8]. Again in this book we will not emphasize these, except some aspects (size and shape dependence) of nano-effects which will be implicitly considered to explain or invoke functionality.

1.2 WHAT ARE FUNCTIONAL MATERIALS?

The world of materials has undergone a revolutionary transformation in the last few decades due to the astounding progress achieved as a result of inter-disciplinary contributions from innumerable physicists, chemists, biologists, materials scientists and engineers. Modern materials research involves a truly multi-disciplinary team where you may find an organic chemist working seamlessly with an electronic engineer to develop a molecular transistor, or a cell biologist inexorably linked with a team of mechanical engineers to develop a new bio-inspired composite for taming adhesion on an aircraft skin. This combination of scientists and engineers with apparently different expertise, experimental skills and languages is the real spirit behind developing functional materials, thus leading to tremendous excitement and a tangible feeling of making something really "unique and novel".

A **functional material** is one that has been artificially designed in the laboratory keeping in mind all the aspects of practical utility. Terms like 'multi-functional materials' or sometimes 'super-materials' are occasionally used to express this meaning more vividly. Many of the recent developments of two-dimensional materials such as graphene and transition-metal chalcogenides (e.g., MoS_2 and TiS_2) are revealing examples with potential applications in nanoelectronics and contiguous disciplines.

What are functional materials? All materials such as wood, concrete, steel, etc., are definitely associated with some functions and, over many decades, incremental changes have occurred to enhance their utility. But these are certainly not examples of functional materials. On the other hand, if wood has a coating which changes colour with relative humidity or temperature, or if concrete changes its colour or gives a visual or electronic warning of imminent crack initiation, they will be considered to have become functional! [3, 9, 10].

The origin of the term 'functional materials' could be understood in a different way, especially from the perspective of an organic chemist. We are aware of a number of organic (carbon containing) molecules in biological systems such as proteins, nucleic acids, vitamins and carbohydrates. Though all are basically carbon skeleton, they perform different functions in biological systems. Even within each class of molecules there are subtle differences in their functions. For example, some proteins are lyophilic and are bound to the lipid bilayer in cell membranes (e.g., caveolin), whereas some have a hydrophobic core to preserve their tertiary structure and a hydrophilic surface to make them soluble in body fluids (e.g., hemoglobin). What makes this difference? Certain groups of atoms present at specific positions along the carbon skeleton can make an organic molecule functional.

A simple aliphatic chain like octane or a simple aromatic hydrocarbon like naphthalene is not a functional molecule from a chemist's perspective. However, if some of the hydrogen atoms in the alkane are substituted by a few hydroxyl groups and ester moieties, it becomes functional. This is the mechanism by which some bacteria can produce polyhydroxy alkanoates, a class of biodegradable polymers. Similarly, if the double bonds in naphthalene are reduced and one of the rings is substituted with six hydroxyl groups, it will become a polycyclic analog of inositol, a second messenger in cellular signal transduction. Thus these groups of atoms which make a simple molecule functional are called '**functional groups**'. This is a good analogy for the terminology 'functional materials' too. Thus, functional substances are classes of materials with one or more functions either present intrinsically or induced during preparation.

1.3 WHERE DO FUNCTIONAL MATERIALS COME FROM?

Functional materials obviously come from atoms and molecules by using different types of interactions in a controllable manner, especially because tuning the chemistry of these atoms and molecules is the primary driving force. However, unlike conventional materials, which come from nature, functional materials are artificially designed or engineered by human intervention. For example, when we make a carbon nanotube by controlling the chemistry in a furnace at temperatures above 1000°C, using a hydrocarbon as a precursor on a selected substrate surface, we are creating a functional material, although the element carbon is available in nature in the form of graphite or diamond with exquisite properties. However, the properties of carbon nanotubes are far superior in terms of functional diversity to that of carbon.

Many kinds of functional materials have been synthesized in the past 20 years. They are the products of human ingenuity, created by modulating diverse types of interactions between atoms and molecules. For this process, our understanding of natural phenomena, however imperfect, is essential.

1.4 HISTORICAL PERSPECTIVES

Although the study of functional materials has emerged as a separate inter-disciplinary field only in recent times, there is evidence of the quest for multi-functionality in more ancient and prehistoric ages. The immaturity in scientific principles, however, precluded ancient artisans from having a precise control over the switchability of functions. But they were aware of certain compositions which can lead to multi-functionality.

A classic example of an ancient functional material is the 'Lycurgus cup' which can change colour on irradiation (see Plate 1, Fig. 1.1), due to the presence of ultrasmall gold and silver particles (now known to be due to surface plasmon resonance) [11]. Other interesting examples are the 'Mayan paintings' which are basically indigo nanocomposites that can withstand corrosive environments; 'Damascus steel', known for its tensile strength, flexibility and toughness, which is possibly a form of a carbon nanotube composite [12]; Tipu Sultan's sword made of special iron-containing nanotubes and other nanostructures of carbon, which is another example of India's ancient mastery over functional nanomaterials; 'faience', the Egyptian ceramic with a quartz core and glazed surface is yet another example, which can mimic precious gems with the changing proportions of the components. Although the synthesis and uses of many such wonder materials has been known for several centuries, after the Second World War our understanding of functional materials underwent a revolution with increased knowledge of thermodynamics, reaction kinetics and phase equilibria, combined with the ability to synthesize materials atom by atom [11–14].

Special attention was given to the relationship of a material's microstructure to its bulk properties, and simultaneously the importance of interfacial phenomena began to gain attention. Nanoscale interface plays a crucial role in controlling the properties of many functional materials. Heterostructures created from nanoscale building blocks can tolerate more defects and strain compared to their bulk counterparts, leading to significant changes in electronic and optical properties.

1.5 LESSONS FROM NATURE

One of the important aspects of functionality, as explained in the definition, is designing materials by looking at nature. Since nature has taken millions of years to evolve into the present form, it makes good sense to look at several wonderful materials available to us and learn how the molecules are organized to introduce functionality in them. An interesting example for functionality in natural systems is the control of floral scents by flowers at different times of the day—some flowers, such as jasmine, release their fragrance (by releasing volatile oils from their petals) at night, while others do so during the day. Other natural examples for functionality include super-hydrophobicity as seen in lotus leaves, tactile behaviour of sea cucumbers, softness and toughness of spider silk, super-adhesive behaviour of gecko feet, strength of clam shells, anti-friction properties of synovial fluid, etc. More recently, a group of researchers have found that drug molecules can be functionalized easily by using naturally available enzymes. How do magnetotactic bacteria sense the magnetic field gradient and position themselves in the open sea in a precisely aligned manner? We now have evidence for the use of single domain nanoparticles of ferrites, although the mechanism is puzzling. The more we understand about such biological structures, the more we are amazed how nature has perfected the design of the functional materials. Hence, there is much for a materials scientist to learn from Mother Nature. Some of these aspects come under bioinspired synthesis or bio-mimetic chemistry, which have been dealt with elaborately in Chapter 4.

1.6 SIGNIFICANCE OF FUNCTIONAL MATERIALS

Functional materials are primarily used for enhancing the quality of our life as they provide unprecedented opportunities for economic growth. They play an important role in making the world more prosperous and environment friendly through fuel-efficient and, damage-resistant buildings, corrosion- and wear-resistant bridges, adaptable e-clothes, etc., without compromising technological advancement and economic growth.

There are several advantages and incentives for developing functional materials:

- Many functional materials work with enhanced energy efficiency and the energy saved could be a strong motive for replacing conventional materials with novel functional materials.
- Reduced emission due to multi-functional catalysts used in the catalytic converters of modern automobile engines is an example of tremendous societal benefits.
- As more and more functions are engineered into the same material (hence the name multi-functional materials), often using nanotechnology, both volume and weight reduction become significant; this in turn provides powerful benefits for aerospace and defence-related applications.
- Functional coatings on aircrafts have the ability to repel ice-particles impinging on them by virtue of their super-hydrophobic (also self-cleaning) nature. Coatings can also have camouflaging properties; their colour can be tuned by electric field due to the electrochromic/photochromic/thermochromic function intrinsic to the coating.
- Many new-generation functional materials that use quantum-caged atoms (QCA) enable efficient solid state lighting (emission confined in a few nm) and are being used by GE, Philips and Siemens in recent times. Typically, these QCA-based nanophosphors are five times as efficient as conventional fluorescent tubes.
- Sunscreens (which use nanosized zinc oxide), self-cleaning windows, stain repellant fabrics, bouncing tennis balls, all these need functional materials illustrating their almost endless benefits to human needs and aspirations.
- New functional materials are required for replacing fossil fuels with renewable materials, leading to a sustainable future which is greener and more effective.
- Suitably designed functional materials could also provide drinking water in an inexpensive manner.

Hence, there are several societal needs for developing new materials to alleviate global problems in the areas of energy, health, ecosystem balance, drinking water and basic resources for human sustenance. Manufacturing advanced functional materials is essential for accomplishing some of the critical needs of each country for its economic growth and prosperity.

1.7 ENGINEERING FUNCTIONS

How do we attach functions to a 'dead' or passive material? Or if some materials already have functional properties, how do we enhance and add more value? How do we tune the functions so that they become much more effective? The answer to these questions is to be found in their chemistry, both at the bulk level and at the surface. There are several approaches for introducing function to a material.

Altering the chemistry of materials

By carrying out various specific reactions on the material in a highly precise manner, a normal material can be converted into a functional material. For example, an insulating oligomer after undergoing a chemical reaction becomes highly conducting and at the same time sensitive to environmental changes, thus attaining the newly found capability of undergoing a resistivity change of several orders of magnitude. Similarly, a doping strategy is used in polyaniline (PANI) films to induce water solubility, chirality, etc.

Surface functionalization strategies

Many materials become functional on attaching a molecule either covalently or electrostatically at the surface. For example, a glass surface can be made to repel water or a gold surface can be made insulating just by creating a self-assembled monolayer (SAM) of some molecules on the surface. Several multilayer strategies produce an anti-reflective coating on many metal/polymer interfaces with important applications in aerospace technology. There are other surface functionalization strategies in the gas phase like plasma treatment to create hydrophilic groups on a polymer, and focussed ion beam to alter the surface chemistry, etc.

Towards multi-functional materials

Another interesting approach to introduce functions is the layer-by-layer assembly (LBL) approach, where a molecular layer is brought in contact with another material by making use of their specific interactions like electrostatic, covalent, van der Waals and H-bonding. An increased understanding of the manipulation of selected molecules and clusters at the nanometre level has led to a number of advanced functional materials and accordingly many stimuli-responsive materials have been developed by these methods. One of the important advantages of adopting the LBL approach to make functional materials is its capability for inexpensive manipulation and templating. This is especially significant for making hybrid and nanocomposites where the ordering of two or more components in a controlled manner is very important. There are several other approaches for developing multi-functional materials, which are analogous to the LBL method. Some of them involve high temperature treatments, laser processing, use of focused ion beams and molecular beams, etc., and many operations like plasma treatment are followed by multilayer formation.

Tuning the functions—as simple as tuning a television

Human life is inexorably linked with the availability of functional materials; our capability to tune the functions empowers us to customize the material for our needs. For example, voice-driven furniture can be designed and personalized with a combination of functional materials endowed with intelligent software control. On the other hand, colour tuning in quantum dots by size (band gap engineering) would lead to interesting optical transitions. Similarly, problems related to the availability of energy resources, quality of health and environmental sustenance are intimately linked to the availability of functional materials, where tuning is important.

1.8 DEMATERIALIZATION

Enhancing the functions of materials contributes indirectly to reduction—in an absolute or relative manner—in the quantity of materials necessary for economic and societal functions. This amounts to performing more functions with less material required for augmenting the multi-functional nature. Normally, we assume that more is better—at least in most economic situations; this logic is opposed by cancer cells which are dangerous when they multiply rapidly. Therefore, it is widely accepted that 'smaller is better, beautiful and more powerful'. Although the original concept of dematerialization was applicable for the field of abstract art, it is becoming increasingly relevant in the area of functional materials too. It indicates the relative reduction in the amount of a material as it becomes more functional; this automatically implies dematerialization. A multi-functional material capable of replacing three different materials and having the same functions illustrates this in a lucid manner. Consumption of less material leads to reduced garbage, a safer environment and landscape conservation, providing benefits to users along the entire materials value chain.

1.9 THE WAY AHEAD—MULTISCALE MODELLING AND COMPUTATION

Since all materials are made of atoms and molecules and we have a mature understanding of interactions at atomic and molecular level, the importance of computational studies and simulation cannot be underestimated. Physical models based on simple systems of atoms, molecules and their organized assemblies need to be understood for developing improved functions for many of these materials. The predictive capability of many quantum mechanics–based materials modelling (atomistic modelling based on *ab initio* or semi-empirical methods, mesoscale and continuum level models, along with appropriate physical laws governing their behaviour) approaches should be used to understand the advantages and limitations of functional materials [15]. Experimental validation of these predictions using many types of designer materials will be extremely useful as illustrated recently by the application of *density functional theory* for storage of hydrogen, or soft polymeric materials and molecular structures using dispersion forces. Molecular dynamics simulations could also be very useful for multi-functional materials in order to understand the kinetics of interaction of the individual components. This is especially significant for handling materials for next-generation solar cells, fuel cells, complex materials in great demand for nuclear fusion, etc. The physical properties of a material can be understood using simple mathematical expressions for classical physics and thermodynamics by the method of *numerical simulation*. Another type includes analytical simulations involving the development of a model based on experimental observations. A good example of the latter is the development of the microstructure of a proton exchange polymer, Nafion, using a model based on small angle x-ray scattering experiments [16].

Despite all these advances, we still require many new and innovative materials to meet the challenge of providing adequate energy, food, clean water and air for each and every one in our planet without compromising the needs of future generations. Consequently, the synthesis and characterization of many new types of advanced functional materials become important. What type of functional materials will be available in the future? Clean solar power would definitely be available along with safe hydrogen-powered, zero-emission vehicles and smart drug delivery systems. Many multi-functional materials would help to generate clean energy, and self-replicating materials will hopefully provide implantable, emotion control chips and artificial organs for humans. The new-found ability to manipulate the genetic code will profoundly influence these materials of the immediate future.

1.10 CONCLUSIONS

Functional materials, if properly translated into economically viable products, offer unprecedented opportunities for technological innovation and national growth. They are key ingredients in shaping our lives, because of their promise in achieving better healthcare systems, protective clothing, integrated electronics systems and smart structures which can respond instantaneously to our needs. Even simple passive materials like textiles (e-textiles) and papers (e-papers) are becoming more functional, with various levels of intelligence and adaptability facilitating unprecedented applications. For instance, ultra-microelectrodes based on single-walled carbon nanotubes (SWCNT), together with state-of-the-art simulations of the brain–machine interface could be useful in developing all types of neuro-prosthetic devices, improving sight, sound, smell and motion, preventing epileptic attacks, enabling spinal bypasses, as well as repairing and even enhancing cognitive capabilities. Could such functional materials with more and more enhanced functions be exploited to steal information, destroy moral and social values and even help one cheat in sporting events? Do we have the moral or ethical right to create some multi-functional material between the animate and inanimate states using nanobiotechnology, with profound philosophical implications? How realistic are the overly optimistic predictions of smart functional materials and their ultimate integration into useful devices based on science fiction books (e.g., *Prey*) and movies (the *Terminator series, Spy Kids*, etc.)? The chapters ahead illustrate these themes using an appropriate technical platform for human prosperity, along with all the excitement and enthusiasm of designing functional materials.

Further Reading

[1] Callister W D and Rethwisch D D, *Materials Science and Engineering: An Introduction*, 8th Edition, John Wiley & Sons, 2010.

[2] Sammes N, Gao W and Li Z, *An Introduction to Electronic Materials for Engineers*, World Scientific Pub. Co., 2011.

[3] Chung D D L, *Functional Materials,* Vols 1 and 2, World Scientific Pub. Co., 2010

[4] Rao C N R, (Ed.*), Chemistry of Advanced Materials*, Blackwell, Oxford, 1992.

[5] Rao C N R and Honig J M, (Ed*s), Preparation and Characterization of Materials*, Academic Press, New York, 1981.

[6] Ozin G A, Arsenault A C and Cademartiri L, *Nanochemistry: A Chemical Approach to Nanomaterials*, 2nd Edition, The Royal Society of Chemistry, Cambridge, UK, 2008.

[7] Pradeep T, *Nano: The Essentials: Understanding Nanoscience and Nanotechnology*, McGraw-Hill Professional Publishing, 2008.

[8] Rao C N R and Govindaraj A, *Nanotubes and Nanowires*, The Royal Society of Chemistry, Cambridge, UK, 2005.

[9] Shahinpoor M and Schneider H–J, (Ed*s), Intelligent Materials*, The Royal Society of Chemistry, Cambridge, UK, 2008.

[10] Addington D M and Schodek D L, *Smart Materials and Technologies for the Architecture and Design Professions*, Elsevier, 2005.

[11] Leonhardt U, News and Views in *Nature Photonics* 1: 207–8.

[12] Srinivasan C, Do Damascus swords reveal India's mastery of nanotechnology?, *Current Science,* 92: 279, 2007.

[13] Zhang *et al.*, Exploiting the reversibility of natural product glycosyl transferase-catalyzed reactions, *Science,* 313: 1291, 2006.

[14] Srivastava S and Kotov N A, Composite layer by layer assembly with inorganic nanoparticles and nanowires, *Acc. Chem. Res.*, 41: 1831, 2008.

[15] Carter E A, Challenges in modeling materials properties without experimental input, *Science,* 321: 800, 2008.

[16] Rohr K S and Chen Q, Parallel cylindrical water nanochannels in Nafion fuel cell membranes, *Nature Materials,* 7: 75, 2008.

Exercises

1. Differentiate between structural and functional materials with selected examples.
2. Can we create cognitive functions in a material? Discuss the pros and cons of this approach.
3. How can we introduce functions in an inert material? What are the chemical strategies available for this?
4. What is dematerialization? What is its philosophical relevance?
5. How does nanotechnology help in making functional materials?
6. What are e-textiles and e-papers? How do they differ from normal textiles and papers?
7. How important is the role of multiscale modelling and computation in predicting the properties of functional materials? Illustrate with an example.
8. Discuss the major challenges in designing and synthesizing functional materials in a chemical laboratory.
9. In order to avoid damage to skin due to sun exposure, cricketers often use a lotion or gel containing nanoparticles of zinc oxide or titanium oxide. Mention the benefits of using these nanomaterials.
10. Mention six non-existing multi-functional materials which could meet the challenge of providing energy, food security, drinking water and clean environment for our future needs.

2

Classification of Functional Materials

This chapter introduces the vast functional diversity of materials, their role in revolutionizing modern technology and their economic impact on society. Materials can be classified based on their function, chemical identity or applications. The role of chemistry in the elegant design of many of these functional materials is illustrated by considering examples with unique properties that originate from custom-designed and self-directing nanomaterials to the more recent meta-materials. This is followed by a discussion of the critical limitations of artificially engineered functional materials. Some of the measures to overcome these limitations in the future are also mentioned.

LEARNING OBJECTIVES

- To realize the functional diversity of synthetic and natural materials
- To differentiate functional materials based on their chemical identity
- To classify materials for various applications based on their properties
- To define the term meta-material and illustrate the design of these with suitable examples
- To discuss various classification schemes of functional materials
- To be aware of the social impact and technological relevance of multi-functional materials
- To understand the limitations of functional materials

2.1 INTRODUCTION

The primary reason for the growing interest in materials research is the need to attain superior combinations for higher performance, lower weight and affordability which are the common demands of almost all technologies. While the development of newer materials with improved performance is always desirable, the focus is now shifting to developing materials which can serve several functions simultaneously, in contrast to the emphasis on structural and engineering materials in the past. Thus, multi-functional materials hold promise for achieving a combination of useful properties as per the criteria mentioned above.

Functional materials embrace several fascinating aspects of both science and engineering and bring out the relationship of matter and its use to society at large. Functional materials are a single group of unique materials ranging from many types of advanced polymers to ceramics and alloys. There has increasing emphasis on how to design multimodal and site-specific functionality, which are in demand for applications ranging from health and medicine to space and defence technology. Hence, it is more difficult to bring the whole class of materials under a common scheme of classification. Possible schemes of classification could be achieved based on their structure, composition, engineering principles, applications, disposal, recyclability etc., rather than differentiating the materials into categories where the focus is on common conceptual aspects.

Functional materials can be classified on the basis of their physical state (monolayers, gels, thin films, etc.), chemical identity (polymers, organic molecules, metals, alloys, ceramics, composites, etc.), chemical relationship between the components of a composite (organic–inorganic hybrids, nanocomposites, meta-materials, etc.) and even applications (optical, electronic, energy storage and conversion). The chapters of this book are organized in such a way that they highlight the most popular types of functional materials instead of strictly following a particular classification scheme discussed here. However, a systematic classification has many pedagogical advantages for beginners. This chapter is intended to provide readers with an overview of the vast expanse of the field of functional materials and the increasing number of challenges in its research, development and commercial implementation.

2.2 CLASSIFICATION BASED ON CHEMICAL IDENTITY

Functional materials can be classified based on the chemical identity of the *constituent phases* [1–3]. For example, a functional material may be a metal/alloy, ceramic, polymer or a composite/hybrid material often in a nanostructured form. We broadly classify them as

- materials with a single phase
- materials with multiple phases, viz., composites made using ceramics, polymers, alloys and their combinations.

The single-phase materials may be grouped as nanomaterials or bulk material, depending on the properties of interest such as quantum confinement.

Another way of classifying functional materials is as *organic, inorganic* and *hybrid* (which means organic-in-inorganic or inorganic-in-organic) *materials* with several unique characteristics (Table 2.1). When we combine hard ceramic materials with soft organic (or polymeric) materials, many new hybrid materials form. Some well-known examples include monolayer-protected nanoclusters, polymer-capped nanoparticles/nanowires and functionalized nanotubes.

Functional materials can also be classified as (i) intelligent, (ii) semi-intelligent and (iii) stupid materials, which might encompass polymers, gels, ceramics, alloys and a variety of hybrids of all these types. Intelligent: (smart) materials themselves are further classified as passively smart, actively smart and very smart structures based on the extent of intelligence, which will be further discussed in Chapter 5.

Functional nanomaterials can be classified in a variety of ways. On the basis of chemical nature, they can be categorized as metals, semiconductors, dielectrics, alloys, polymers and composites. On the other hand, they can be zero-dimensional dots, one-dimensional wires, two-dimensional films or three-dimensional structures. Quantum dots and metallic nanoparticles capped by bifunctional molecules and polymers can also be considered as functional materials with tunable properties [2].

Organic functional materials

A great variety of organic and polymeric materials have interesting properties that are useful for functional applications such as novel light emitting diodes and field-effect transistors.

Table 2.1 Classification of functional materials based on composition and function

Basis of Classification	Types of Materials	Examples	Applications
Chemical composition	Organic	Conducting polymers	Light emitting diodes, Field-effect transistors
	Inorganic	CdSe, Au, Pt nanoclusters	Catalysis, Medical diagnostics
	Organo–inorganic	Poly (3-octyl thiophene)-CNT /Si	Biomedical applications
Intelligence	Passively smart	$BaTiO_3$	Electronic nose
	Actively smart	$PbZrO_3$	
	Very smart	Multi-functional ceramics	
Dimensionality	Quasi zero-dimensional, one-, two- and three-dimensional	Quantum dots, semiconductor nanowires and thin films	Nanoelectronics
Functionality	Mono-, bi- and multi-functional	Amino acids, α-hydroxy acids	Molecular electronics, supramolecular assembly

When we consider the myriad extended and molecular organic species, small organic molecules and oligomers available for the design of functional materials, it is clear that the variety of combinations providing both flexibility and processibility as thin films is huge. A few host–guest and donor–acceptor types of organic materials are revealing examples, and many of these are important for biological applications like tissue engineering and biomedical electronics.

Inorganic functional materials

Many traditional functional materials are purely inorganic, as represented by ZnO or more complex oxides like $BaTiO_3$ and $PbZrO_3$, where the functional aspects are a result of the peculiar structure. Shape memory alloys like Ni-Ti (Nitinol) are purely inorganic systems, as also are a variety of nitrides, carbides and superconducting oxides. The phase diagram and associated structural changes as a function of composition or external parameters like temperature, solvent and pressure, provide valuable thermodynamic insights into the mechanism of their function, and to some extent, the structure–property correlation can be successfully made in many stimuli-responsive materials. The jet engine is an illustrative example where a variety of inorganic materials (even ceramic–metal composites known as cermets) are elegantly combined to provide multi-functionality.

Organo–inorganic hybrid materials

Recent technological breakthroughs and the demand for materials with newer functions have led to the concept of 'hybrid materials' in which a combination of two or more materials yield properties different from that of the individual constituents. Organo–inorganic hybrid materials are systems that have salient features of both organic and inorganic systems, viz., ease of functionalization and structural integrity, respectively. These materials are prepared to enhance various properties of the inorganic component including stability and processibility. For instance, inorganic nanoparticles can be introduced into the matrix of a host-conducting polymer either by some suitable chemical route or by an electrochemical incorporation technique. However, each synthesis opens the way to a group of materials with complementary behaviour between two components. Chemical origin as well as the special properties, viz., colloidal stability, optical, catalytic and electrochemical properties, magnetic susceptibility, etc., always add new dimensions to the resulting hybrids like the case of polymer–carbon nanotube composites, illustrated in Chapter 8.

Hybrid materials consist of a structural component called the 'matrix' which will host a second component (filler in polymer) used to tune or enhance its properties. Hybrid materials can be classified in a number of ways, based on whether the matrix is organic or inorganic, crystalline or amorphous; whether the guest entity is a simple molecule, a macromolecule, particle or fibre, and whether the type of interaction between the guest entity and the host matrix is strong or weak. Polymer–clay nanocomposites come under this category when inter-layer van der Waals interactions are controlled to obtain unique properties. Organically modified silica and silicates (Ormosil) also come under this category. Well-known examples include naturally available composites such as cellulose and lignin. Soft interactions such as H-bonding and π-stacking interactions, where the bond energy is of the order of 20–50 kJ/mole, are preferred to strong covalent interactions as tunability is better in the former. Hybrid materials could in turn be classified into different types, as illustrated in Figs. 2.1 and 2.2, respectively, where properties drastically undergo changes depending upon whether we have inter-penetrating networks or covalently connected chains or blends.

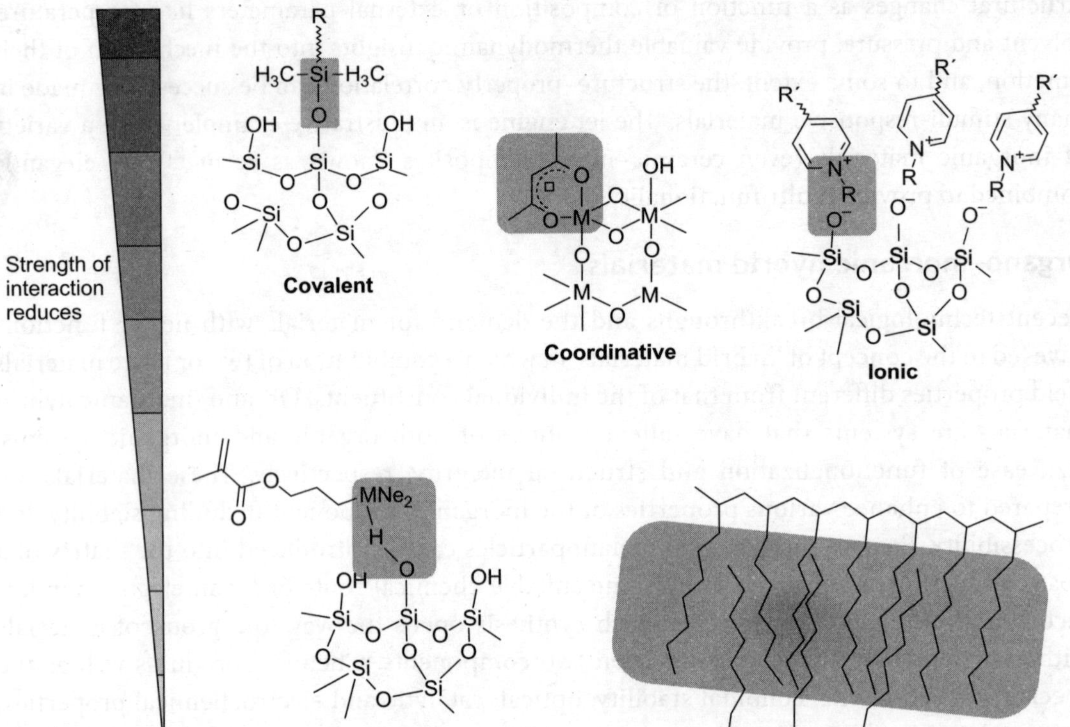

Fig. 2.1 Various types of interactions between common functional groups arranged in the order of their strength [Reproduced with permission from John Wiley & Sons: Kickelbick Guido, *Hybrid Materials: Synthesis, Characterization and Applications*, 2006]

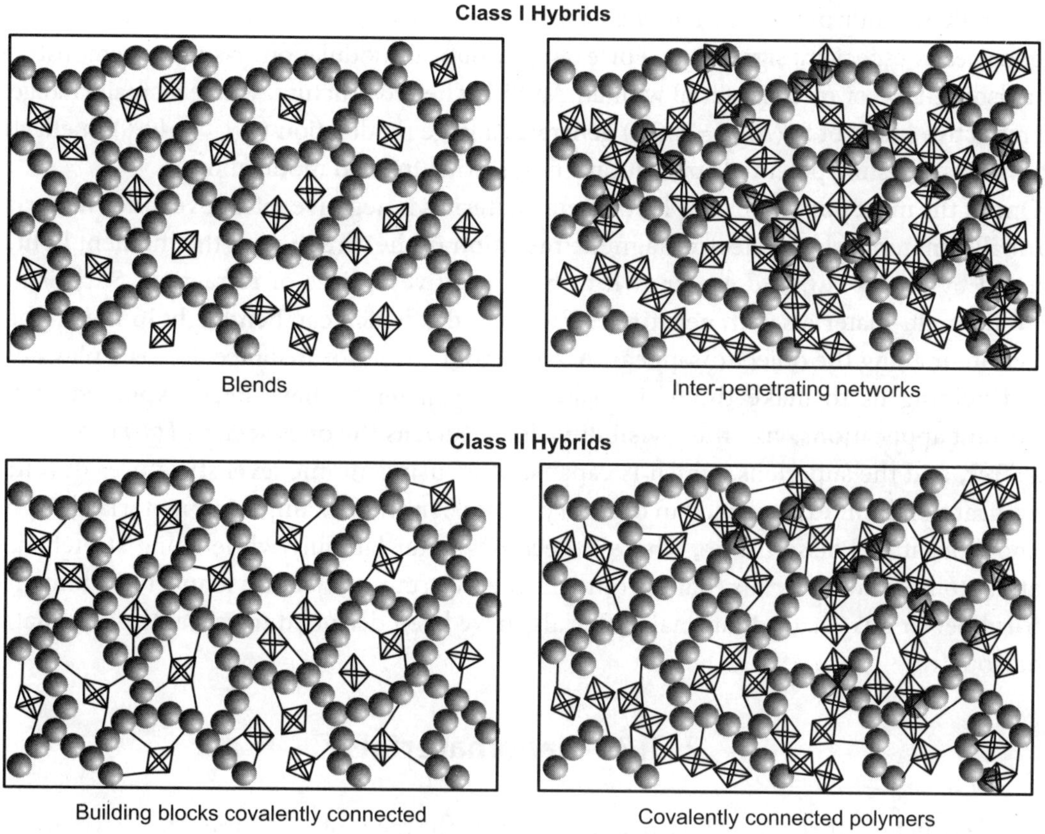

Fig. 2.2 Different types of hybrid materials. Spheres and tetrahedra schematically represent two different materials making the hybrid network [Reproduced with permission from John Wiley & Sons: Kickelbick Guido, *Hybrid Materials: Synthesis, Characterization and Applications,* 2006]

2.3 CLASSIFICATION BASED ON FUNCTIONS AND APPLICATIONS

2.3.1 Meta-materials

The term 'meta-materials' was coined by Rodger M Walser of the University of Texas at Austin in 1999 to indicate certain unusual properties of artificially created materials [3]. According to the original definition, meta-materials are macroscopic composites having a synthesized, three-dimensional, periodic, cellular architecture designed to produce an optimized combination of two or more responses to a specific excitation. They are artificial structures repeated by micron-sized elements specially designed for unique properties. These materials can in turn be classified based on their exotic properties, and their capacity to scale responses from microwave to optical frequencies is especially significant. For example, optical modulation has been demonstrated for a fishnet-type of meta-material with an Ag/Si/Ag heterostructure, where a small change in the refractive index of Si ($\Delta n_{Si} \approx 1.6\%$) generates a large modulation ($\Delta n_{eff} \approx 40\%$) in effective behaviour suggesting potential applications in fast switching and modulation.

One of the most popular examples of meta-materials is negative refractive index materials. Normally, materials bend electromagnetic radiation in the direction of the incident light, as dictated by Snell's law, and are known to have positive indices of refraction. Surprisingly there are meta-materials with negative refractive index which can bend light in the opposite direction, making the object disappear. A 2-nm gold cover, for instance, forms a plasmonic shield helping us to make things invisible. These materials have been exploited in two important applications, viz., the invisibility cloak, such as the ones seen in *Harry Potter* and *Star Trek,* and the superlens, which is capable of focusing atomic level structures devoid of the diffraction limit experienced in ordinary lenses. Another example is a material designed to show negative Poisson ratio, where it becomes fatter laterally while being stretched, in contrast to normal materials that become thinner. Certain polymeric foams (also known as anti-rubber or auxetic or dilational materials) have been designed to reveal this fascinating behaviour.

2.3.2 Nanomaterials

These are structures that have at least one dimension in the range of 1–100 nm. They have attracted much interest as a result of their peculiar and fascinating properties, as well as their unique applications that are superior to that of bulk counterparts [4]. For example, in electronics, the ever-increasing complexity in microprocessor and memory chips means that every two years there is doubling of the chip density. This brings the individual electronic components, with dimensions of 100 nm or less, into the low-dimensional regime, facilitating the manifestation of novel electronic and optical properties. This was demonstrated in the 1970s with the fabrication of quantum well and superlattice devices. Nanomaterials range from zero-dimensional atomic clusters (quantum dots) to three-dimensional structures, where *at least one dimension is in the nanometre range.* In comparison, atoms, clusters, quantum dots and nanoparticles are defined as *zero modulation dimensionality* (0D) systems which can have any aspect ratio ranging from unity to infinity.

When the size of a particle becomes comparable to one of the critical length scales characteristic of its chemical constituent for a specific application, it exhibits exotic properties different from its bulk counterpart. For example, for electronic applications, when the size of the conductor becomes smaller than the mean free path of the electrons in that material, it can even offer a 'zero resistance' path for electronic conduction, resulting in an exotic conduction mechanism called *ballistic conduction*. Many of the single-walled, CNT-based electronic devices make use of ballistic transport and Coulomb blockade. Thus, achieving multi-functionality is much simpler in the case of nanomaterials, which has led to an upsurge in a separate field—'functional nanomaterials'.

Wires, rods, belts and tubes in the nanometre range are classified as *one-dimensionally modulated* (1D) and this way of classification provides a good system to investigate the dependence of electrical, thermal and optical or mechanical properties on the dimensionality (size and shape). Some of the established examples include size-dependent excitation or emission, quantized or ballistic conductance, Coulomb blockade or single-electron tunnelling (SET) and metal–insulator transition. Many of these properties play an important role when interconnects and active components are fabricated in nanoscale electronic, optoelectronic, electrochemical and electromechanical devices (MEMS/NEMS). The most important two-dimensional (2D) layers with thickness in nanometre range and consisting of ultrafine grains are *two-dimensionally modulated.* This class includes insertion materials such as graphite and layered-type dichalcogenides, and oxides of the transition metals Ti, Nb, Ta, Mo, W and V. Some of these materials are extremely useful for making rechargeable Li batteries, as we will discuss in Chapter 6. Some materials also function as solid lubricants because of their layered character and low frictional properties.

The last class comprises *three-dimensionally modulated* microstructures or nanophase framework, where cross-linked channels allow ion insertion if the size of the channels is sufficiently large to accommodate the ions. For example, 3D-zeolitic solids containing aluminum, silicon and oxygen with regularly spaced pores within the molecular framework can have nanopores, enabling them to be useful in adsorbing small molecules, ions or gases—just as a sponge sucks up water. Many fascinating multi-functional catalysts of variable utility to the petroleum industry come from this class of materials.

2.3.3 Super-materials

The word 'super-materials' is often used for a class of materials with superior or enhanced functional properties. They often have an amazing combination of useful functions and they are also known as multi-functional materials. They could be ceramic like $BiFeO_3$ or polymeric like polyvinylidene difluoride (PVDF), or a hybrid of both; some are also endowed with intelligence, that is, they are highly sensitive to what happens in the environment. For instance, sensitive skin used for aircrafts with in-built camouflaging capability, and anti-acoustic coating to cancel noisy neighbours are interesting examples of super-materials. The word super-materials, like 'super-heroes', implies that extraordinary feats are possible with these materials. In order to propel humanity to the next stage of evolution, such materials, however, need to overcome issues related to the brain–machine interface.

Multi-functionality is attained when the properties of the material are suitable for many applications, including optical, electronic, magnetic, energy and electromechanical systems. The property of a multi-functional material can be tuned by applying external stimuli such as electric field, heat, mechanical shock/vibration, irradiation and magnetic field. Hence, some of these materials are also known as stimuli-sensitive or adaptable materials. The tunability arises from reversible variations within the material, which could be a change in phase, domain size (in the case of composites), morphology or superlattice structure. *Thus, a common criterion for a material to exhibit multiple functions is that the changes induced by any external stimulus should be 'reversible', that too within a reasonable 'response time'.* For example, if a 'shape memory' material requires one year to 'remember' its original shape after a thermal shock, it would not be useful for making any device. Most of the materials will of course change a little with a change in the environment. Expansion/contraction of a metal with increase/decrease in temperature is a good example. But stimuli-sensitive materials are those which show a non-linear response, i.e., a small change in environmental stimuli causes a large change in their properties. The complexity of classifying functional materials can be appreciated simply by considering the case of *multiferroics*. Multiferroics are defined as single-phase materials ($BiFeO_3$ is a good example) which simultaneously possess two or more ferroic properties, viz., ferromagnetism, ferroelectricity and ferroelasticity. Typical multiferroics belong to the group of the perovskite transition metal oxides, including rare earth ferrites like $LuFe_2O_4$. Although this definition sounds simple, there are several categories of multiferroics based on the origin of their multi-functionality like charge ordered, geometrically frustrated, magnetically driven multiferroics.

For example, a typical insulating material could be switched to a conducting state by applying a tiny electromagnetic/magnetic field. Consider, for instance, the case of zinc oxide (ZnO). Normally, it is an electrical insulator with resistivity of the order of 10^{12} Ωcm. However, if there is an environmental stimulus like lightning, it acts like a good conductor to transmit all charges. Lightning normally generates a field gradient of 10^3–10^6 V/m, which can turn the stubborn insulator into an efficient conductor. It is important to note that this change is reversible, which makes ZnO, a functional material, extremely useful for varistor (variable resistor) applications. Self-replenishment of ZnO towers where repeated lightning can heal cracks in the materials is an interesting example. Hence, materials with these multiple functions will play an important role in making smart structures. Some of these stimuli-sensitive materials with selected applications are given below (Fig. 2.3).

One of the important characteristic features of functional materials is the tunability of interfacial phenomena since most of the actions often occur at physical interfaces. Interfaces, of course, are the domain of materials scientists. It will be exciting to see over the next few years, just how far, and in what ways, scientists and engineers will modulate interfacial behaviour for developing many of these materials. For instance, the mere presence of a monolayer of certain molecules on the surface can stop the surface reconstruction of many semiconductors, and the monolayer can help pin the interface down to atomic level. Precise atom-by-atom control of monolayer structures and the dynamic responses have important consequences for the development of functional materials and architectures.

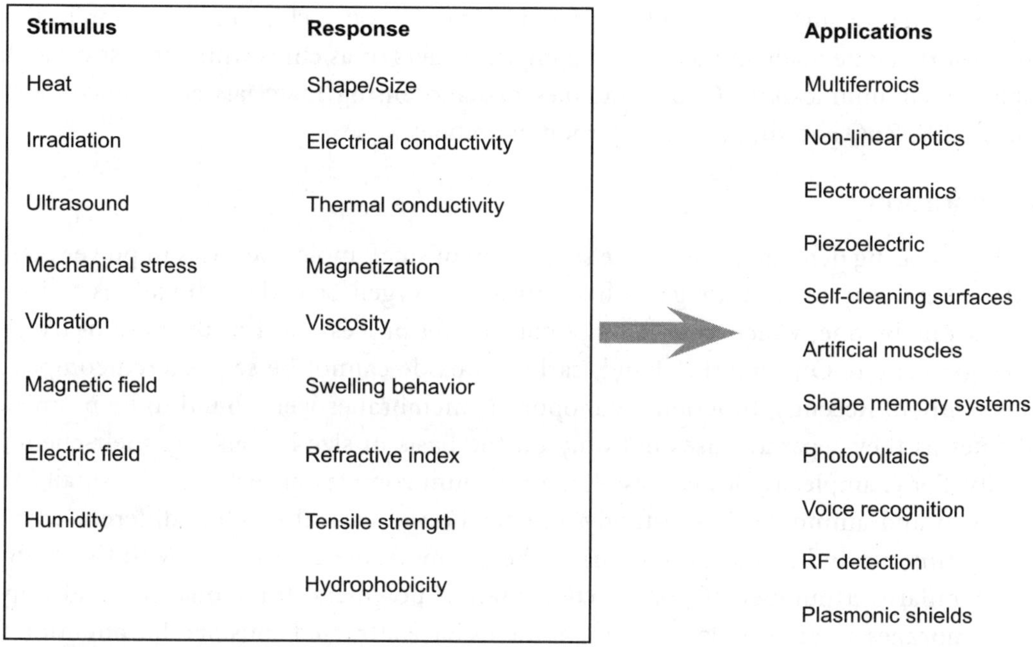

Fig. 2.3 Classification of stimuli-sensitive materials based on their response to different types of external stimuli and their applications

2.4 TECHNOLOGICAL RELEVANCE

Many functional materials are technologically important due to their immense application potential to enhance the quality of human life and economic development [4]. Nanotechnology has enabled the design of many multi-functional materials and components, especially for aerospace, defence and electronic applications.

Catalytic converters

Automotive catalysts contain precious metals like platinum, rhodium and palladium to speed up the chemical reactions of pollutants like nitrogen oxide, carbon monoxide and hydrocarbons to produce non-toxic emissions. By using nanoparticles of precious metals—instead of large particles—less metal is required to produce the same surface area over the ceramic base of the catalyst. Thus the new generation catalytic converters use only 70%–90% of the precious metals to purify automobile exhausts.

Chemical sensors

Due to the large surface-to-volume ratio, low surface energy barrier and good thermal and mechanical stability, nanostructured chemical sensors can offer higher sensitivity, robustness and lower power consumption for defence, medical (e.g., lab-on-a-chip) and space applications. These sensors can be made in the form of compact wafers or as chips with wireless capability suitable for communication. Good examples of nanosensing materials are semiconductor nanowires like ZnO and single-walled carbon nanotubes.

Gas separation

There is increasing demand for effective separation of small molecule gases in power plants. The traditional way to separate gases like nitrogen, oxygen or carbon dioxide is to freeze them out one by one, which is an energy-consuming process, and in the case of oxygen, it is dangerous too. On the other hand, carbon dioxide cannot be sequestered completely by this method. Recently, functional nanoporous membranes were found to be promising candidates as they separate gases not only on the basis of size but also by their chemical reactivity. For example, a porous crystal of an iridium complex absorbs several small gases like oxygen and ammonia. Interestingly, the gas-bound crystal exhibits different colours (red for ammonia and green for oxygen) as the gas molecule coordinates with the iridium centre. Similarly, a number of porous coordination polymers, functionalized and doped silica membranes and molecular sieve membranes have attracted considerable attention for gas separation.

Photocatalytic degradation of air pollutants in self-cleaning systems

The extent of air pollution has been constantly increasing with increasing industrial activities leading to smog formation. Recently, some semiconducting oxide nanoparticles are being used to catalyze photodegradation of these air pollutants. For example, TiO_2 nanoparticles, when stimulated by sunlight, can convert harmful air pollutants like carbon monoxide, nitrogen oxides and volatile organic compounds (VOCs) into environmentally acceptable products like calcium nitrate and carbon dioxide.

Novel systems for hydrogen generation and storage

Hydrogen offers the potential for a truly clean fuel. As hydrogen-powered vehicles and fuel cells are being developed, there is a high demand for efficient ways to separate and clean hydrogen. Nanomembranes that can separate hydrogen from gas streams, creating a clean hydrogen feed, are being developed. Similarly, a number of systems based on functionalized carbon nanotubes and metal hydrides are used to store hydrogen molecules.

Solar energy conversion

Polymer-based organic photovoltaics are considered as cheaper alternatives to silicon solar cells. So a number of efforts are being made to improve their performance. Recently, more efficient devices have been obtained by forming composites of carbon nanotubes with conjugated polymers, wherein efficient hole transportation and exciton dissociation cause enhanced performance. The principle behind the improved efficiency is the high conductivity along the tube axis of carbon nanotubes combined with the chemical and physical properties of conjugated polymers used in the photoactive layer, as explained in one of the later chapters.

Bio-mimetic membranes

Biological membranes in animal and plant cells are the most effective natural systems to separate ions in response to light, concentration gradients and voltage gradients. Such efficiency cannot be attained in the removal of small ions for potable water using conventional filtration methods. So recent efforts are focused on mimicking the functions of biological cell membranes to prepare 'bio-mimetic membranes'. For example, liquid crystals of fatty acid esters (similar to lipids) immobilized in a porous nitrocellulose membrane have been found to mimic lung walls with selectivity to CO_2/O_2 and water permeability. A number of bio-mimetic membranes can be prepared by simple combinations of carbohydrate chains, ion-exchange groups, water and lipid-like substances. Such membranes can also be used as 'drug meters' to measure concentrations of antibiotics, antioxidants, antiviral and psychotropic substances [5].

2.5 CONCLUSIONS

How much difference will the development of functional materials make in improving water quality, agriculture, nutrition, health, energy and the environment in developing countries? Most people agree that nanotechnology could answer this question positively since functional materials can be harnessed to solve some of the world's most pressing problems including global warming, environmental pollution, lack of pure drinking water in some areas, sustainable development of energy sources, eradication of poverty, development of new drugs and new diagnostic tools for accomplishing health for all. Transportation alone accounts for about 80% of global warming and functional materials used in electric vehicles can significantly reduce gas emissions. Many of the new functional materials can positively contribute to the attainment of the United Nations Millennium Development Goals (MDGs) by strengthening the economic growth of developing countries like India and China. However, there are also doubts that some of these materials cannot be developed and deployed within a time frame of 10 years, and that some materials may not be acceptable socially, culturally and environmentally, despite their critical impact. Some are too expensive and hence cannot be affordable to people, especially from developing countries, to realize their full benefit.

The MDGs aim to promote human development and encourage social and economic sustainability through

- energy storage, production and conversion
- agricultural productivity enhancement
- water treatment and remediation
- disease diagnostics and screening
- drug delivery systems
- food processing and storage
- air pollution and remediation
- construction
- health monitoring and vector and pest detection and control

It is widely believed that many of the above objectives would be accomplished much more effectively and faster if suitable functional materials are developed in the coming years.

Over the last few decades, an amazingly diverse range of functional materials have been developed ranging from ultrasoft and self-healing to super-hard and extraordinarily tough materials using different type of chemistry. Some are still to be developed completely while few others are commercially available. Many of these functional materials are expensive due to the small scale of preparation and lack of information on durability and degradation modes. However, more research is expected to bring the cost down so that these could be affordable to facilitate rapid commercialization. The MDGs goals are intimately linked with many of these critical materials for human sustenance in the foreseeable future, and hence we will see more rapid advances in many of these materials.

Further reading

[1] Butt H-J, Graf K and Kappl M, *Physics and Chemistry of Interfaces*, Wiley-VCH Verlag GmbH & Co., KGaA, Weinheim, 2003.

[2] Ball P. *Made to Measure*, Princeton University Press, New Jersey, 1997.

[3] Chaturvedi P, Hsu K, Zhang S and Fang N, Metamaterials: Design and Function, *MRS Bulletin* 33: 915, 2008.

[4] Triennial Review of the National Nanotechnology Initiative Committee to Review the National Nanotechnology Initiative, A Matter of Size: National Research Council ISBN: 0-309-66138-2, 2006; available at: http://www.nap.edu/catalog/11752.html.

[5] Shimomura S, Higuchi M, Matsuda R, Yoneda K, Hijikata Y, Kubota Y, Mita Y, Kim J, Takata M and Kitagawa S, Selective sorption of oxygen and nitric oxide by an electron-donating flexible coordination polymer, *Nature Chemistry*, August 2(8): 633–37, 2010.

Exercises

1. What are meta-materials? Illustrate the concept of designing these with two examples.
2. Explain the importance of recyclability in materials preparation.
3. Mention a few functional materials which could solve some of the pressing problems of humanity?
4. Explain the term 'multiferroics' with the help of suitable examples.
5. How do ZnO-based lightening arrestors function? Why are they considered self-healing?

6. Explain the advantages of 'lab-on-a-chip'.
7. What are intelligent materials? How are they further classified?
8. What is a hybrid material? How can hybrid materials be subdivided based on composition?
9. Consider the combination of materials used in making a modern jet engine (*J. Am. Ceram. Soc.*, 74: 463, 1991) and explain why they are considered to be multi-functional.
10. Is there a difference between organo–inorganic materials and organic-in-inorganic materials? Explain with the help of examples.

3

Molecular Self-Assembly

This chapter discusses the basic thermodynamic framework of self-assembly, followed by a review of common synthetic protocols and key challenges in achieving systematic control at the molecular level. The fundamental driving force for self-assembly is delineated by suitable theoretical arguments, and after discussing classification and experimental techniques, the chapter finally concludes with relevant applications.

LEARNING OBJECTIVES

- To appreciate the importance of self-assembly in chemistry and nature
- To distinguish between self-assembly, self-organization and directed assembly
- To have a broad idea of different types of adsorbents, adsorbates and interactions responsible for molecular self-assembly in terms of collective behaviour
- To realize the challenges in various synthetic protocols using self-assembled monolayers and multilayers
- To indicate the key limitations of self-assembled monolayers as a synthetic strategy for producing nanostructured materials
- To understand the applications of self-assembly in areas like biosensors, molecular electronics, MEMS, preparation of biomaterials and corrosion prevention

Fig. 3.1 Patterns on the skin of the leopard and zebra are examples of self-assembly in nature [Adapted from www.freenaturepics.com]

Tiresome classes? Lengthy sessions? Finished all your assignments for the day? Frustrated at the big mess of books and papers around you? Now, imagine how cool it would be if your study-table instantaneously self-assembles into a home theatre and your sit-erect chair unfolds into a flat sofa! This is indeed a promise that 'self-assembly' researchers offer to young students! Given above are beautiful examples of self-assembly in nature. It is a natural human tendency to look for 'symmetry in dissymmetry'; 'order in disorder': what is random at a larger scale can be ordered at a smaller scale and vice versa. This is the power and beauty of self-assembly. The objective of this chapter is to provide a glimpse of the various aspects of self-assembly, its thermodynamic basis and the means of exploiting this phenomenon to synthesize functional materials.

3.1 INTRODUCTION

'Assembly' means grouping of similar objects for a common purpose and 'self-assembly' indicates groups formed by an internal motivation dictated by the 'self' or consciousness. When we use the qualifier 'self' to specifically describe the term 'assembly', we should immediately become cautious about the existence of another type of assembly, often quoted as 'directed assembly'. The difference between the two can be easily appreciated by observing the way in which school children organize under different circumstances: they assemble in the order of their classes every morning for prayer; they also assemble into groups in leisure or games periods. Have you ever wondered at the difference between these two? The former is a 'directed' assembly dictated by school management and the latter is 'self-assembly' simply governed by the common likes and dislikes among a group of friends! Currently, the term 'self-assembly' is used frequently, misleading one from the actual spirit of the subject. For instance, 'self-assembled furniture'; the furniture does not assemble by themselves and actually represent furniture that can be dismantled to fit into any space!

A more formal and convenient definition of self-assembly is given by Whitesides and Grzybowski [1]: "Processes ranging from the non-covalent association of organic molecules in solution to the growth of semiconductor quantum dots on solid substrates have been called self-assembly". Thus the usage of the term 'self-assembly' will be limited to, as described by Whitesides, "Processes that involve pre-existing components (separate or distinct parts of a disordered structure), which are reversible, and can be controlled by a proper design of the components". 'Self-assembly' is thus not synonymous with 'formation' as there could be a big difference in the thermodynamic driving force. It actually represents the natural tendency of many physical systems to reach patterns and structures of lowest free energy by exchanging energy.

3.1.1 What is self-assembly?

Self-assembly or self-organization is a process that occurs at several levels in nature, ranging from terrestrial to extra-terrestrial strata. Biological systems reveal the highest order of self-organization; their ability to gain internal ordering is in fact related to the level of intelligence. For example, cells get organized in a directed manner to form tissues and tissues get organized to form organs, as reflected in many organisms. Even in the inanimate world, self-organization occurs continuously.

Sometimes, the terms 'self-assembly' and 'self-organization' are differentiated on the basis of time scales; the former refers to the immediate coming together of the components, while the latter refers to the improvement in orderliness of a system with time. In other words, self-organization is a process in which the internal arrangement of a system improves with respect to time without any external intervention. The system spatially evolves without being guided or managed by an external agency.

Self-organization (irrespective of spatial or temporal) normally occurs in open systems, where their complexity increases with time. The dynamic outcomes of self-organization have been proved to play a crucial role in many areas of chemistry, mathematics, economics and human behaviour, such as phase evolution, cellular automata, crowd behaviour and market growth. In chemistry, self-organization is synonymous with self-assembly. Hence, we should ignore the differences between them, and concentrate on understanding the properties of the materials synthesized using self-assembly.

3.1.2 Energetics of self-assembly: working against entropy considerations!

The apparent origin of self-assembled monolayers can be attributed to Zisman's work in 1946, wherein he prepared a monomolecular layer of a surfactant by adsorption on a clean metal surface. The primary emphasis, though, was on the relationship between the wetting angle and the molecular structure. This was followed by a few isolated studies of the chemisorption of similar molecules on different metal surfaces until 1983, when Nuzzo and Allara showed that organosulphur compounds such as dialkyl disulphides (R_2S) can form oriented and highly ordered monolayers on a gold surface from dilute solutions. Following this discovery, it was found that sulphur compounds like long chain alkane thiols can also form highly organized assemblies on a gold surface. Since then, a large number of substrates and organic molecules have been investigated, although monolayers of alkane thiolates and disulphides on noble metal surfaces constitute one of the best studied and thoroughly characterized systems.

Chaos or disorder is accepted as a law of nature, and we are curious to see how the peculiar scenes of self-assembly in natural systems take place. Molecules generally prefer to exist in random motion (collision) with their neighbours, irrespective of whether they are in a liquid or gas phase. The scientific basis for this natural behaviour is offered by the Second Law of Thermodynamics, which states, "for a process to be spontaneous, its free energy change should be negative". For an endothermic process, this is possible only if the change in entropy is positive, which means that spontaneous processes are always accompanied by an increase in entropy. The free energy change of a process is related to entropy by the following expression:

$$\Delta G = \Delta H - T\Delta S$$

where ΔG is the free energy change, ΔH is the enthalpy change, ΔS is the entropy change and T is the temperature.

Hence, if we say a group of molecules is organized, we really observe a system that has overruled the entropy requirements of nature. But the most fascinating aspect is that they still survive and are stable! For example, in the case of alkanethiol molecules self-assembled on gold surfaces, ΔH is about 56 kcal/mol while $T\Delta S$ is only 2–3 kcal/mol. *How does this happen? What is the driving force?*

Molecular interactions are classified as strong or weak based on the free energy changes associated with them (Chapter 2). It is the cumulative effect of a collection of weak interactions that brings about the magic of self-assembly! To appreciate the importance of weak interactions, let us have a close look at the process of digestion in our body. The proteins we consume are assimilated within four hours, whereas in the laboratory, you may have to boil the protein for about 24 hours in a 20% HCl solution to achieve its complete breakdown! Similarly, the process of converting the fatty acids into carbon dioxide and water, which requires harsh reaction conditions in the laboratory, like extremes of pH, high temperatures and corrosive chemicals, is elegantly managed in physiological conditions.

How do enzymes achieve accelerated rates for chemical transformations which are otherwise difficult? The key is self-assembly! It is the assembly of the active site of an enzyme with a specific substrate, as explained by the preliminary 'lock and key' mechanism, that is responsible for such wonders. For example, the rates of hydrolysis of ionized phosphate mono- and di-esters were found to be enhanced 10^{15}–10^{17} times when catalyzed by alkaline phosphatase enzyme extracted from *Escherichia coli*. The case of enzymatic catalysis has been highlighted mainly because almost all types of interactions categorized under self-assembly are involved in achieving overall efficiency [2]. The approximate time scales (and corresponding energies) of various processes following the self-assembly of an enzyme with its substrate can provide valuable insights.

Weak interactions are in fact more advantageous, as they can evolve with time, leading to better organization. For example, consider the self-assembly of alkanethiols on a gold surface. You can easily observe the increase in ordering of the monolayer with increasing length of the alkyl chains, as depicted schematically in Fig. 3.2. While the interaction energy between the gold and sulphur atoms of the thiol molecules remains the same, it is the increasing interchain van der Waals interaction that makes the monolayer more and more ordered. There are many other weak interactions like hydrogen bonding and hydrophobic interactions which serve as driving forces for self-assembly.

The versatile nature of weak interactions governing self-assembly renders many beneficial properties to the resulting system, including:

- Excellent reversibility with an ability to reconfigure
- Synergistic behaviour
- High and conformal coverage
- Accurate control over the level of organization
- Variability with respect to the nature of the solvent

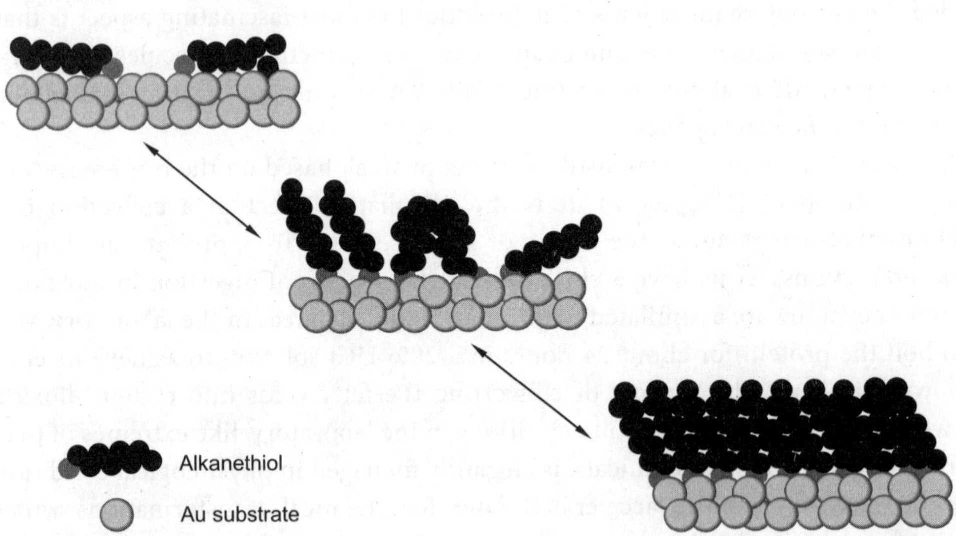

Fig. 3.2 Self-assembly of alkanethiols on a gold surface

3.2 CLASSIFICATION OF SELF-ASSEMBLED MONOLAYERS

Self-assembly is ubiquitous in an enormous number of systems and it is hence difficult to achieve a general classification. Nonetheless, it has been attempted here to obtain a considerably broader view of the phenomenon, unlike the more common classification schemes adopted in books and review articles. It is quite common to use the term 'self-assembly' for the organization of molecules on a solid substrate from the liquid or vapour phase. Actually, 'self-assembly' means far more then the simple solid/liquid and solid/vapour interfaces. Familiar examples of self-assembly which we have discussed in the last section like enzyme/substrate assembly do not in this classification. Hence, we begin by classifying self-assembly as 'interfacial' (i.e., at the junction of two phases) and 'homogeneous' (within a phase) and proceed by introducing various types of interfaces and interactions responsible for the assembly (Fig. 3.3).

3.2.1 Interfacial self-assembly

Self-assembly can occur in a number of interfaces such as solid–liquid, liquid–liquid and liquid–air. Of these, the solid–liquid interfaces are the most common systems investigated for self-assembly, owing to ease of experimentation, reproducibility and lower cost of fabrication. The most familiar example, the self-assembly of thiols on Au surfaces, has already been described (Fig. 3.2). Here, better control of ordering is possible due to the rugged nature of the double layer formed at the solid–liquid interface. The reconstruction of the surface structure

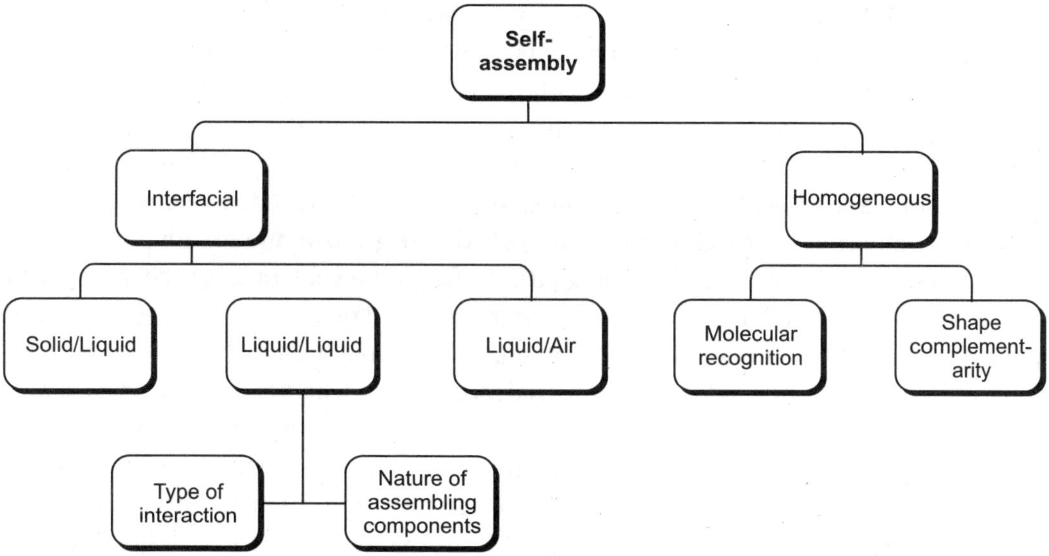

Fig. 3.3 Interfaces and interactions responsible for molecular self-assembly

of the solid on assembling a group of foreign molecules is supported by the rest of the lattice in its bulk.

In contrast, liquid–liquid interfaces are more dynamic in nature, which demands that the assembling molecules themselves be *amphiphilic*. A good example is the self-assembly of lipid molecules at oil-water interfaces. Liquid–air interfaces have an even higher level of complexity, as one can envision the degrees of freedom, a molecule would possess at such interfaces. Hence, assembly at air–liquid interfaces is normally achieved by 'directing' long chain molecules floating on a liquid using a perpendicular force called the Langmuir–Blodgett (LB) technique. But there are rare cases of 'self-assembly' at liquid–air interfaces using acid–base interactions between molecules floating on the surface of a liquid and those dissolved in the liquid.

Irrespective of the nature of the interface, self-assembly can be further classified based on the type of interactions between the assembling components and the chemical nature as demonstrated below.

Adsorbate–adsorbent interaction

The simplest classification of molecules capable of self-assembly is on the basis of the nature of interaction between the components, as illustrated by the strong chemisorption of thiol on Au on the one hand, and alkyltrichlorosilane on a hydroxylated surface via long-range interactions (i.e., physisorption) on the other. There are also many types of weak interactions that can aid self-assembly, as summarized in Table 3.1.

Chemical nature of the components

A number of components are available for self-assembly at the solid–liquid interface although the choices are limited for the other two types of interfaces. Depending on the nature of organic molecules, we can classify them as a monolayer of fatty acids, monolayer of bifunctional molecules, monolayer of all organic adsorbates, multilayers of diphosphonate, monolayer of organosulfphur molecules, and so on. From an electrochemistry perspective, the self-assembled monolayers (SAMs) can be classified into two types: the redox inactive SAMs (e.g., simple alkanethiols on gold) and the redox active SAMs (e.g. alkanethiols with pendant redox groups like ferrocene containing thiol on gold). As far as the substrates are concerned, they could be classified as metal or semiconductor, and also based on their structure (single crystal or polycrystalline), orientation of the substrates and functional groups.

SAMs can further be divided into two forms depending on whether an ordered structure is formed on the surface (alkanethiolates on Au surface) or not. In the covalent type, extensive chemisorption-driven reconstruction on the surface can occur, as in the case of alkanethiol adsorbed on silver. An ionic form of bonding can occur in the chemisorption of carboxylic acids on basic oxide surfaces are less table, where carboxylate salt is formed; however, these structures are less stable.

Table 3.1 Types of interactions that aid self-assembly

Bond type	Examples
Covalent bonds that can be formed and broken reversibly	Disulphides (RSSR, ribonuclease); vanadate and borate esters
Inorganic metal–ligand bonds	Metal salts; organometallic complexes; zinc fingers
Hydrogen bonds	Nucleotide base pairs; amide hydrogen bonds in proteins
Electrostatic interactions involving charges	Salt bridges in proteins; cadmium arachidate bilayers
Electrostatic interactions involving dipoles	Crystalline IC_4H_4CN
Hydrophobic interactions	Micelles; Langmuir–Blodgett monolayers on water; lipid bilayers, hydrophobic cores of proteins, inclusion complexes of cyclodextrins
Aromatic π-stacking and charge transfer	Nucleic acids
van der Waals interactions	*n*-Alkane crystals; urea inclusion complexes

3.2.2 Homogeneous self-assembly

Self-assembly can occur in two different scales, ranging from macroscopic (visible to the unaided eye) to molecular (nanoscale level) [4]. In this secion, we will discuss the most prevalent type of self-assembly in biological systems, viz., self-assembly of molecules in homogeneous solutions.

The driving force for the self-assembly of two or more molecular entities in a homogeneous phase is the presence of complementary shapes, as in the case of enzyme/substrate interactions discussed in an earlier section or due to molecular recognition depending on the functional groups of the assembling components. For example, Fig. 3.4 shows a beautiful assembly of molecules in the aqueous phase simply by molecular recognition induced by hydrogen bonding interactions.

These self-assembled structures have been demonstrated for a number of applications. An interesting example is the control of the Diels–Alder reaction in molecular capsules. This was achieved by Fujita and coworkers who made capsules of coordination complexes of Pd (II) with internal volume of 0.9 nm^3 [5]. Normally, the Diels–Alder reaction between anthracene and phthalimide yields two major products. However, if this reaction is carried out within these capsules, the reaction preferentially yields the 1,4-product. Similarly, a number of capsules and cages have been synthesized by homogeneous self-assembly and are often denoted as 'supramolecular structures'. Other interesting examples of homogeneous self-assembly are the molecular plug–socket connectors made by Stoddart and coworkers [6] and molecular

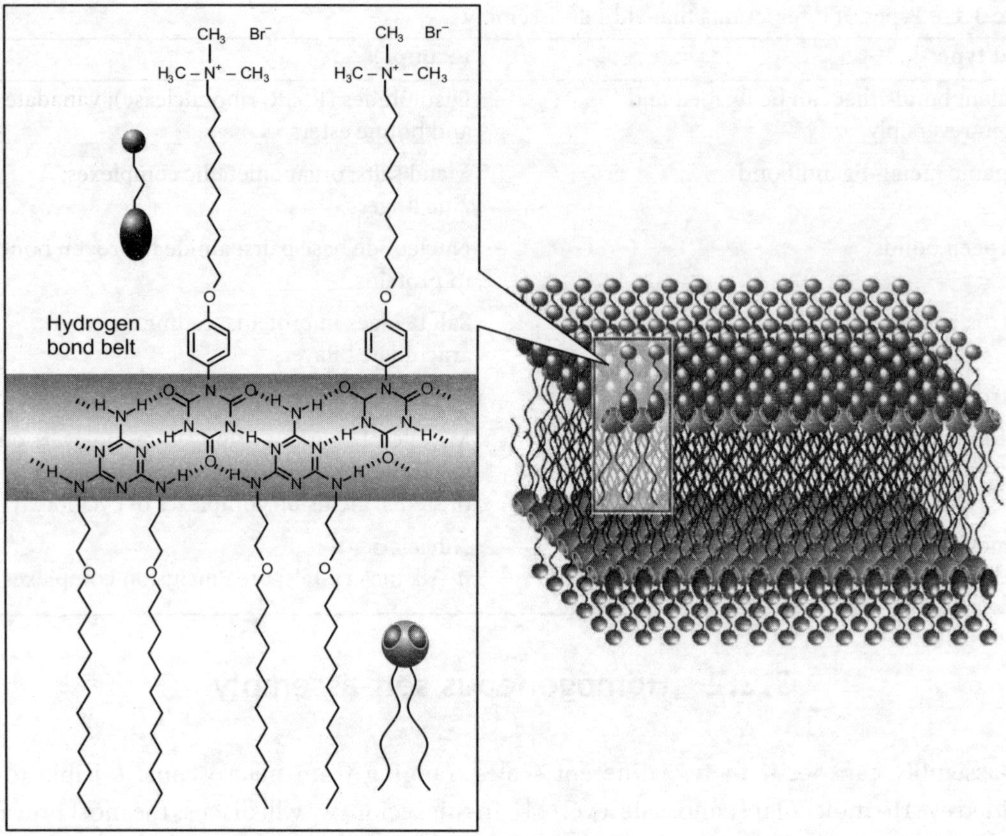

Fig. 3.4 Formation of lipid bilayer by self-assembly of lipid molecules through hydrogen bonding interactions [Reproduced from: Ariga K, Hill J P, Lee M V, Vinu A, Charvet R and Acharya S, Challenges and breakthroughs in recent research on self-assembly, *Sci. Technol. Adv. Mater.*, 9(1): 014109, 2008, under the terms of the Creative Commons Attribution-ShareAlike Licence]

nanovalves serving as gatekeepers at the entrance of cylindrical mesoporous silica to trap and release luminescent molecules [7].

3.3 SYNTHETIC PROTOCOLS AND CHALLENGES

Since molecular self-assembly by definition involves soft methods (without any energy-intensive process such as microwave, high electric and magnetic fields, high temperature, etc.), we must be careful about the choice of synthetic procedures. Although many cases of spontaneous self-organization are seen in nature, it is difficult to achieve a level of control in the laboratory using biological and geophysical systems. Hence, essentially this has to be contrasted with methods that chemists and physicists adopt in the laboratories to control self-ordered structures. Solid state physicists and electrochemists control the concentration of species to obtain self-similar structures (fractal formation). In many cases, diffusion-limited aggregation occurs under the strong driving force of the concentration gradient. In some other cases, self-assembly and self-organization are used even for structures prepared at high temperature (chemical vapour deposition, molecular beam epitaxy, etc.). We will consider methods that are either strictly under equilibrium conditions (self-assembled monolayer formation) or close to equilibrium. Organizations of structures (self- or externally-driven) which are in the metastable state are not considered here.

The following methods are commonly adopted to prepare materials using molecular self-assembly:

- Wet deposition or solvent-assisted self-assembly
- Vapour phase deposition
- Langmuir–Blodgett method
- Inverse self-assembly
- Sequential self-assembly

3.3.1 Wet deposition

The most convenient and extensively employed preparation methodology for SAMs is from a dilute solution. In a typical formation procedure, substrates are immersed in a millimolar solution of the desired molecule in a solvent such as ethanol or *n*-hexane, based on its solubility. The time of monolayer formation varies from several minutes to hours depending on the system under study. The longer incubation period generally allows the molecular film to assemble in a crystalline-like solid phase and also affords the possibility of desorption of physisorbed and chemisorbed contaminants from the gold surface into the solution, as shown in Fig. 3.5.

The substrates are taken out from the solution, washed several times with the same solvent and then dried; sometimes, annealing is conducted to get better organization. In this process, a mixture of two different thiol molecules can also be used to obtain mixed SAMs which can form domain structures. The domain sizes can be tuned simply by altering the proportion of the mixed monolayers, as shown in the case of a mixture of methyl and ester terminated thiol SAMs on Au substrates in Fig. 3.5.

3.3.2 Vapour phase deposition

Unlike the above case, where the solvent plays an important role, the preparation and characterization of SAMs in vapour phase have been reported in rare cases. For example, Crooks and coworkers prepared SAMs by passing a 10% saturated *n*-alkanethiol vapour (mixed with N_2) over Au (111) substrate for several hours at low flow rate (0.5 ml/min), and the comparison

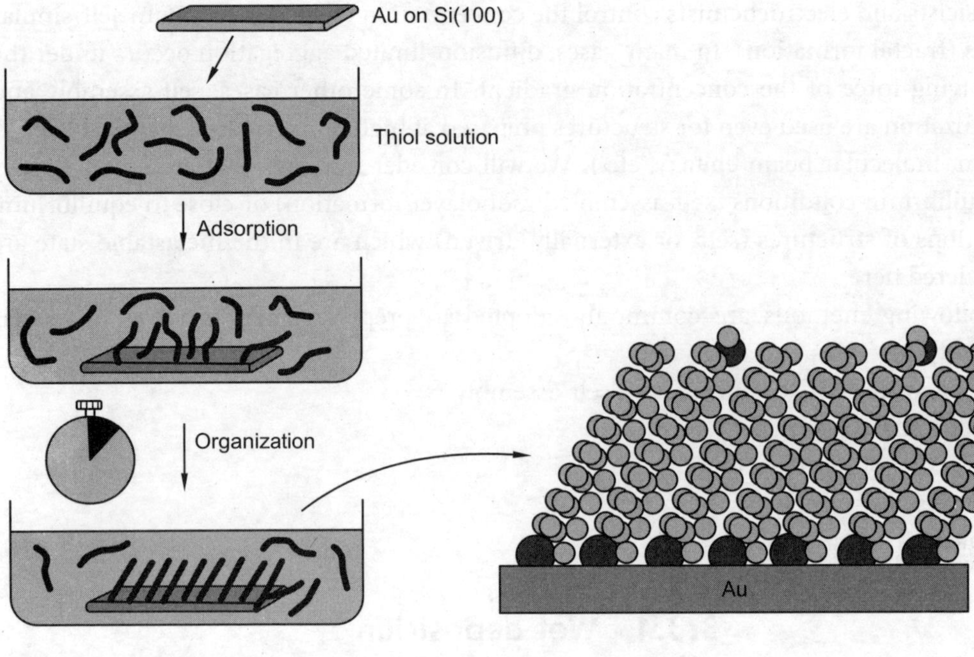

Fig. 3.5 *(see also Plate 1)* Solution-route synthesis of alkanethiol self-assembled monolayers on a smooth gold surface [Courtesy: Prof. Bo Liedberg, Linkoping University, Sweden]

with SAMs from the solution indicates similar structures and packing densities. Nevertheless, these vapour phase deposited SAMs act as poorer mass transfer barriers than those from the solution phase, especially when the molecule contains a long hydrocarbon chain.

3.3.3 Langmuir—Blodgett and Langmuir—Schaeffer techniques

Thin films of molecules on solid substrates can also be formed by forcing the monolayer floating on a liquid surface by external pressure to climb on solid support. This technique is called the Langmuir–Blodgett (LB) technique if the solid support is kept perpendicular to the subphase and Langmuir–Schaeffer technique if the solid is kept parallel to the subphase. Figure 3.6 provides a schematic representation of the principle behind the LB technique.

3.4 LIMITATIONS OF SELF-ASSEMBLY

Despite the simplicity and elegance of molecular self-assembly as a means of producing interesting monolayer or multilayer structures, they have several limitations with respect to preparing functional materials. The prominent issues are discussed below.

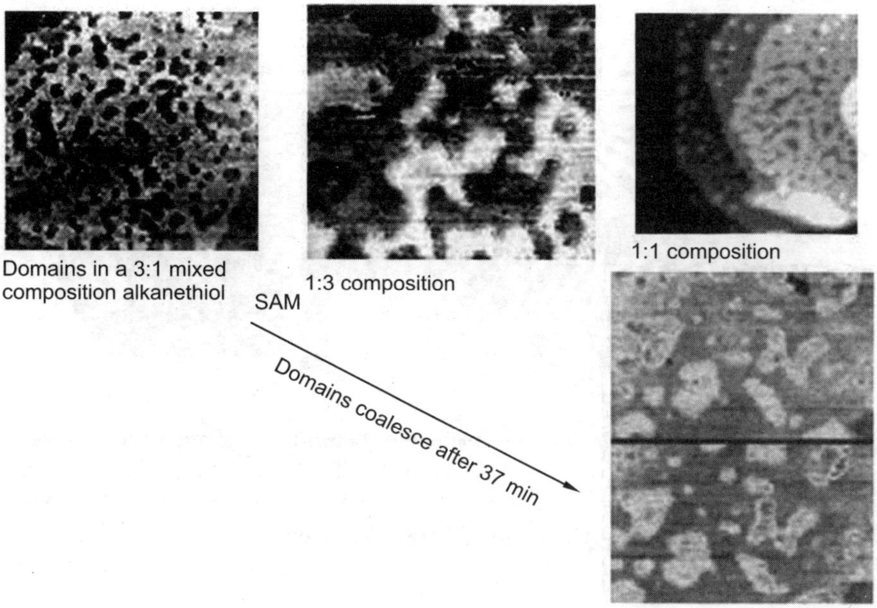

Fig. 3.6 Formation and coalescence of domains in mixed SAMs of alkanethiols with different chain lengths on a gold surface [Courtesy: Prof. Bo Liedberg, Linkoping University, Sweden]

Stability

One of the major limitations of SAMs is their poor oxidative stability. Many SAMs of long-chain thiols, even on a platform like Au (111), are not stable for more than a few days on exposure to air, and hence special precautions are needed while storing them. The stability of SAMs in general decreases from Au to Ag to Cu for long-chain thiols, amines and carboxylic acids, with the quality of the substrate playing an important role. In certain cases, the solvent used for the preparation of SAMs as well the concentration of the solution are critical.

Specificity of interactions

Another major limitation of SAMs is the high substrate–molecule selectivity since only selected substrates (metallic, semiconducting and even insulating) like Au, Ag, Cu, Pt, carbon, Si and glass could be used for preparing SAMs. Certain polymeric and amorphous materials could be functionalized (plasma, chemical treatment, etc.) to overcome this difficulty.

Other processing limitations include difficulty in scaling up for large area industrial applications, sensitivity to a number of experimental conditions and impurities limiting its reproducibility and lack of control over the kinetics of assembly (for example, multilayers are formed necessitating extensive washing and careful annealing) although some of these could be alleviated by a sequential step of SAM formation. Simple repetitive structures are formed by systems slowing down when approaching equilibrium configuration while many

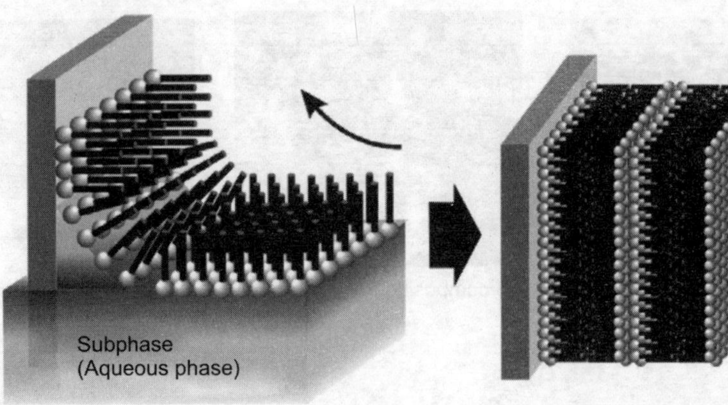

Fig. 3.7 Schematic representation of the principle behind the Langmuir–Blodgett technique [Reproduced from: Ariga K, Hill J P, Lee M V, Vinu A, Charvet R and Acharya S, Challenges and breakthroughs in recent research on self-assembly, *Sci. Technol. Adv. Mater.*, 9(1): 014109, 2008, under the terms of the Creative Commons Attribution-ShareAlike Licence]

different possibilities of complex structures are formed by dynamic systems far away from equilibrium.

3.5 APPLICATIONS OF SAMS

Since nature abounds with a variety of self-assembled structures, it is possible to look at some of them and learn the rules of rational design of self-assembled systems for many applications. Some of the selected applications are discussed here.

3.5.1 Biosensors

Specific interaction of biomolecules like proteins, enzymes and nucleic acids with certain ligands and substrates is exploited in biosensors to detect the concentration of the latter. The working principle of a biosensor involves the immobilization of biomolecules on an electrically or optically conducting substrate, which can create a signal when the biomolecule binds to its substrate in the analyte solution. The biomolecules can be immobilized or assembled on the substrate by several ways: direct physisorption, layer-by-layer assembly (Langmuir–Blodgett and Langmuir–Schaefer) or self-assembly. Among the various immobilization strategies, self-assembly prevails as the most useful method due to the ease of formation, preservation of biological activity of the molecule after assembly and stability of the films. Thus, the principal application of self-assembly is to prepare reproducible platforms for biosensing [8,9]. A simple construction of a glucose sensor is shown in Fig. 3.8.

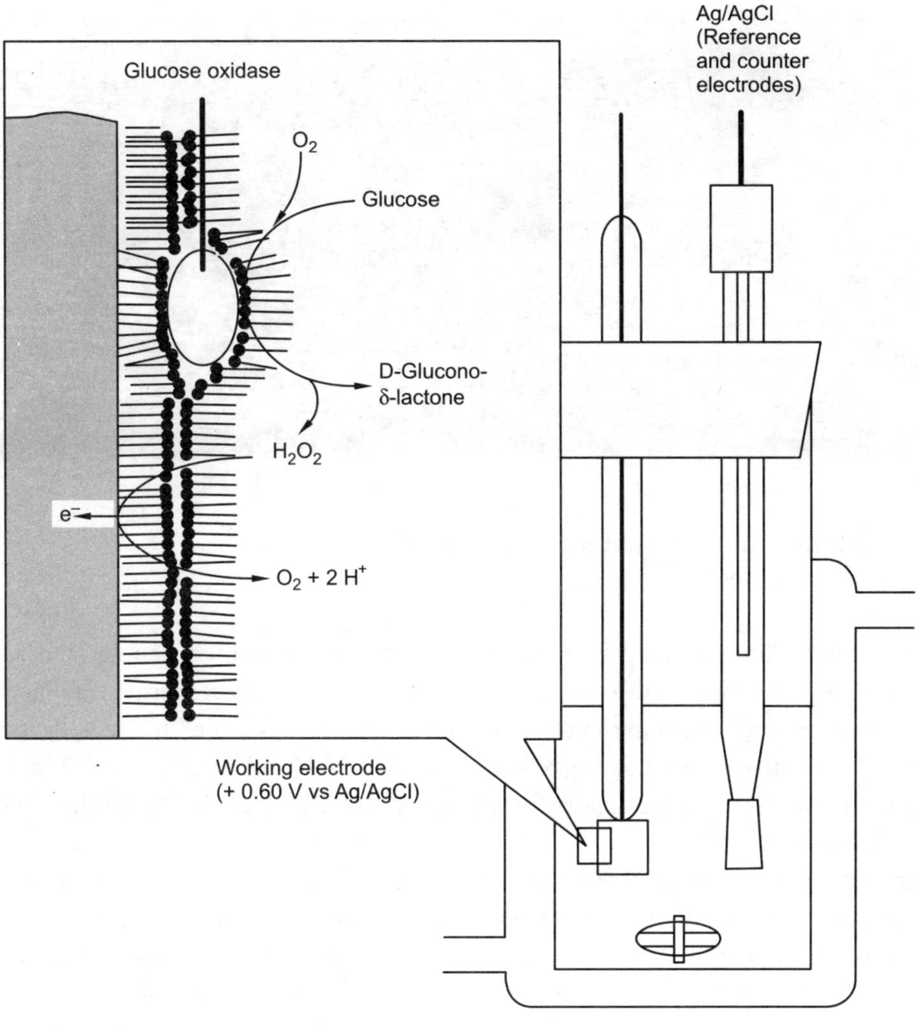

Fig. 3.8 A simple construction of a glucose sensor [Reproduced from: Ariga K, Hill J P, Lee M V, Vinu A, Charvet R and Acharya S, Challenges and breakthroughs in recent research on self-assembly, *Sci. Technol. Adv. Mater.*, 9(1): 014109, 2008, under the terms of the Creative Commons Attribution-ShareAlike Licence]

3.5.2 Microelectromechanical systems (MEMS)

This is a fast emerging technology that enables the fabrication of machines invisible to the unaided eye! Using a process called micromachining, it is now possible to assemble a whole set of machinery on a silicon chip hardly the size of a few grains. A few examples of MEMS devices are shown in Fig. 3.9. Despite their promising applications, the MEMS devices suffer

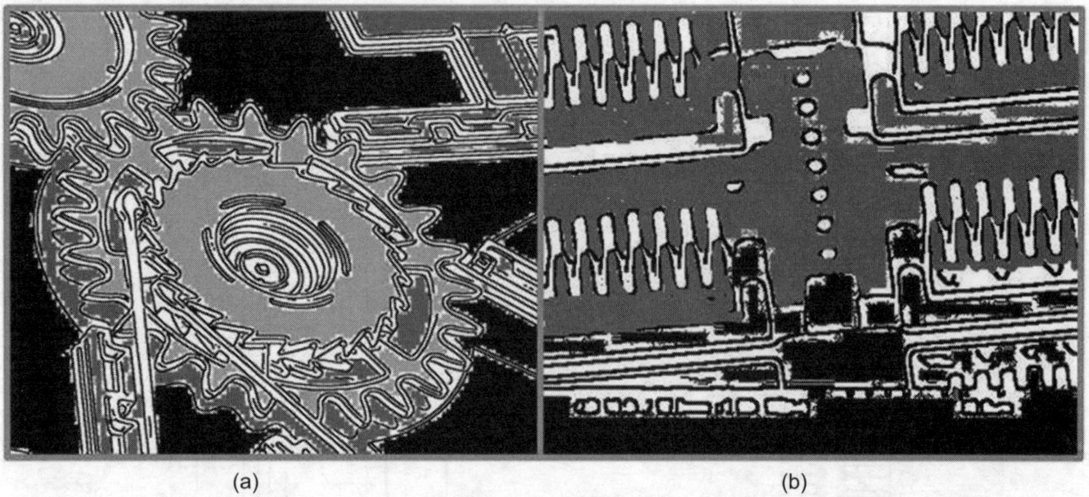

Fig. 3.9 (a) Microelectromechanical gears and (b) brush-type connectors [Courtesy: www.memx.com]

from serious limitations created by a process called 'stiction', which denotes the adhesion of microdevice components with one another due to high surface energy, capillary forces, etc. An elegant way of reducing stiction in microdevices has been to use self-assembled monolayers as 'anti-stiction coatings'. For example, SAM of octadecyl trichloro silane (a silane with a long alkyl chain) was found to convert a hydrophilic Si (100) surface to a perfectly hydrophobic surface.

Self-assembly not only helps in reducing the mechanical damage of the MEMS structures, but can also be used to assemble the components: the solder material itself can allow self-assembly of the MEMS components. In brief, the components are coated with gold at one end and allowed to come into contact with a pyrex substrate containing bumps of a self-assembling solder, viz., a bismuth alloy. In order to minimize surface energy, the gold-capped silicon components gradually assemble themselves on the solder bumps, giving rise to the electronic device.

3.5.3 Anti-reflection coatings

When light falls on a surface, part of it is reflected, while the rest is transmitted/absorbed. To improve the performance of optical devices, reflection of a part of the incident light must be minimized. For example, consider a photovoltaic device with silicon as the photoactive electrode. The performance of the device could be considerably improved by minimizing the reflectivity of the silicon surface. Periodic optical microstructures with anti-reflection properties are abundant in nature. *Have you observed the striking blue colour of the eyes of a Morpho butterfly?* This arises from the anti-reflective nature of multiple layers of cuticle and air, which act as natural photonic crystals. Similarly, there are many nocturnal insects which use arrays of non–close packed bumps of sub-300 nm size as anti-reflection coatings. Lithography is not a reliable option to fabricate these coatings because it is limited by either low resolution or small sample size, in addition to being costly. On the other hand, self-assembly serves as an elegant, cheap, high throughput alternative to lithography to fabricate periodic, anti-reflective microstructures, as shown in Fig. 3.10.

3.5.4 Molecular electronics

In an earlier section, we discussed how SAMs can improve MEMS fabrication. This section deals with yet another fascinating application of SAMs. With the help of self-assembly, it is now possible to create molecular machines, electronic components and connectors [10]. For example, Paul Weiss of Pennsylvania State University has studied the switching behaviour of the molecule oligo(phenylene ethynylene) (OPE). When OPE is attached to a self-assembled monolayer, it can adopt one of two states—one vertical and one at an angle. The molecule can conduct electricity only when it is in the vertical state, as followed by a technique called *scanning tunnelling microscopy* [11]. Many such molecular switches have been fabricated using

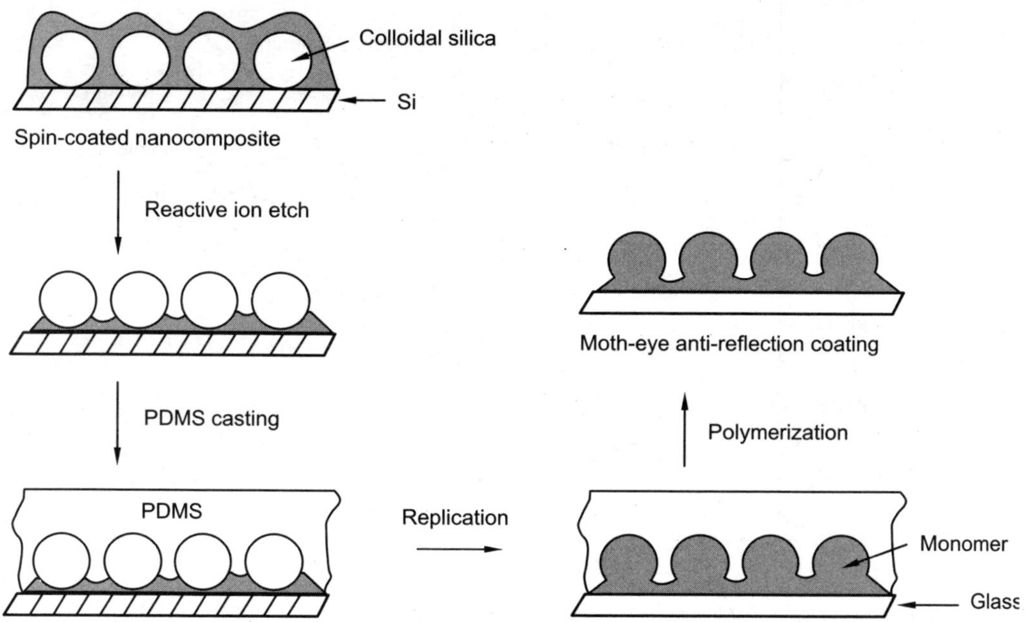

Fig. 3.10 Non–close packed arrays of silica nanoparticles, self-assembled in a matrix of poly (ethoxylated trimethylolpropane triacrylate) [Reproduced with permission from the American Institute of Physics: Linn N C, Sun C-H, Jiang P and Jiang B, Self-assembled biomimetic anti-reflection coatings, *Appl. Phys. Lett.*, 91: 101108, 2007]

molecules that can shift between two configurations at random. This field is called 'molecular computing'.

'Chemical computing' is a method in which molecules are used to create the world's densest data storage medium [12]. For example, teams of scientists in Caltech, Pasadena and University of California, Los Angeles, have made a molecular electronic device that mimics dynamic random access memory (DRAM) in today's computers. We are aware of the integrated circuits made of silicon chips. However, there is a limit to how small and how many integrated circuits can be fabricated on a silicon chip, as given by the famous Moore's law (Fig. 3.11).

The realization of storage devices of the size of a human white blood cell is expected to be attained only by 2020, using solid state components. This has now been achieved using a monolayer of two-state [2] rotaxanes sandwiched between 400 silicon and 400 titanium nanowires arranged in a cross-hatched pattern. A single bit of data can be stored at the point where silicon and titanium nanowires cross each other trapping about 100 [2] rotaxane molecules between them. This means that the complete electronic memory circuit contains 160,000 bits at a density of 10^{11} bits/cm^2. A single bit is only 15 nanometres wide or about 10,000th the diameter of human hair. By contrast, the densest memory devices currently available are approximately 140 nanometres wide.

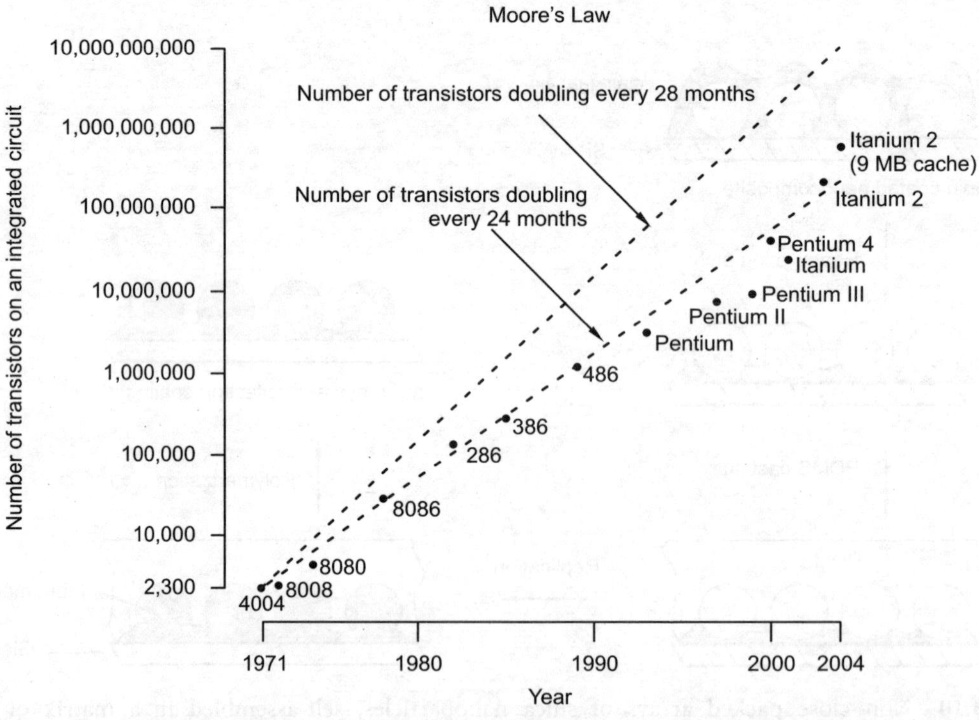

Fig. 3.11 A schematic presentation of the change in component density with respect to time, revealing Moore's law [Reproduced from: http: en.wikipedia.org/wiki/File:Transistor_Count_and_Moore%27s_Law_-_2011.svg under the terms of the GNU Free Documentation Licence]

3.5.5 Micro-patterning of nanomaterials

As the size of a material is brought down to the nanoscale, its surface energy increases. Hence nanoparticles or clusters tend to coalesce. It is the process of self-assembly that enables the synthesis of nanomaterials in the solution state stabilized by appropriate capping molecules. The advantage of self-assembly for the synthesis of nanoparticles has been extended further to aid the two- and three-dimensional organization of pre-formed nanoparticles. Such effective organizations are normally achieved by using bifunctional molecules as capping agents (Fig. 3.12).

3.5.6 Tissue engineering and drug delivery

Self-assembly has gone far beyond the horizon of our imagination and is now applied in tissue and organ engineering. A patient undergoing external dialysis could soon receive a new kidney made in the laboratory from his or her own cells, instead of waiting for a donor organ which their immune system may reject! This is the level of challenge faced in tissue engineering. When biotechnologists failed to replicate the structural complexity of living tissues, self-assembly researchers showed that complex tissues can be built bottom-up by creating what they call living Legos. These are nothing but biocompatible gels of various shapes studded with cells, which can self-assemble into complex structures similar to those found in living systems (Fig. 3.13). Another interesting outcome of self-assembly is the facility of drug delivery (Fig. 3.14).

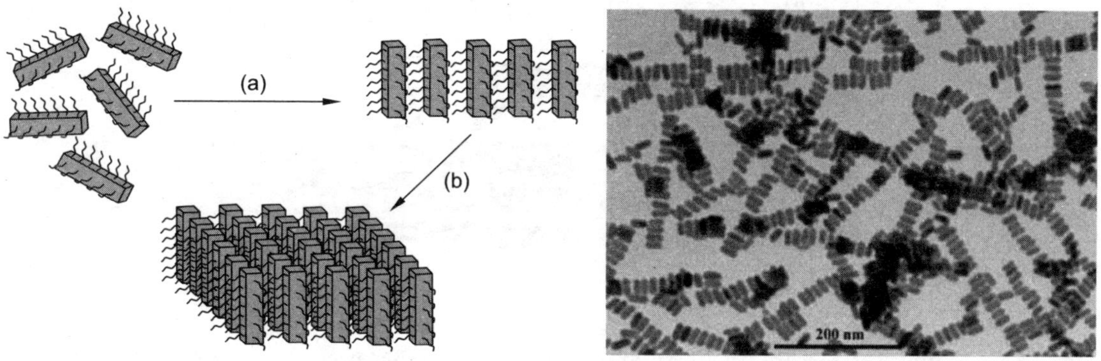

Fig. 3.12 (a) Mesoscale assembly of crystalline hybrid nanoparticles through face-specific adsorption of organic molecules and (b) Higher order assembly resulting in a 2D superstructure formation; TEM image showing ordered chains of prismatic $BaCrO_4$ nanoparticles prepared in a microemulsion [Reproduced with permission from Wiley-VCH Verlag GmbH & Co. KGaA: Cofen H and Mann S, Higher order organization by mesoscale self-assembly and transformation of hybrid nanostructures, *Angew. Chem. Int. Ed.*, 42(21): 2350, 2003]

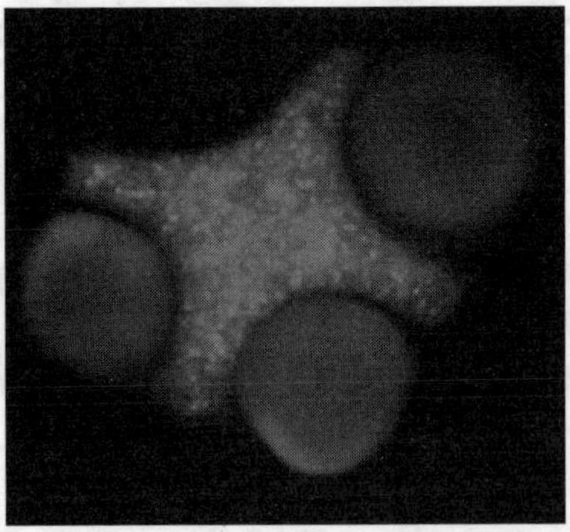

Fig. 3.13 *(see also Plate 2)* Living Legos: Polymer building blocks studded with cells, self-assemble into structures whose complexity mimics that of human tissues. The cross-shaped gel contains cells stained green; rod-shaped gels which are about 200 microns across contain cells stained red [Reproduced with permission from the National Academy of Sciences, USA: Du Y, Lo E, Ali S and Khademhosseini A, Directed assembly of cell-laden microgels for fabrication of 3D tissue constructs, *Proc. Natl. Acad. Sci.*, 105(28): 9522, 2008]

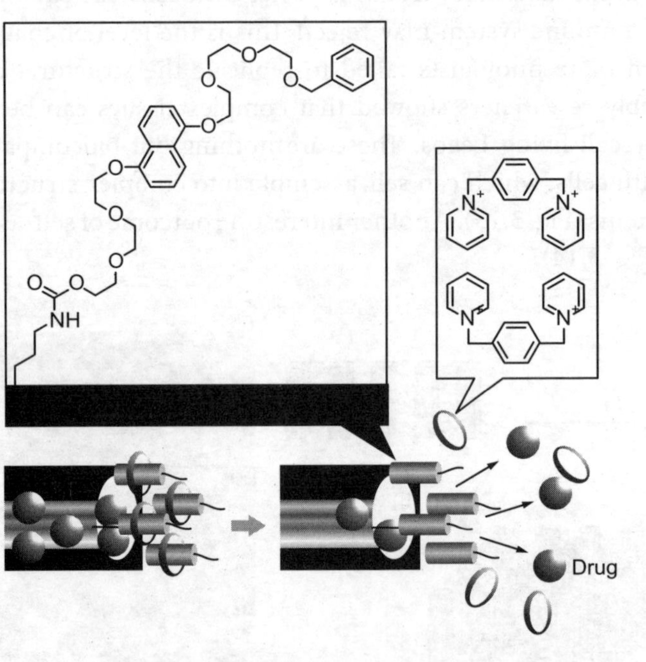

Fig. 3.14 Nanovalves for drug delivery are created by tethering pseudorotaxanes at the entrance of cylindrical pores of mesoporous silica filled with drug molecules. Here, a molecule of 1, 5-dioxynaphthalene derivative acts as a gate post and the pseudorotaxane acts as the gatekeeper which releases the drug molecules off the pores when treated with a reducing agent $NaCNBH_3$ [Reproduced from: Ariga K, Hill J P, Lee M V, Vinu A, Charvet R and Acharya S, Challenges and breakthroughs in recent research on self-assembly, *Sci. Technol. Adv. Mater.*, 9(1): 014109, 2008, under the terms of the Creative Commons Attribution-ShareAlike Licence]

3.6 CONCLUSIONS

Self-assembly is a powerful approach to organize molecules, atoms and supramolecular systems to achieve certain useful functions. The mere presence of a monolayer self-assembled on a metallic surface like gold can make it insulating. Similarly, a hydrophilic silicon surface on a super-hydrophobic non-wetting surface can be achieved by self-assembly. Many of the properties of the material could be manipulated by self-assembly, and bifunctional molecules ensure a layer-by-layer approach to create many multi-functional materials. One of the unique advantages of self-assembly is in tuning electrostatic, covalent and van der Waals interactions using these molecules. Self-assembly with multiple points of contact produces more stable structures. In some cases, rigid spacers can be placed in between self-assembled systems and molecular level corrugation can also be obtained by mixed self-assembled monolayers.

Further reading

[1] Whitesides G M and Grzybowski B, Self assembly at all scales, *Science*, 295: 2418, 2002.

[2] Thomas W J O, Ratajczak H and Rao C N R, *Topics in Molecular Interactions*, Elsevier, Amsterdam, 1985.

[3] Benkovic SJ and Schiffer SH, A Perspective on enzyme catalysis, *Science*, 301: 1196, 2003.

[4] Ariga K, Hill J P, Lee M V, Vinu A, Carvet R and Acharya S, Challenges and breakthroughs in recent research on self-assembly, *Sci. Technol. Adv. Mater.*, 9: 014109, 2008.

[5] Fujita M, Tominaga M, Hori A and Therrien B, Coordination assemblies from a Pd(II)-Cornered square complex, *Acc. Chem. Res.*, 38: 369, 2005.

[6] Rogez G, Ribera B F, Credi A, Ballardini R, Gandolfi M T, Balzani V, Liu Y, Northrop B H and Stoddart J F, *J. Am. Chem. Soc.*, 129: 4633, 2007.

[7] Nguyen T D, Liu Y, Saha S, Leung K C-F, Stoddart J F and Zink J I, Design and optimization of molecular nanovalues-based on redox-switchable bistable rotaxanes. *J. Am. Chem. Soc.*, 129: 627, 2007.

[8] Chaki N and Vijayamohanan K, Self-assembled monolayers as a tunable platform for biosensor applications, *Biosens. Bioelectron.*, 17: 1, 2002.

[9] Wink T H, van Zuilen S J, Bult A and Bennekom W P, Self-assembled monolayers for biosensors, *Analyst*, 122: 43R, 1997.

[10] Reed M A, Zhou C, Muller C J, Burgin T P and Tour J M, Conductance of a molecular junction, *Science*, 278: 252, 1997.

[11] Evans J, Chemists switch over to molecular computing, *Chemisry World*, 28 November 2005.

[12] Milgrom L, Chemical computing creates world's densest data storage medium, *Chemistry World*, 24 January 2007.

EXERCISES

1. Using the concepts of self-assembly, explain why some proteins are lipophilic while others are hydrophilic.

2. Explain base-pairing in DNA and RNA molecules.
3. While a double-stranded DNA molecule can be easily denatured by heating, the secondary structure (i.e., folding) of a protein requires special chemical treatment. Explain in the light of the energetics of self-assembly. Also explain the reversibility of these processes.
4. Illustrate the term self-organization with examples. Is there any difference between self-assembly and self-organization?
5. Define molecular self-assembly, mentioning its thermodynamic prerequisites.
6. Distinguish between directed assembly and self-assembly using suitable examples.
7. What are MEMS and NEMS? Why are they important? How does a SAM on silicon help in the fabrication of MEMS?
8. Explain the advantages of making a biosensor using self-assembled monolayers.
9. How is the concept of self-assembly useful in molecular electronics?
10. Why does a long-chain thiol form a self-assembled monolayer on an Au or Ag surface?
11. Compare and contrast the preparation of molecular films for electronic applications by SAM and LB films as two separate techniques.

4

Bioinspired Materials

This chapter provides an insight into bioinspired (bioid) materials and processes from a functional perspective, illustrating many surprises in materials of biological origin, perhaps due to the slow pace of evolutionary engineering. Precise organization over a large length-scale and structural hierarchy yielding unusual physicochemical properties are highlighted using selected examples. The chapter then introduces the art of biomimicry with interesting case studies. Finally, the discussion spills over into other interesting research themes, including 'bionics' and biomineralization, to identify the plethora of opportunities for chemists to make an impact on information technologies by bioinspiration.

LEARNING OBJECTIVES

- To define bioid materials and understand the related terms 'biomimetics' and 'bionics'
- To understand natural processes in biological organisms with relevance to materials science in general and hybrid composites in particular
- To define biomineralization and see how minerals prepared in the laboratory differ from similar minerals prepared by living organisms
- To illustrate the concept of synthesizing hierarchical structures and functionally graded materials based on similar natural materials
- To list the advantages and disadvantages of synthesis inspired by biomaterials
- To analyze natural composites like bone and cartilage in terms of design of materials and microstructure generating extraordinary multi-functional properties
- To explain the super-hydrophobic and self-cleaning behaviour of surfaces similar to the lotus leaf and to learn how to make artificial super-hydrophobic surfaces after a study of natural systems

Have you ever wondered how pine cones open up after falling off the tree, or how a shark with its massive body swims effortlessly in water at a speed of about 60 miles an hour, or how a wet penguin survives temperatures of –20°C immediately after leaping out of the water? There are many such secrets in nature, far beyond our imagination! The quest for an understanding of such intricacies and attempts to reproduce them in the laboratory has opened up an interesting area of materials science, called 'bioid materials' (abbreviated as bioid materials).

There are two excellent examples of bioinspiration in the textile industry. One is a fabric design inspired by pine cones, which has small flaps that open up when you start sweating and closes when your skin returns to its normal humidity. The other is a super-fast swimsuit with features similar to that of shark skin to reduce drag and win you a gold medal in the Olympics!

The objective of this chapter is to take the reader on a safari into the world of bioid materials. We do not promise to provide a comprehensive review of the whole field. Instead, we do ensure that after expediting through this chapter, your mind will not fail to grasp inspiration from the biological systems around you!

4.1 INTRODUCTION

Novel functional materials can be developed in two broad ways: one is an intuitive design based on logic and scientific reasoning and the other involves lessons from nature [1–3]. Natural systems have evolved with increased levels of organization (molecular tectonics, for example) and complicated mechanisms to achieve maximum efficiency, shorter response time and reversibility. Many materials found in nature reveal amazing combinations of properties that are normally not seen in artificially prepared materials; this could be the consequence of their struggle for survival among more competent living organisms along the evolutionary trail. If we categorize biological systems on the basis of their level of smartness, we can immediatly make out that those at the lower end of the food chain have the most intricate mechanisms to protect themselves from predators. For instance, a lion or a tiger need not change its colour and shape as there is hardly any need to protect themselves from more ferocious animals. So, the art of creating bioid materials is exactly the art of learning big things from small creatures!

4.1.1 What are bioid materials?

The term 'bioid materials', has been used in different contexts by different authors. The most common context is *materials prepared by exploiting biological interactions or naturally available biological molecules* [2–4]. For example, if you mix, say, a batch of nanoparticles capped with single-stranded DNA molecules with another batch of nanoparticles capped with DNA molecules with a base sequence complementary to that of the former batch, there is a possibility of the nanoparticles getting organized due to the hybridization of the single DNA strands to form duplexes, as shown in Fig. 4.1. The assembly can then be called a 'bioid assembly'. This property of DNA molecules has also been used to assist the self-assembly of gold nanorods with remarkable consequences [5].

Another related term is 'biomimetic materials', which could be defined as materials similar in structure/function to biological systems, which essentially means chemistry at a higher level of organization and dynamics. The approach is to observe natural processes and mimic them in an artificial environment. The definition is not very sharp and often overlaps with the earlier definition of bioid materials, which are used interchangeably. On the other hand, there is a class of materials called 'biomaterials', which are nothing but materials designed for biological applications [2]. For example, there are polymeric materials (e.g., polyglycolic acid) which can support bone cell and tissue growth and assist bone regeneration. The bioid materials discussed in this chapter mean something more and stand apart from all the existing classes of biomaterials, often used in medicine textbooks. We use the definition *'Bioid materials are materials which can perform biological functions with the level of organization and dynamics (smartness) inherent in natural systems; it is not just* ***mimicry*** *of biological systems; instead, it is all about* ***inspiration*** *drawn from exotic natural phenomena!'*

Many of these materials are endowed with special features:

- Frequent use of molecular (organo–inorganic) constituents—supramolecular tectonics to make hybrid materials of diverse properties in identical units

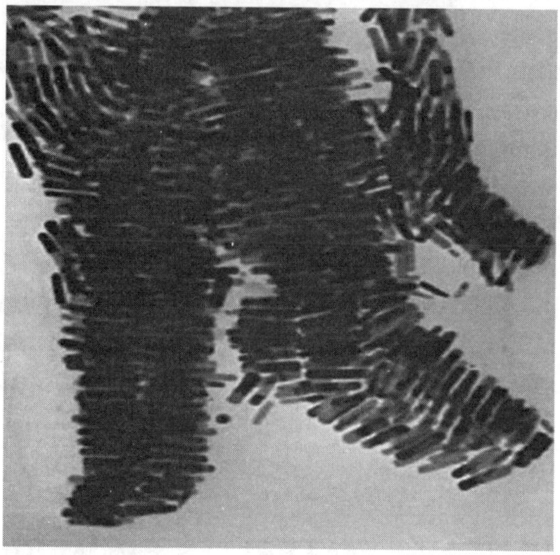

Fig. 4.1 TEM image of large bioinspired self-assembled aggregates of aligned gold nanorods formed by interparticle duplex linkages using surface-attached complementary 21-base pair oligonucleotides [Reprinted with permission from the Royal Society of Chemistry: Dujardin E, Mann S, Hsin L-B and Wang CRC, *Chem. Commun.*, 14: 1264, 2001]

- Ability for self-diagnosis and self-repair based on environmental changes
- Precise shape and orientation control, often by protein mediation of structural motives
- Stimuli-sensitive, variable properties like fatigue resistance and resilience
- Interfacial composition tuning using hard and soft materials for durability
- Sensitivity and critical dependence on the presence of water
- Precise spatial and functional hierarchical control, often using mediators

Many of these characteristic features are abundant in natural materials, with various levels of perfection contributing to the extraordinary combination of properties, as illustrated by auricular cartilage and bone which display interesting changes in length scales and composition for flexibility and toughness (functional hierarchy). For example, hollow, laminated rods of collagen and calcium in the bone handle both compressive and bending forces, but cancellous and spongy ends provide more elastic properties. Engineering analysis of many of these natural structures with the help of computer modelling and simulation has given powerful insights, enabling scientists to incorporate many of the above characteristics in their design [3].

4.2 CLASSIFICATION OF BIOID MATERIALS

How do we classify bioid materials? Can it be done on the basis of the type of organism, or their functions, molecular interactions or their response times?

Unlike the classes of materials discussed in other chapters, the classification of bioid materials appears to be very complicated. One simple scheme of classification is based on their applications:

- Stimuli-sensitive materials
- Super-hydrophobic materials
- Super-adhesive materials
- Super-hard and lubricating materials
- Low-drag materials
- Camouflage materials

There are several other classifications based on different parameters including their mechanical nature (soft, hard and hybrid), chemical composition (molecular, organic, inorganic, polymeric, organo–inorganic, etc.), and electrical and optical properties, However, for convenience, we have adopted a classification based on their functions, which is intimately linked with their chemical nature.

4.3 FUNCTIONAL MATERIALS FROM BIOMIMICRY

It is almost impossible to replace the biosynthetic pathways of living organisms with laboratory analogues in the duplication of hierarchical materials with all the subtle morphological and microstructural details. Hence, many materials chemists use a hybrid approach of preparing synthetic, but biocompatible, matrices like polylactic acid or copolymers of glycolic and lactic acid to prepare artificial grafts for skin, blood vessels, muscles, etc. [1]. In this section, we will introduce specific examples and illustrations for each of the above classes of bioid materials. In other words, we will see how functional materials can be designed from biomimicry, enabling a more efficient multi-functional performance.

4.4.1 Stimuli-responsive materials

The ultimate goal of biomimetic research is the development of materials that can respond to sensory needs like touch (tactile response), in which materials really come alive! There can be different degrees of tactile stimuli, based on intent. Imagine that your chair shapes itself into a bed realizing what is in your mind, based on the pressure exerted by your body, indicating that you are done for the day! How would it be if the material of your bicycle hardens only when you touch it, and otherwise remains flexible like a soft toy that can be carried in the school bag instead of being left in the parking lot! There is plenty of room for imagination in the world of bioid materials, many of which can lead to interactive smart systems rivalling concepts seen in science fiction movies.

Many systems in nature are touch-sensitive; the touch-me-not plant and electric eel are common examples. Recently, scientists at Case Western Reserve University designed a polymer that can switch its rheology instantaneously, inspired by an aquatic species called the sea cucumber. What is so special about the sea cucumber? It has the amazing ability to flatten itself to slip through minute crevices, and to transform instantaneously into a hard and rigid creature to defend itself against predators! How does this happen? The skin of a sea cucumber is made up of an ultrafine network of cellulose 'whiskers', which when encountered by a predator stick together with the help of some molecules released by the surrounding cells, making it hard and rigid (viscosity regulation). A team of researchers isolated stiff cellulose fibres from the skin of tunicates—creatures with skin similar to that of sea cucumbers—and combined them with a rubbery polymer mixture (Bingham plastic) to create a rigid material, which could soften in the presence of water and harden as the solvent evaporates [6]. By replacing rigid metallic electrodes implanted in the human body with flexible stretchable polymeric electrodes, the risk of tissue damage is reduced. In the above example, the rigidity of the material changes with external stimulus; other properties commonly observed in biological systems, that respond quickly to external stimuli, include size, shape (as in the case of a touch-me-not plant) and electrical conductivity (as in the case of an electric eel).

In a similar manner, an American scientist, who experienced problems due to excessive perspiration and discomfort in summer, was inspired by the functioning of a pine cone. A pine cone unfolds after falling from the tree to eject its seeds. When he explored the mechanism behind this, this led to the development of a new type of smart fabric. How does it work? Pine cones are firm and closed when they are attached to the tree; as they ripen, they fall from the tree to release the seeds. The scales of the cone consist of layers of two materials with different thermal coefficients of expansion. When the cones dry out and the humidity reduces, one layer expands more than the other, allowing the seeds to be released. Inspired by this mechanism, researchers designed a smart fabric with small flaps made of layers of two different materials, which open outwards when the body temperature rises and humidity increases as one starts sweating. Fortunately, the process is highly reversible; the flaps close when the body returns to the normal temperature [7]. The same principle can be used to design fabrics that change their shape based on body temperature.

4.4.2 Super-hydrophobic materials

Most of us become 'hydrophobic', that is, 'afraid of water', in winter. How much are you afraid of water? If you are just mildly afraid you will be categorized as 'hydrophobic'; if you are extremely afraid, then you are 'super-hydrophobic' in which case, you would never want to take a bath at all! This is true for certain materials too and they are called super-hydrophobic materials.

The wettability of a material is described quantitatively by a parameter called *contact angle,* defined as 'the angle at the interface of a solid and a liquid'. This is the key factor that decides how effective a detergent is in cleaning soiled clothes. This is again the factor that ensures that the mercury droplet in a thermometer rolls without wetting the glass walls. Figure 4.2 offers a depiction of the principle of wetting and contact angle.

Surfaces with a water contact angle above 150° have excellent water repulsion properties and those with contact angle less than 20° (ideal limits are 180° and 0°) are extremely hydrophilic. What is the key factor deciding the wettability of a material? Is it the roughness at the molecular

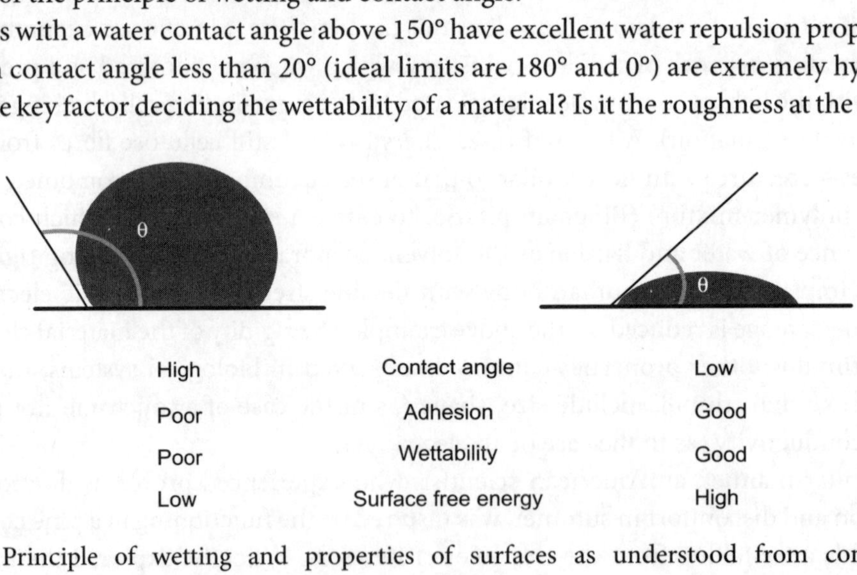

Fig. 4.2 Principle of wetting and properties of surfaces as understood from contact angle measurements

level or chemistry of the specific functional groups? Nature offers excellent roadmaps to tune the wettability of a material which has just been synthesized in a test tube. Let us begin with the classical example of lotus leaves. Most of us would have played with it in our childhood by rocking a water droplet on its surface. But you may not have been aware of its relevance or reason for inspiring materials scientists to make materials which can ease the toil in cleaning wet floors and toilets. Lotus leaves have not only inspired materials but have also resulted in concrete 'systems', which will be discussed in the next chapter on smart materials.

What makes a lotus leaf super-hydrophobic? The surface of the leaf looks perfectly smooth to the unaided eye, but it actually consists of an arrangement of corrugations in the micro and nanoscales that can trap air in their crevices, rendering the surface super-hydrophobic. Figure 4.3 shows the SEM images of the surface of a lotus leaf and compares it with an artificial super-hydrophobic coating with a similar microstructure.

Other examples of super-hydrophobic natural materials are ducks' wings and the water strider. *Like water off a duck's back* is a famous idiom. Earlier it was believed that there is a waxy coating on the wings of ducks that prevents them from getting wet. Recently it was realized that the presence of microstructures that can trap air makes them hydrophobic and that there is no such artificial coating.

The effect of surface roughness on wettability was quantified by Cassie and Baxter [8], as described by the following expression. The effective contact angle of a liquid on a composite surface is given by,

$$\cos \theta_c = \gamma_1 \cos \theta_1 + \gamma_2 \cos \theta_2$$

where, θ_1 and θ_2 are the contact angles of components 1 and 2 with real fractions, γ_1 and γ_2, respectively. Interestingly, when one of the components is air, which has a contact angle of 180°, the expression becomes,

$$\cos \theta_c = \gamma_1 (\cos \theta_1 + 1) - 1$$

Thus, with a smaller γ_1 and larger θ_1, it is possible to get very high contact angles, that is, super-hydrophobic surfaces. Accordingly, surfaces with water contact angles greater than 150° and lower than 20° are described by many as super-hydrophobic and super-hydrophilic, respectively, although other diagnostic criteria such as hysteresis and low rolling angle are also important to describe the extent of hydrophobicity. The hierarchical surface structures in lotus leaves and other leaves prevent dirt and even bacteria from adhering to them.

Super-hydrophobicity or 'lotus leaf effect' has attracted tremendous attention due to its wide applications related to the development of water-repellent and stainless coatings, self-cleaning and anti-fouling surface design and lab-on-a-chip devices. In many of these applications, it is of immense importance to externally control the interaction of liquids with a super-hydrophobic surface, including the modification of contact angle, droplet mobility and degree of penetration of liquid [9].

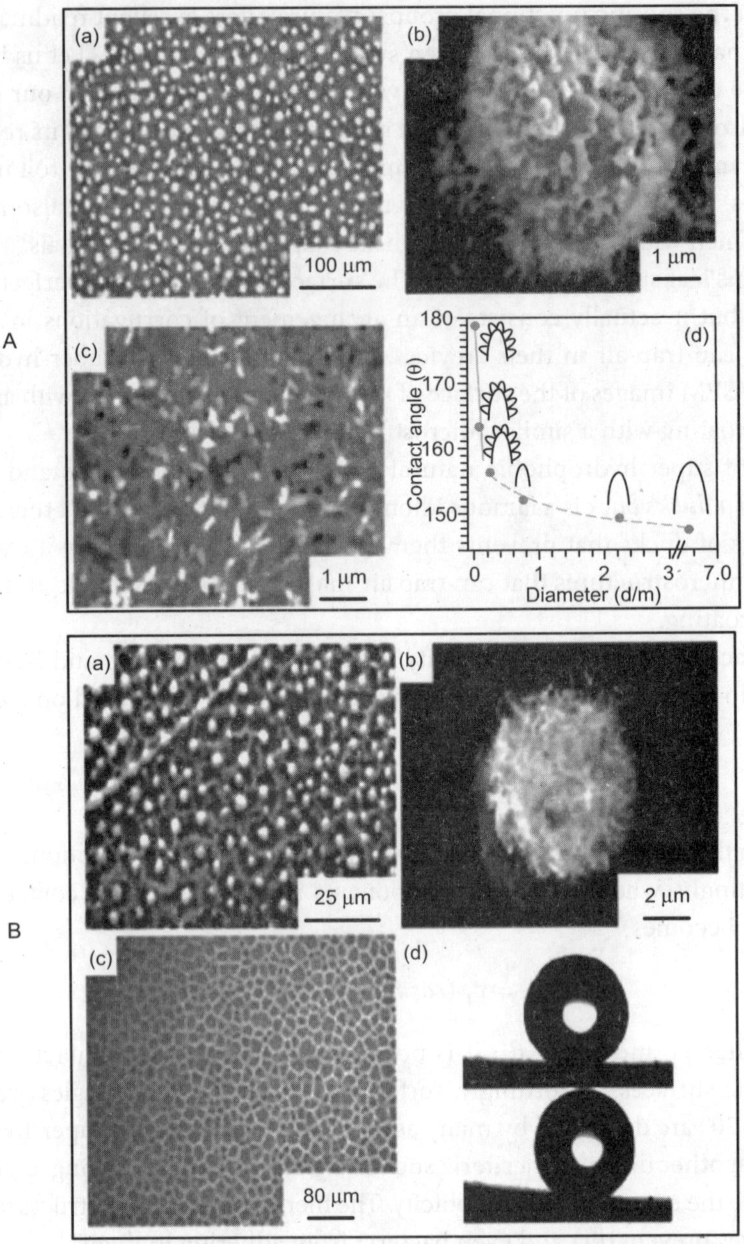

Fig. 4.3 *(see also Plate 2)* A: SEM image of a lotus leaf surface; (a) every epidermal cell forms a papilla with a dense layer of epicuticular waxes; (b) SEM image of a single papilla; (c) SEM image of the lower surface of a lotus leaf; (d) calculated contact angle versus the size of papilla. B: SEM images of lotus-like polymer film: (a) network of papilla; (b) single papilla; (c) large area honeycomb structure and (d) rolling of water droplet on the surface of the lotus leaf–inspired polymer film [Reprinted with permission from John Wiley & Sons: Feng L, Li S, Li H, Zhang L, Zhai J, Song Y, Liu B, Jiang L and Zhu D, Super-hydrophobic surfaces: From natural to artificial, *Adv. Mater.*, 14(24): 1857, 2002]

Water strider

Fig. 4.4 *(see also Plate 3)* A water strider walking on water [Reproduced from http://en.wikipedia.org/wiki/File:Water_strider_-_strider_surface_tension.jpg under the terms of the GNU Free Documentation Licence]

Have you noticed a water strider gracefully skipping on the surface of water like an Olympic skater? Yes, this insect can pack about 15 times its weight and remain afloat! Earlier, this was thought to be due to the presence of a waxy layer on the insect's legs, which along with surface tension keeps it afloat. Later in 2004, it was discovered that the insect's legs are made up of microscopic hairs that can trap tiny air bubbles, which in turn make them super-hydrophobic. This could help the design of water-resistant textiles and small aquatic devices with reduced drag and fast propulsion properties.

Why are we interested in super-hydrophobic materials? Because they can make it possible for us to enjoy rains without getting wet and winter without the accumulation of fog on our car windows and spectacles, and get rid of dirt with just a gentle tap instead of scrubbing with corrosive detergents. Surprisingly, it is now possible to control the wettability of a surface with an electric switch; this emerging research area is known as 'electro-wetting' [6]. Plenty of applications use a range of super-hydrophobic materials that will make life easier and spare us the time to do more fruitful and enjoyable things.

Nevertheless, there are certain limitations in commercializing these super-hydrophobic materials: functional fatigue with time, lack of reversibility in electro-wetting materials, scale-up issues, slower response that limits switching applications. New super-hydrophobic surfaces are being developed with a view to overcome some of these limitations.

4.4.3 Super-adhesive materials

Next in the line-up of bioid materials are those with interesting adhesive properties, mimicking the efficiency observed in biological systems. Have you ever wondered at the elegance with which a gecko climbs up a steep surface without slipping? Or how burrs cling to your pet's skin? Nature knows the trick of exploiting simple forces to hold bulky creatures. A number of creatures, including insects, spiders and lizards, have the unique ability to cling and detach easily from steep surfaces. Although the morphologies of their feet are quite different, all of them have in common, hierarchically arranged hairy structures called 'setae'. The higher the body mass of the animals, the more minute are the setae, as illustrated in Fig. 4.5.

The gecko has a complicated hierarchical structure in its feet. It begins with soft ridges called lamellae, 1–2 mm in length located on the toes, containing hairs (setae) 30–130 μm long and 5–10 μm wide, which spread into several branches (spatulae) of length, width and

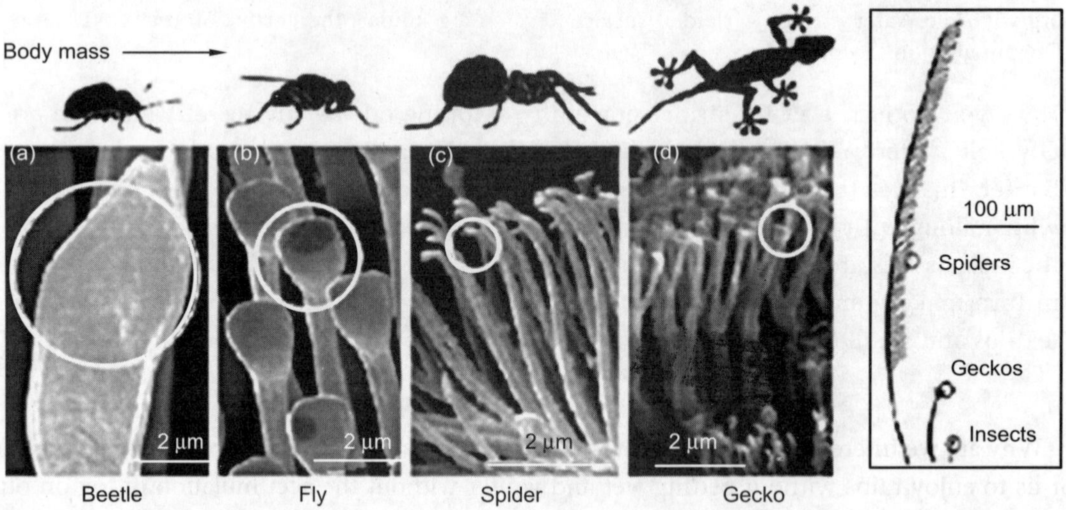

Fig. 4.5 Scaling of the microstructure of the hairy attachment pads of a beetle, fly, spider and gecko [Reprinted with permission from Arzt E, Garb S and Spolenak R, From micro to nano contacts in biological attachment devices, *Proc. Nat. Acad. Sci.*, 100(19): 10603–606; 2003]

thickness—500 nm, 200 nm and 10 nm, respectively, as shown in Fig. 4.6. The setae are made of β-keratin that has a tensile strength of 20 GPa and the spatulae are oriented at an angle with respect to the contacting surface to allow them to hang and peel off easily.

The clinging ability of a gecko can be understood from the vertical force required to pull it down from a nearly vertical surface. A force of 20 N has to be applied to pull down a lizard, which hardly weighs a few grams, from a vertical surface; it is roughly equal to the force required to pull a 5-kg bag across a floor with a frictional coefficient of 0.3! The excellent adhesion of gecko feet increases the coefficient of friction to almost unity, which makes it difficult to pull down a lizard sticking to a surface. Thanks to this knowledge, just 1 m^2 of a super-sticky material called 'Gecko tape', inspired by gecko feet, can hold the weight of an average family car!

Fig. 4.6 (a) A gecko looking top down (left) and bottom up (right); (b–e) Hierarchical structures of a gecko foot at different scales [Reprinted with permission from Elsevier: Gao H, Wang X, Yao H, Garb S and Arzt E, Mechanics of hierarchical adhesion structures of geckos in *Mechanics of Materials*, Elsevier, 2005]

Another major breakthrough is the design of Velcro, based on the clinging mechanism of burrs to animal fur. One day, the inventor of Velcro, George Mestral, found his dog in big trouble with the burrs that were clinging to its fur [10]. When he examined the burrs under a microscope, he found that they consist of a number of hook-like structures which latched on to the soft fur of his dog. This led to the invention of Velcro, a very popular adhesive tape used everywhere now!

4.4.4 Super-hard materials

Super-adhesive and non-wetting behaviour are not the only interesting properties prevalent in natural systems; many materials are known for their hardness. For example, spider silk is five times stronger than a high-grade steel of the same diameter, and its toughness is equal to some of the toughest known materials such as Kevlar, an aromatic polyamide fibre. Kevlar is synthesized at high temperatures and corrosive environments and, once prepared, it is difficult to dispose due to its non-biodegradability. A spider, however, has a far better machinery that can function at room temperature and ambient conditions to produce a material that has excellent mechanical strength and is biodegradabe as well! The dragline silk of the golden orb-weaving spider is the most studied. It is a natural polypeptide of the scleroprotein group encompassing collagen (found in ligaments) and keratin (found in nails and hair). The composition, however, differs with the type of spider species and its diet, the major amino acids being glycine (42%) and alanine (25%). The same species can weave silks of different strengths, depending on whether it is meant for trapping prey or for supporting the eggs.

In general, the elasticity of spider silk is due to its glycine-rich regions where a sequence of five amino acids is continuously repeated. For example, Capture silk—the most elastic spider silk—has 43 such repeating blocks and can be stretched 2–4 times its original length (> 200%), while Dragline silk with nine repeating blocks can be stretched only to about 30% of its original length.

This composition exists as a liquid crystalline fluid until it reaches the spinnerets of the glands, as shown in Fig. 4.7. While passing through the narrow tubes, the protein molecules align and partially crystallize parallel to the fibre axis through a self-assembly mechanism where the polyalanine regions link together via hydrogen bonds to form pleated β-sheets (highly ordered crystalline regions). These β-sheets act as cross-links between the protein molecules and impart high tensile strength to the silk with promising applications ranging from seat belts to parachutes.

The unique features of spider silk are:

- High tensile strength (1.6 GPa)
- Light weight
- Eight times more extensible than Kevlar

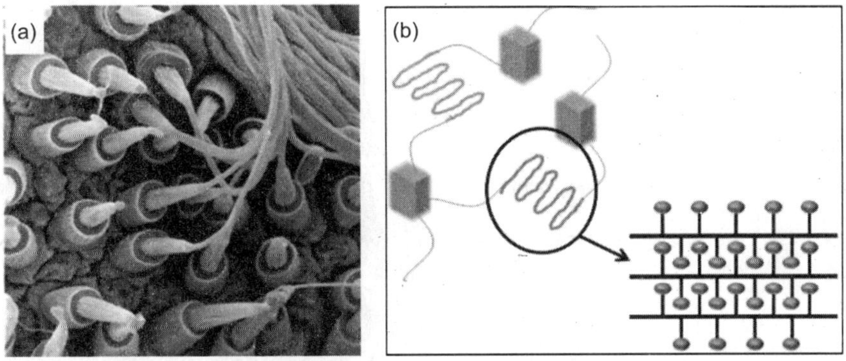

Fig. 4.7 (a) Generation of spider silk from fluids propelled from the ducts of a spider [Figure Courtesy: Tina Carvalho/Microangela]; (b) β-pleated sheets and glycine-rich crystalline regions in spider silk

- Five times tougher than Kevlar
- Biodegradability
- Biocompatibility

Surprisingly, the combination of strength and flexibility has been rare in synthetic materials, until recently, when researchers were inspired by spider silk and reinforced commercially available polyurethane elastomers with clay nanoparticles to yield strong and flexible composites [11].

Usually, when we think of spider silk, only its mechanical properties come to mind. It has yet another interesting property—its ability to hold and trap water from air! If we closely observe spider silk on a winter morning, we can see water droplets lined up in the knots! This property has been mimicked recently by a Chinese research group to prepare a polymer for harvesting fog [12]. Their work briefly involves coating nylon fibres with poly(methylmethacrylate)/N,N-dimethyl formamide-ethanol which forms knots when dried up

4.4.5 Low-drag materials (super-lubricants)

Another beautiful example of bioinspired design is that of lubricating materials. We are amazed by the wonderful properties of the thick, slippery fluid found in the cavities of synovial joints responsible for the frictionless movement of bones, called the 'synovial fluid'. The main function of this fluid is to serve as a lubricant in a joint or tendon sheath and to nourish the cartilage (Fig. 4.8). The synovial fluid consists of albumin, fat, epithelium and some leukocytes, the deficit of which could lead to severe health problems like arthritis. Think of a non-stick utensil coated with a material inspired by the synovial fluid to get rid of the screeching noises arising from the tug of war between the spoons and the frying pan! Synovial fluid has the lowest frictional coefficient known for any material and the closest material to this is Teflon. Similarly, the interface between collagen and the 100-times-stiffer hydroxyapatite in the

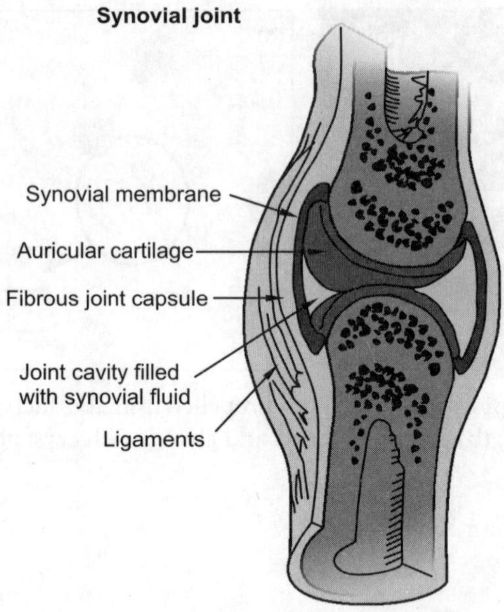

Fig. 4.8 Structure of a synovial joint [Reproduced from http://en.wikipeida.org/wiki/File:Joint.png under the terms of the GNU Free Documentation Licence]

bones is formed via epitaxial crystallization of mineral in a phosphorylated collagen template revealing intriguing interfacial compositions.

Designing natural composites becomes easier if we look at the hierarchical structure of cellulose aggregates in wood or collagen aggregates in cartilage or tendon, which are engineering marvels. An astounding variety of collagen fibrils exist in cartilage, tendon and bone despite having similar amino acid composition (coils of helical polypeptide having 300-nm length) illustrating the control of architecture over a wide length scale. For example, in bones, the orientation controls elastic modulus and fracture strength associated with hydroxyapatite mineral while in tendons (which are elastic, yet sufficiently stiff), the longitudinal orientation provides nonlinear stress–strain behaviour, which also makes it fatigue-resistant. Bone is anisotropic and its tensile strength could be 148, 49 and 39 MPa in the longitudinal, tangential and radial directions and water plays a central role in controlling its elasticity. It has been reported that an athlete who runs 10 miles every day normally uses each Achilles tendon 6 million times, without any performance degradation. Similarly, auricular cartilage is a functionally gradient material (FGM) exhibiting high strength and stiffness, and outstanding frictional and wear characteristics; its tensile modulus can vary from zone to zone to about 40 to 1 MPa with an endurance capability of a million cycles, all due to hierarchical structures [3].

Another class of fascinating materials designed by bioinspiration is well known to win gold medals for swimmers and skiers. We can also learn from nature how to play sports and compete with minimal energy. The fastest shark is known to swim at a speed of 60 miles an hour, almost

15 times faster than the fastest Olympic swimmer. What makes this speed possible? You will understand if you get a closer look at the shark, without being eaten! The trick lies in its skin. Sharks have the toughest skin due to the distinctive protrusions present on the surface, which actually offer them the best hydrodynamics [13]. The company Speedo has designed a low-drag swimsuit based on the morphology of shark skin. Water is actually channelled through small grooves in the fabric to create microvortices which facilitate hydrodynamics.

Another classic example of a low-drag system is penguin feathers. Can we survive a temperature of –20°C immediately after stepping out of ice-cold water? Penguins can, because of the unique morphology of their feathers which make them excellent thermal insulators. Penguin feathers consist of many small hooks, similar to Velcro, that cling together when the penguin dives into water, making them thin and streamlined. When the penguin wants to climb a shore, the feathers unzip and spread immediately, almost with an umbrella-like click, to offer the warmth of an excellent blanket. How does this happen? When the penguin dives into water, the feathers are compressed by the water pressure, and inflate immediately when out of water, trapping air amidst the shafts of circular cross-sections (barbs) and perpendicular fibres (barbules). Researchers are trying to exploit these properties to design effective thermal insulating fabrics, especially for military and defence applications.

4.4.6 Materials for camouflage

In addition to the above classes of materials, there are natural systems which can change their colour according to their mood and environment. You might have watched a chameleon sitting on your salad at a picnic lunch! Some animals change colour with the seasons; that is why we are not able to observe a hare for an entire season. There are many beautiful examples of camouflaging animals with colour changing ability: chameleons, rabbits and even the octopus.

Every species has its own camouflaging mechanism. If we consider reptiles, amphibians and fish, their colouration is decided by biochromes in their skin cells. Some of them change their overall colour (like cuttlefish), while others reveal patterns (like chameleons). The mechanism is complex. In simple terms, the colouring pigments are surrounded by muscles which can expand and contract. When the muscles contract, the pigments are squeezed to the top and the colour is revealed. Thus, an animal changes its colour by contracting all the chromophores with a certain colouring pigment, thereby suppressing the ones with other colours. Even within this class of animals, the stimuli and purpose of camouflage differ from species to species. For instance, nudibranches, a small sea creature, can alter its colour by changing its diet, and some parasitic species like the fluke can take the colour of their host!

The widest range of colours and patterns can be noticed in chameleons. The chromatophores in their skin cells help them to do so. Chameleons primarily change colour to express mood rather than to blend with the environment. Octopus, squid and cuttlefish constitute another interesting class of animals exhibiting brilliant camouflage mechanisms. Their sophisticated skin allows them to hide from hungry predators in the ocean. Octopus skin is made up of a group of proteins with super-reflective properties which offer dynamic camouflage ability. A deeper understanding of the composition and optical properties of these proteins will provide a new way to make super-reflective materials!

The colour changing ability of furry animals is rather more interesting. Most hares, and animals like the arctic fox, are capable of changing their colour from brown in summer to white in winter. The fur of the animal is a dead tissue similar human nails, and the composition cannot be tuned by the animal. To change colour, the hare has to create a whole new coat of fur according to the season! There are many unravelled camouflage mechanisms in nature which could in the future provide revolutionary ideas to a materials scientist.

4.5 BIONICS: BIOINSPIRED INFORMATION TECHNOLOGY

In this section, we will learn how biological systems have infuenced various branches of industry and economy to move from an electronic perspective to a field known as 'bionics'. Although the history of bionics dates back to the period of Leonardo da Vinci, the definition of bionics was proposed only about 15 years back by Neumann: *Bionics is the science of systematic transfer of construction, process and evolutionary principles of living systems into technical applications.* Another simple definition: 'Bionics is learning from nature for the creation of independent technical solutions'. The latter definition emphasizes that bionics, unlike biomimetics, does not copy from nature. Instead, it is all about using the principles of living systems to achieve technical solutions.

Let us consider, for example, how we can solve the problem of vortex formation at the wings of airplanes using bionics. If we observe the winglets of a gliding bird, we notice the blended texture of the tips, which avoids vortex formation when it glides. Thus, by the introduction of blended winglets, the aerodynamics of flights can be considerably improved (Fig. 4.9). Similarly, looking at butterfly wings, we can design three-dimensional photonic crystals, whose refractive index will be regularly varied over a length-scale comparable to the wavelength of light to obtain photonic band gap materials.

From boxfish to aerodynamic cars!

The boxfish is a square-shaped bony creature found mostly in coral reefs, sea weeds and lagoons. Nature has designed it so elegantly that it can withstand the harsh environment present in these locations. The outer skin of the boxfish consists of numerous hexagonal bony plates which offer rigidity and strength to survive collisions/high pressure, and allow it to manoeuvre through confined spaces. Another interesting feature is that tiny vortices that form along the armour plate structures on its skin stabilize the fish in any position and keep it safely

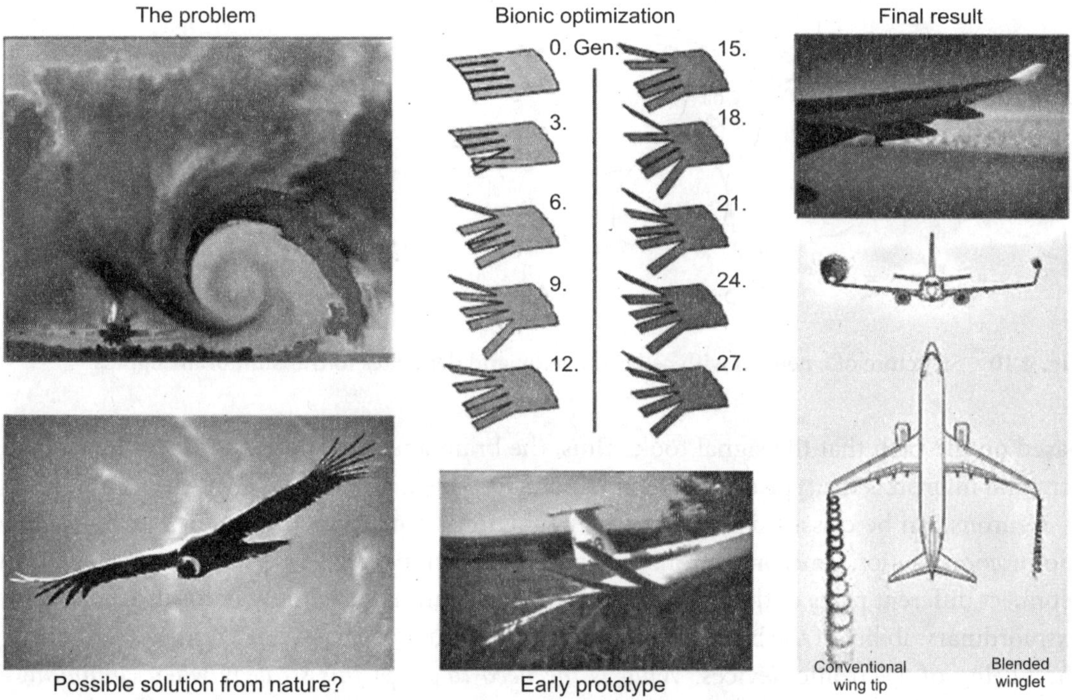

Fig. 4.9 *(see also Plate 3)* Bionic approach to minimize energy loss due to vortex generation at the wing tips of airplanes [[Reprinted with permission from Neurohr R and Dracomirescu C, Bionics in Engineering—Defining new Goals in Engineering Education at "Politehnica". International Conference on Engineering Education (ICEE-2007), September 3–7, 2007, Coimbra, Portugal.]

on course, even in areas of high turbulence. Thus, the fish need not move its fins in the process and can conserve its strength, resulting in the least possible energy consumption. Now, you must already be visualizing your dream car! That is exactly what DaimlerChrysler achieved in 2005. By mimicking the fish's boxy frame and scale structure, strength, stability and light weight, a streamlined profile was reproduced in their new car model to achieve speeds of about 190 km/hour and fuel economy of 30 km/L!

Similarly, the complicated processes of signal processing and information/exformation occurring at the brain have inspired the development of better electronic devices. The human brain is the best electronic device ever known. It can distinguish between several types of audio signals and can locate your loved ones even in a big crowd. *How is it possible?* The brain has special cells called *neurons* which are responsible for its intelligence. A neuron has a unique structure, with branches (axons) and dendrites extending from a central cell body, as shown in Fig. 4.10. The axon conducts electric signals used to convey information to the brain. Though all these signals are identical, the brain determines what type of information is being received,

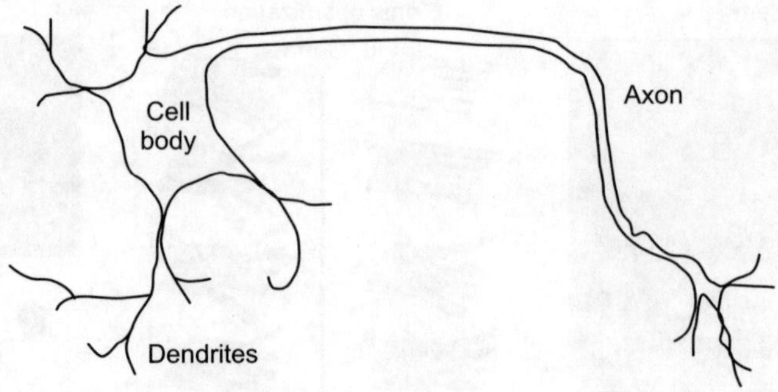

Fig. 4.10 Structure of a neuron with cell body, axon and dendrites to transmit brain signals

based on the path that the signal took. Thus, the brain analyzes the patterns of signals being sent and interprets the type of information being received.

Neurons can be classified based on their functions: sensory neurons (for perception and motor coordination), motor neurons (for muscle function), relay or projection interneurons (connect different parts of the brain) and local interneurons (used only in local circuits). This extraordinary ability of the brain to separate signal from noise has been mimicked to improve the fidelity of electronic devices. *What is the need to adopt this strategy when computing is so advanced these days?* Despite the advances in computing, there are certain tasks that a program written for a common microprocessor is unable to perform. For example, in 2006, an intelligent crop protection system was required by the government of USA to protect crop fields from seasonal plague. The system required a flying vehicle that could inspect crop fields by flying over them, and also not be controlled by conventional computation. So a neural network was adopted. It is a parallel system of computation capable of resolving paradigms that linear computing cannot.

An artificial neural network (ANN) is a mathematical model based on neural networks present in biological systems consisting of an interconnected group of artificial neurons through which the information is processed. In most cases, ANN is an adaptive system that changes its structure based on external information that flows through the network during the learning phase. Similarly, the signal-to-noise ratio of electronic systems like digital telephones, theatre sound systems and CD players can be improved by using the 'inhibitory coupling' mechanism of neurons. Specifically, neuronal networks in the brain operate by a method called 'inhibitory coupling', in which activation of one neuron momentarily suppresses the level of activity in other neurons in the network. This reduces clumping of information and provides better clarity. Interestingly, the neurons in the human brain often fire irregularly and slowly despite the many signals they need to encode. Individual neurons often take ten milliseconds or more between firings. However, they still manage to provide the best noise filtration system. This type of model helps to give many simulation challenges in the modelling of functional materials.

4.5 BIOMINERALIZATION—EN ROUTE TO NANOTECHNOLOGY

Biomineralization is a process in which minerals are deposited in an organized fashion in the matrix of living organisms in order to harden or stiffen existing tissues. Examples include silicates in algae, carbonates in invertebrates and calcium phosphates and carbonates in vertebrates. Bone, enamel, shells of oysters and clams and spines of sea urchins are examples of biominerals, where, the biomineralization mechanism can cause doubling of toughness and ductility without loss of stiffness on water absorption. For example, calcium carbonate ($CaCO_3$) is one of the most abundant biominerals found in different crystallographic (polymorphic) forms, namely, aragonite, calcite, vaterite and even amorphous forms. For example, the spines of sea urchins are composed of Mg-containing calcite occluded by about 0.05 wt% of organic macromolecules (mostly proteins) [14]. The process of biomineralization has been duplicated in the laboratory by using acidic macromolecules isolated from the shells of molluscs, which when attached to a substrate induces $CaCO_3$ nucleation and controls the structure, morphology, crystal orientation and spatial confinement of the inorganic phase. This resulted in doubling of toughness and ductility without loss of stiffness on water absorption by the mollusc.

In another interesting experiment, organic macromolecules with disordered head groups were self-assembled (see Chapter 3) on Au or Ag substrates to induce formation of an amorphous $CaCO_3$ film. When part of the SAM was made to organize using the tip of an atomic force microscope, the ordered phase acted as a nucleation centre and catalyzed phase transition from amorphous to crystalline $CaCO_3$. Thus, a deeper understanding of biomineralization has led to many developments in the hierarchical assembly of materials. In nanotechnology, the method of building controlled architectures of materials is commonly known as the bottom-up approach. Nevertheless, there are still many processes in biological systems which are not clearly understood. A few such questions would be:

- While synthetic calcite crystals can be cleaved along their lattice planes, why does the spine of a sea urchin fracture like glass?
- What was the chemical nature of the first mineral crystals formed in bones and teeth?
- What controls the initial deposition of mineral crystals?
- Is there a common mechanism for biomineralization?
- How can the functions of matrix proteins be verified?
- Are these matrix proteins multi-functional?

All such questions can be answered by analyzing the various mechanisms and conditions of biomineralization [15].

4.6 ADVANTAGES AND LIMITATIONS

Many naturally occurring hierarchical structures act as a guide for new materials technology, where property tuning could be easily carried out by controlling experimental parameters. One of the main advantages of this approach is the use of soft chemistry routes (rather than the 'heat-and-beat' approach of chemists working on traditional ceramic materials); equilibrium structures can be prepared 'in situ' and at ambient temperature and pressure, which will have moderate thermal and chemical stability. Ultrasoft cell membranes with exceptional ion-transport and selective gating properties illustrate the advantages of this approach.

Many structural, morphological and compositional variations, including defects, can be tuned easily in the laboratory by altering the chemistry, unlike in naturally occurring materials. For example, molecular to macroscopic length-scale variation can be effectively tailored with implicit advantages for potential end-use applications. Further tuning of the mechanical properties by controlling both the soft matrix as well as the hard inorganic components is also possible, as illustrated by the microstructural control in natural composites like the hierarchical structure of cellulose aggregates in wood or collagen assemblage in cartilage or tendon. Many natural materials can offer valuable insights as model systems for how properties can be controlled.

There are also several limitations for this approach. Many biomaterials augmenting body functions are heavy, especially when we make them in the laboratory, despite being engineering marvels. Nature, of course, uses only a limited number of constituents like proteineous materials (having a handful of elements like C, H, N, O, S, P, etc.) and a selected few inorganic compounds (like calcium carbonate, silica and phosphates) to form organo–inorganic composites of unlimited structural control and mechanical properties. In contrast, many of our materials, with a similar performance level, are bulky and heavy in comparison to what nature has made and refined by slow evolutionary engineering. Rapid development of many implants like intraoccular lenses have benefited millions of people, but these are undoubtedly not as durable as the original natural lens.

Performance deficiencies arising from functioning over a narrow temperature range for engineering applications is another major limitation. Manipulation is more on length-scale as it is much more difficult to control the events in time (e.g., defect dynamics) as most structures are formed at a very slow rate. Consequently, the economic viability of the commercial production of many of these materials is questionable. Similarly, although a broad range of functions are seen in biological systems (especially in living organisms), only limited functions of special interest are looked at by materials scientists. Only a limited number of solvents can be used for the synthetic approach, which limits the chemistry. Durability, corrosion in the real environment, higher cost, etc., are some of the other limitations of this class of remarkable materials.

4.7 CHALLENGES AHEAD

Some of the materials developed by this approach are too expensive to be used in everyday applications. Artificial organs developed by tissue engineering are a revealing example. Many of the self-healing materials developed thus far lack durability and resistance to corrosion in the body environment. In many cases, the immediate priority is to develop active materials matching both mechanical and biological properties, enabling faster cellular regeneration and fusion. A more fundamental understanding of the interactions between in vivo and in vitro biological structures is expected in the near future with the help of more accurate computer modelling and simulation studies. We need to learn many more new rules of adhesion, strength and precise control of components to match the performance levels of natural materials, so many bioceramics and bioactive glasses can be made for clinical applications. This approach holds promise for generating a variety of extraordinary functional materials for use in high-performance adhesives, artificial body parts and biomedical implants, smart filtration systems, wear-resistant and low-friction joints and bearings, selective and ultrahard coatings with inbuilt molecular recognition capability, improved spacecraft, etc. We need to learn much more about selectivity, atom-economy of synthesis, environmental impact and reuse of many of these materials from nature [16–17].

4.8 CONCLUSIONS

Many naturally present materials of biological origin, such as spider silk, shells, and spines, reveal amazing mechanical strength, toughness, lustre and thermal stability. Many of these hybrid, hierarchically designed materials perfected by nature tempt us to create similar materials in the laboratory. The more we study these materials, the more our amazement and interest to test our knowledge in designing something equivalent, if not superior.

Recent developments in the field of biomaterials that range from simple embedded implants to more complex functional materials that control biological interactions are expected to have a major impact on various fields of medicine, including diagnostics and patient care. For example, active grafts and implants no longer act as foreign bodies but help to grow new cells like skin, cartilage or blood vessels by interfering with cellular function.

More recent innovations in bionanotechnology, coupled with stem cell research and genetic engineering, are expected to generate many active 'almost-living' biomaterials of adjustable properties to suit each one personally, or 'designer biomaterials' for everyone. Cost-effective fabrication techniques for many of these functionally gradient materials are expected to be evolved, based on expected breakthroughs in ongoing modelling and simulation studies of several research groups working on biomaterials in various parts of the world.

Further reading

[1] Gray H B, Stiefel E I, Selverstove J and Ivanobertini V, Eds., *Biological Inorganic Chemistry*, University Science Books, 2007.
[2] Mann S, *Biomometic Materials Chemistry*, Wiley–VCH, 1996.
[3] Hierarchical structures in biology as a guide for new materials technology committee on synthetic hierarchical structures, Commission on Engineering and Technical Systems, *National Research Council*, 1994; available at http://www.nap.edu/catalog/2215.html.
[4] Dujardin E and Mann S, Bio-inspired materials chemistry, *Adv. Mater.*, 14: 775, 2002.
[5] Dujardin E, Hsin L B, Wang C R C and Mann H, DNA-driven self-assembly of gold nanorods, *Chem. Commun.*, 1264, 2001.
[6] Capadona J R, Stimuli-responsive polymer nanocomposites inspired by the sea cucumber dermis, *Science*, 319: 1370, 2008.
[7] Dawson J, Vincent J F V and Rocca A M. How pine cones open, *Nature*, 390(6661): 668, 1997.
[8] Bormashenko E, Why does the Cassie-Baxter equation apply? *Colloids and Surfaces A: Physicochemical and Engineering Aspects*, 324: 47, 2008.
[9] Kakade B, Mehta R, Durge A, Kularni S and Pillai V K, Electric field induced superhydrophobic to superhydrophilic switching in multiwalled carbon nanotube papers, *Nano Lett.*, 8: 2693, 2008; Sato O, Kubo S and Gu Z-z, Structural color films with lotus effects, superhydrophilicity, and tunable stop-bands, *Acc. Chem. Res.*, 42: 1–10, 2009.
[10] VELCRO; available at http://www.velcro.com/index.html.
[11] Nanotechnology News; available at http://www.azonano.com/news.asp?newsID-3593.
[12] New materials inspired by water-catching properties of spider webs, IdeaConnection; available at http://www.ideaconnection.com/innovation-in-business/New-Materials-Inspired-by-Water-Catching-Properties-o-00132.html.
[13] Wainwright S A, Vosburgh F and Hebrank J H, Shark skin: function in locomotion, *Science*, 202: 747–49, 1978.
[14] Douglas T, A bright bio-inspired future, *Science Perspective*, 299: 1192, 2003.
[15] Bolskey A L, Biomineralization: Confllicts, Challenges and Opportunities, *J. Cell Biochem.*, 72: 83, 1998. Mann S, Hannington J P and Williams R J P, Phospholipid vesicles as a model system for bio-mineralization, *Nature*, 324: 565–67, 1986.
[16] Burns J W, Boom time for biomaterials, *Nature Materials*, 8: 411–13, 2009. Vincent J F V, *Structural Biomaterials, Princeton University Press*, Princeton, New Jersey, 1990. Baeuerlein E, *Handbook of biomineralization: Biomimetic and Bio-inspired Chemistry*, Wiley–VCH, 2007.

Exercises

1. Classify bioinspired materials citing examples.
2. What is the need for designing bioinspired materials? Illustrate with suitable examples.
3. Explain how a water strider walks on water.
4. Illustrate how spider silk has 'biologically found structural hierarchy over wide length-scales' to generate properties superior to Kevlar.
5. What is special about the surface of a lotus leaf? How can we create an oxide surface that is artificially self-cleaning and super-hydrophobic?

6. With suitable examples demonstrate that 'nature is parsimonious in its use of constituents' for its synthesis.
7. What are functionally gradient materials (FGM)? Give an example to illustrate the concept of FGM existing in living organisms.
8. Explain the cellular synthesis of materials. What are the main benefits of using biological cells as templates for making materials?
9. Considering calcium carbonate as an example, demonstrate the important advantages of bioinspired synthesis. How does this approach vary with a chemical approach of preparing calcium carbonate?
10. Name four general limitations of bioinspired synthesis of the present generation of materials.
11. Define three different criteria to identify a super-hydrophobic surface. How are self-cleaning abilities generated on some of these surfaces? Explain using the lotus leaf as an example.

5

Smart Materials

This chapter introduces the basic concept of smart materials and explains various criteria for smartness in materials. After identifying both available as well as emerging synthetic tools and challenges, it provides several realistic examples to illustrate the importance of smart materials and systems. It finally concludes with a description of the impact of artificial intelligence on current technologies and integration of these materials and devices in our day-to-day life.

LEARNING OBJECTIVES

- To understand the concept of intelligence and smartness in materials
- To identify various criteria for smartness
- To classify materials according to their level of smartness
- To explain specific systems of different levels of intelligence, with suitable examples
- To illustrate how smart gels can be tuned to undergo volume transitions as a function of pH, temperature, electric field, etc.
- To explain the working of shape memory alloys and smart electroceramic materials with illustrative examples
- To explain the meaning of terms like smart cloths, smart shoes and smart rooms in terms of qualitative reasoning
- To be aware of the technological challenges and limitations of smart systems

Fig. 5.1 The common poorwill is a bird which normally resides in high rolling prairies, foothills and deserts at elevations of around 4,000 feet. It is known for its distinctive sound and ability to enter a temporary daily hibernation called torpor [Reproduced from http://en.wikipedia.org/wikipedia.org/wiki/File:Phalaenoptilus_nuttalliiDF28N04B.jpg under the terms of the GNU Free Documentation Licence]

One day, an ornithologist identified a bird in a rock crevice. When he picked up the bird, there was no heartbeat and its body temperature was 60°F, but it was alive! After remaining in this condition for 88 days, in contrast to its normal temperature of 106°F, the bird flew off when the atmospheric temperature rose above 66°F. This type of a temporary hibernation in birds is called 'torpor'. The common poorwill becomes torpid when the atmospheric temperature becomes 35–66°F and uses only 10 g ounces of stored fat over a period of 100 days to keep itself alive. An amazing level of 'smartness' is displayed by this little bird in conserving its energy resources!

Rejuvenation is one of the important criteria of smart materials. The objective of this chapter is to take the reader gradually through the essential components of smartness, namely, sensing, adaptability and reversibility, and give a glimpse of how to make a material smart at our own will!

5.1 INTRODUCTION

'Smartness' is one of the key features that differentiates a natural (living) system from an artificial one. Every living system has evolved with different levels of smartness in order to move up in the food chain—to become a predator rather than be a prey, or at least to succeed in the struggle for survival. Fortunately, unlike in animals, the philosophy of 'kill or die' does not exist among human beings owing to our ability to think and respond to the mental conditions of a fellow human being. On the other hand, the lifestyle of animals is based purely on the conditions of supply and demand of food. Hence, the smart responses of animals and plants are more spectacular, faster and at a higher level of complexity than in humans.

Dog's nose versus human nose

Sniffer dogs used by detective agencies have a sense of smell 2,000 times higher than that of humans. They are known to distinguish scents even if they are masked by other odorous substances. They can even detect a drop of blood dried over a period of 10 years. Now, with the advent of nanotechnology and self-assembling strategies, it is possible to mimic their functions and create electronic noses. At present, artificial noses mimicking the capability of the human nose are available. The human nose consists of a layer of mucus that dissolves the incoming scents, and separates the odours so that they arrive at the receptors at different speeds. The pattern is then interpreted by the brain to distinguish the smells. Mimicking this, an electronic nose can be constructed with an array of about 20 sensors which can detect different types of molecules and send the signal to a computer, although a human olfactory epithelium contains millions of receptors.

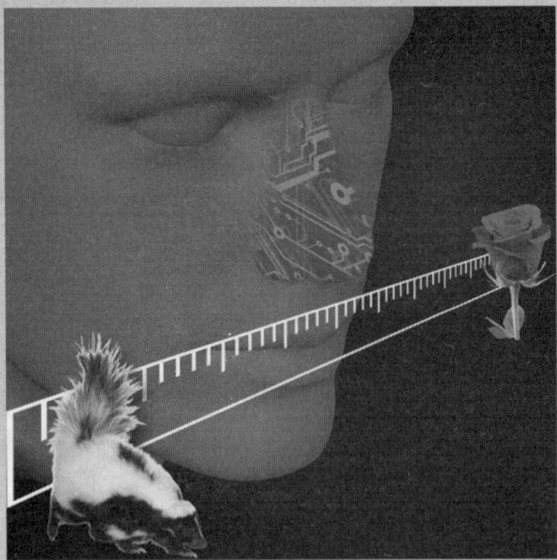

Fig. 5.2 Electronic nose that mimics human nose, fabricated at CAMSS, NC A&T which can distinguish between specific components of an odour [Adapted from: http://www.commons.wikimedia.org]

Consider a simple example. Suppose we are at risk of getting infected by some microorganism, such as a virus; we do not have any camouflaging mechanism (see *Chapter 4*) to stop or divert the virus from attacking us, although internally there are antigens which can fight them once they enter our body, aiding a gradual recovery. Under similar circumstances, cuttle fish can change its colour and shape once it senses a predator and an octopus can spit a poisonous liquid to drive away its enemies. Similarly, if we compare the sense of smell of a human nose with that of a dog's, we will immediately remember the number of eatables your pet dog has stolen from hidden containers.

Figure 5.2 shows an interesting comparison of the human nose with a dog's nose, along with a smart system called 'artificial nose', built on the basis of these concepts. This is the level of smartness we are trying to introduce in materials around us. This concept, cumulatively called 'artificial intelligence' in embedded materials, is the major drive for all future technologies.

5.1.1 What are smart materials?

The definition of smartness in materials is not very different from that of smartness in living systems: it is always understood as '*the ability to assimilate, correlate and coordinate external happenings and respond in a synchronized fashion*'. In *Webster's Third International Dictionary of the English Language,* the word 'smart' is defined as [1]:

> *'Having or showing mental alertness and quickness of perceptions, shrewd informed calculation, or contrived resourcefulness, marked by or suggesting brisk vigour, speedy effective activity or spirited-liveliness.'*

In other words, smart materials can be defined as materials that can sense as well as adapt to changes in environmental conditions such as temperature, pressure, illumination, shock and electric/magnetic field—conditions which are easy to spot in living organisms. They are functional materials endowed with intelligence.

What distinguishes a smart material from a functional material? In other words, why should smart materials be discussed in a separate chapter? Any material is considered to be useful only if it 'responds' to some controllable stimuli, but a 'smart' material is one which is described by the following adjectives when it responds to an external stimulus:

- High magnitude of response
- Instantaneous response
- Reversibility
- Sensitivity and specificity

The idea of achieving smart materials relies on the art of translating the level of intelligence prevalent in natural systems into synthetic materials and systems, which have been essentially passive so far. Although the concept of 'artificial intelligence' has encountered innumerable debates and controversies, like any other new concept, modern systems indeed require self-controlled smart materials, which can respond in a predictable manner.

5.1.2 Significance of smart materials

Over the past 20 years, there has been an enormous development in the design of functional materials like piezoelectric, magnetostrictive and electrostrictive materials. Now we expect the materials to be smart enough to take care of themselves and the device they are incorporated in to respond to changes in the environment. The design of multi-functional materials has undoubtedly revolutionalized many industries by making the device components light-weight and compact (rubbery ceramics). However, their design is based on the prediction of the environmental conditions in which they have to function. Thus, when these conditions become unpredictable and fluctuate, as in the case of air transport, space exploration and underwater expeditions, many materials suffer serious fatigue and break down.

An appropriate example is the tragedy involving Air Florida in 1982, which crashed into a nearby river after taking off from National Airport, Washington DC, because its surface and sensors got covered with snow. This mishap could have been avoided if the aircraft's surface had been made of a smart material or skin capable of de-icing itself. Similarly, there are many issues awaiting solutions from smart materials and structures in the case of space travel.

In our daily life, the higher the level of smartness of materials around us, the better would be the ease and cost of living. Imagine self-cleaning toilets, walls, floors and tiles that keep themselves clean and dry and save us the hastle of scrubbing. Thanks to the advent of glasses with tiny bumps on their surface—their density and spacing closely resemble the morphology of a lotus leaf—water droplets roll off the surface keeping it clean and dry. A number of products have appeared in the market, based on the lotus effect (Fig. 5.3). Another innovative idea is 'self-bleeding paint' which keeps automobiles scratch-free; they start flowing whenever there is a break (also self-healing) in the continuity of the coating.

The demand for smart materials and systems is increasing infinitely for high-end industrial applications, right from healthcare, packaging and architecture to aeronautics. Consider an engineering structure such as a bridge, a building or a pipeline—especially those exposed to corrosive environments—where sustainability demands regular inspection and further repair in the case of damage. By and large, the maintenance cost of such structures even exceeds the original cost of construction, in addition to being time consuming. Nevertheless, attempting a design to minimize the damage could possibly compromise the performance. This is where the inception of smart materials and systems make a tremendous difference in architecture. Similarly, an interesting class of smart materials, called 'shape memory alloys', has

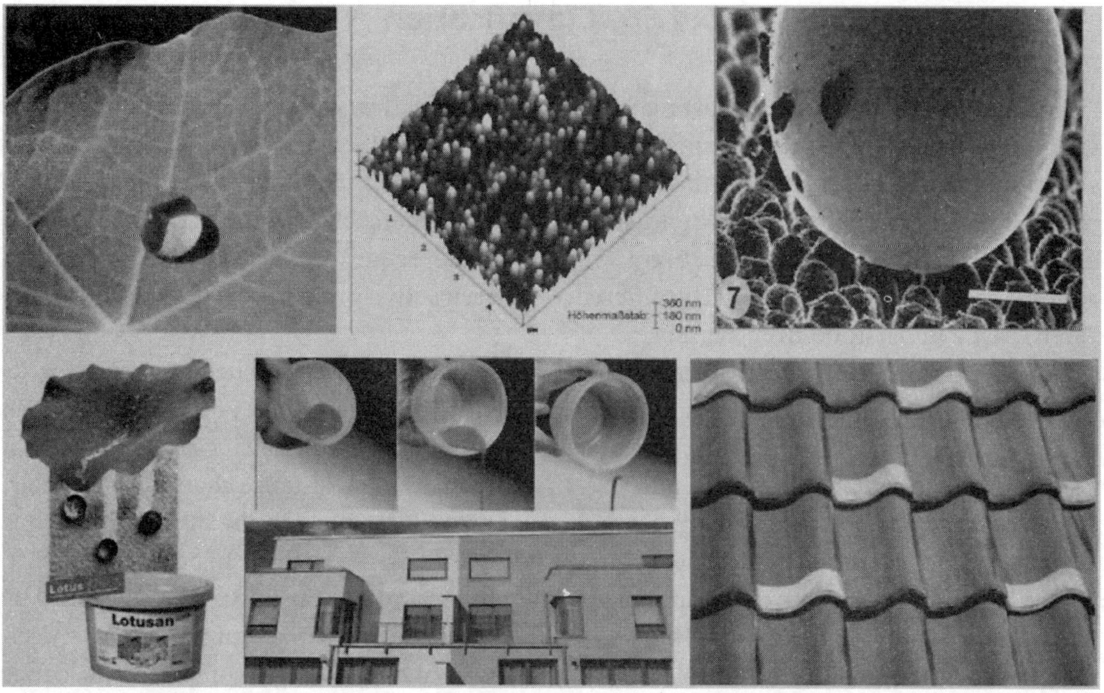

Fig. 5.3 *(see also Plate 4)* A water drop resting on a lotus leaf surface; its cross-sectional images by AFM and TEM (top) and demonstration/application of super hydrophobic surfaces [Reproduced with permission from John Wiley & Sons: Kickelbick G, *Hybrid Materials: Synthesis, Characterization and Applications,* Wiley-VCGH]

been successfully exploited to tailor the aerodynamics of flights. Recently, Boeing introduced 'variable geometry chevrons (VGCs)', utilizing compact, light-weight and robust shape memory alloy actuators, which tune the shape of the chevrons at the trailing edge of a jet engine in order to optimize acoustic and performance criteria in multiple flight conditions.

The packaging industry is yet another important area of application of smart materials. Labels on the packaging that can sense the quality of edible contents, coupled with an electronic 'use by date' indication or colour changes are of immediate requirement. This is not uncommon in nature: we are familiar with the banana skin that changes colour when the fruit is ripe. 'Smart' surveillance becomes still more critical in medicine and healthcare: think of a surgical implant that is smart enough to sense infection or shape-changes and repair itself without the need for invasive surgery; or an implanted glucose sensor that triggers the release of insulin from an inbuilt reservoir in diabetic patients or clothes which can generate antiseptics as and when required. There are numerous yet-to-be-explored opportunities in these industries to bring smartness from 'bench to bedside'.

5.1.3 Classification

The range and applicability of smart materials is so vast that they cannot be brought under one general classification. Generally, smart materials can be classified as passively smart, actively smart and very smart, based on their degree of smartness [2]. *Passively smart materials* can respond to an external stimulus in a useful manner by themselves without the need for an actuating mechanism, whereas *actively smart materials* require an actuator component to respond to a particular stimulus. The difference between actively and passively smart materials can be easily understood from Fig. 5.4.

An example of a passively smart material is a ceramic varistor used in a lightning arrestor. Its operating principle is based on the sudden decrease in electrical resistance of the material when struck by high-voltage lightning, as otherwise it is a stubborn insulator. Zinc oxide (ZnO) is a common varistor employed for this purpose. In addition, as the resistance change is reversible, the material can be operated through several cycles without fatigue. On the other hand, active smartness is not exhibited by a single material—it is usually a system that can be actively smart. A typical example of an actively smart system is the suspension of a car electrically controlled by piezoelectric sensors and actuators. The role of suspension in a car is to maximize friction between the tyres and the road in order to isolate the vibrations from the passenger compartment. This is achieved by a combination of piezoelectric materials which drive the suspension springs.

On the other hand, a very smart material responds to an external stimuli by changing one or more of its property coefficients (which we call 'learning'), thus tuning its sensing and actuating functions in space and time to optimize its future behaviour. Its performance can get better and better with time! This concept has been illustrated by developing tunable transducers based on elastic non-linearity.

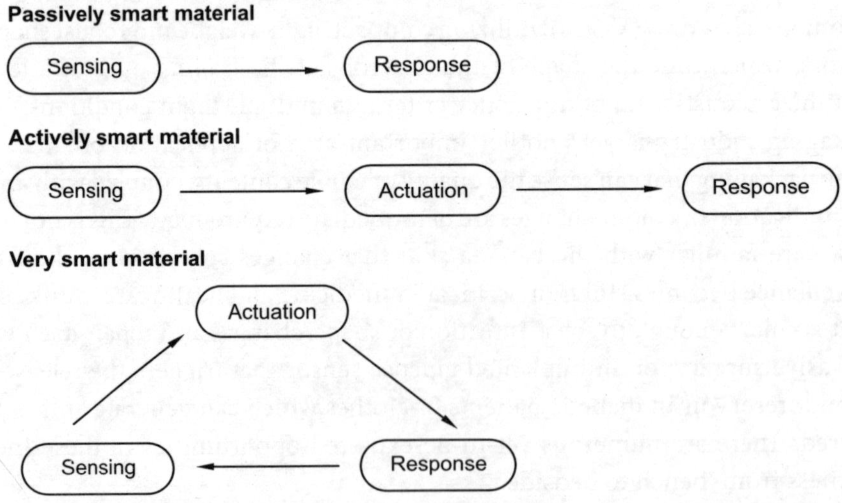

Fig. 5.4 A scheme of classification of smart materials based on the degree of smartness

Table 5.1 A list of dynamic variables which manifest smart behaviour in materials

Dynamic variable	Smart material
Colour	Photochromic Thermochromic
Light emitting	Electroluminescent Fluorescent Phosphorescent Shape memory alloys
Shape	Polymers/Gels Piezoelectric Dielectric elastomers
Electrical response	Conducting polymers Electroceramics Electrostrictive Electrorheological fluids Magnetorheological fluids
Rheology	Thermoelectric
Temperature	Smart composites
Self-diagnostic	Self-assembling materials

Smart materials can also be categorized on the basis of external stimuli, the type of response, physical state and chemical nature. A simple classification based on the type of response is provided in Table 5.1. Sometimes there could be an overlap between two classes of materials. For example, electroceramics, electrorheological fluids and electrostrictive materials respond to an applied electric field by making corresponding changes in their optical/magnetic, mechanical properties and shape, respectively, while magnetostrictive materials change their shape in an external magnetic field. Conversely, piezoelectric materials are capable of generating an electric potential in response to an applied mechanical stress. Many of these show 'non-Newtonian behaviour as their viscosity changes with an applied shear stress. On the other hand, smart gels and shape memory alloys are materials at a higher stratum of artificial intelligence, which can perform a wide range of functions by a combination of responses to given external stimulii, including reversible swelling and phase changes.

5.1.4 Criteria for smartness

It is difficult to list the criteria for smartness from a general perspective, since every class of smart material requires a unique approach. However, there are certain important common features, which almost all classes of smart materials share:

- One of the essential pre-requisites for smartness is the ability of a material to exhibit *multi-phasic behaviour*, i.e., it should be capable of existing in more than one stable phase (some single phase materials are also smart) as can be understood from its phase diagram. The different phases can be due to:
  - different crystal structures if the material is crystalline
  - different conformations in the case of a polymeric material
  - different compositions in the case of a multi-component smart system
- The second requirement is that the *energy difference between phases* be within a limit accessible by an external perturbation such an electric/magnetic field and irradiation, so that even a minor perturbation could bring about a phase change. For example, all piezoelectric, electrostrictive, magnetostrictive and shape memory materials undergo at least two phase transformations, leading to complex domain wall changes which is the actual orgin of sensing and actuation capabilities.
- The third and the most important criterion is *reversibility in the phase changes*—this is possible only if the various phases do not differ much in chemical composition, namely, stoichiometry of the components.
- A point that could be considered as the fourth criterion for smartness is that there should be *no time-dependence in the material's properties*; this decides the swiftness of its response to an external stimulus.

Nevertheless, for a material to be 'very smart', it should have non-linear properties unlike 'simply smart' materials with linear responses. Self-recovery, self-adjustment, self-diagnosis and several other features of living organisms could also be used at least qualitatively, to decide if a materials smart (or not).

5.2 SMART TOOLS TO IMPART INTELLIGENCE

What endows such unusual properties to a specific class of materials? Why are certain materials smarter than others? Is it just their chemical identity or are there additional factors to be considered while designing a smart material? Though, in this section, we will not go into the details of manipulating materials, we will take a glimpse of the tools required to make a dumb material smart. The two most common strategies to impart smartness in materials are *molecular design* (nanotechnology) and chemical *functionalization*.

Molecular design relies on the central dogma of material science, 'Size does matter'. Akin to the increasing level of intelligence seen down the food chain in biological systems, materials also get smarter as they become smaller. However, the reason is not complicated, as in the case of biological systems. The magic begins when the size of the material is brought down to a critical value with reference to the length-scale corresponding to the motion of electrons, phonons or polarons in that material. For example, gold which is yellow in colour in its bulk form, can display a range of colours from purple to blue when the size of its particles is within 1–10 nm. There are many more such examples, even in natural systems, to illustrate smartness in nanoscale materials; while designing, constituents could be selected to impart intelligence.

Functionalization is another strategy to introduce smartness in a passive material, that is by attaching chemical functional groups on the surface of the material. The nature of the functional group determines whether the material is going to be actively, passively or very smart. If a nanoparticle is functionalized with a hormone which can specifically bind to the receptor present on the surface of a tumour cell, it can be targetted towards the cancerous cell/tissue for diagnosis or treatment. Similarly, even bulk surfaces modified with molecular recognition units like antibodies and enzymes can become smart enough to detect pathogens and metabolites present in body fluid. For example, glucose sensors can detect blood glucose levels by attaching glucose oxidase enzyme to graphite electrodes.

5.3 REPRESENTATIVE EXAMPLES

There are innumerable examples for commercially successful smart materials and systems ranging from domestic to industrial applications. Yet, certain materials tend to enthuse the scientific community due to their fundamental properties and the way in which they are relayed to achieve inherent smartness[2]. A few representative examples of such materials are presented to demonstrate the recent advances in smart materials and systems.

5.3.1 Shape memory materials

Can you envision a shirt where the sleeves roll up when it just gets warm enough? Or trick spoons which twist when you try to stir your coffee or tea? Or a 'smart spring' that can reduce hot water flow from a shower when the water gets hot enough to hurt.

Shape memory materials can 'remember' their shape even after a series of deformations and immediately get back to their original state the moment the deformations are removed. How does this happen? Materials do not have brains like humans to 'remember' things. What is meant by 'memory' in materials science? Before finding the answer to this question, let us try to understand the phenomena that is common to all these shape memory materials.

Some materials exhibit a memory effect with respect to thermal perturbations, some with mechanical and yet others with pH changes. There is something in common, however, to all these materials. It is clear that the basic requirement is that the material should undergo a 'reversible' phase transformation with respect to an external stimulus. For example, if a material shaped at one temperature gets deformed at another temperature, it reverts back to its original

Nitinol sculptures

Artists have used the shape memory properties of Nitinol to make sculptures that change shape! A sculpture named '*Hope–Despair*' was made by French artist, Olivier Deschamps, featuring a woman holding a baby. When it is cold, the figure of the woman is seen lying down on the ground with the baby in front of her; when it is warm, the woman will be kneeling, holding the baby up to the sky.

Applying a similar principle, an artist–scientist pair designed another sculpture called 'Onibaba' (or magical reeds). A bunch of Nitinol wires were planted on the floor of a building. When visitors approached, the reeds rose to reveal the pathway; when they left, the reeds fell back to cover the ground.

Another interesting example of a Nitinol-based smart material is a robot called 'Stiquito'. Stiquito is a small, inexpensive, six-legged robot used in universities and high schools since 1992 for teaching the basic concepts of electronics. It simply consists of a number of Nitinol wires which can expand and contract with change in temperature, simulating muscular action. The IEEE Computer Society Press has published three books containing instructions for building the Stiquito robot.

Terfenol is another related material containing terbium and iron based on magnetostriction. Both Nitinol and Terfenol were invented in the Naval Ordinance Laboratory (NOL), Maryland, now disestablished.

shape as soon as the initial temperature is reached. Similarly, some materials undergo enormous elastic deformations with changes in mechanical stress and revert back to the original shape when the stress is removed—a phenomenon called *superelasticity*, analogous to shape memory. Although the inception of this concept dates back to the late 1930s, the actual realization of its industrial significance followed the observation of this peculiar behaviour in Ti–Ni alloys in the 1960s. Later, the memory effect was observed in other classes of materials such as polymers and ceramics. However, till date, the Ti–Ni alloys remain the most popular commercially—despite being costly—due to their excellent shape memory performance, mechanical properties and the resulting ease of processing, and are known by the trade name 'Nitinol'.

The interesting shape memory properties are not only exploited in science and technology but also in arts and architecture. For example, Nendo, a Japanese company has designed a lamp based on the shape memory alloy called 'Hanabi' (meaning 'fire flower'). When the lamp is turned on, the heat of the bulb makes the shape memory alloy spread open like a blooming flower, which closes when turned off.

Irrespective of whether a mechanical or thermal stimulus is used, the fundamental principle behind the shape memory effect is the switching of the material between two phases, namely, austenite and martensite, in the solid state. Metals and alloys are well known for their physical properties like tensile strength, ductility, malleability and thermal and electrical conductivity. However, if these alloys are plastically deformed at one temperature, they will recover their original shape on being raised to a higher temperature, generating a displacement or a force. A temperature change of just 10°C is enough to switch the materials from one phase to another, making them promising candidates for several applications like satellite latching, leak-proof coupling, conversion of low-grade heat to mechanical energy, etc. These alloys are also known as MARMEM alloys since their remarkable shape memory effect is based on the physics of *martensitic phase transformations.* The matensitic transition temperature depends on the composition of the alloys, although this could be controlled by a variety of external factors like the application of stress. A few examples of shape memory alloys along with their transition temperature are listed in Table 5.2.

5.3.2 Smart gels and polymers

A gel is a polymer or an organization of long-chain molecules forming a network of fibres similar to a spider's web [3]. Such network structures have voids known as pores which can entrap solvent molecules like water, giving them fluidity and elasticity, by a process called 'gelation'. They respond to changes in environmental conditions by expanding, bending, shrinking, or by similar shape changes, and some of these could be tuned by controlling the chemistry at the molecular level. The extent of swelling of a gel depends on the interactions between the polymer fragments and the solvent molecule and on mutual interactions between the polymer molecules themselves. These factors make the swelling behaviour more dynamic and versatile with respect to external stimuli like temperature, pressure, ionic strength and pH of the solvent medium.

These are actually another class of smart materials belonging to the larger family of *soft matter*. In the last section, the shape memory properties of an alloy in the solid state were

Table 5.2 A list of typical alloys exhibiting shape memory effects and their transformation temperature

Alloy	Composition (at.%)	Transformation temperature range (°C)
Ag–Cd	44 Cd	– 190 to – 50
Au–Cd	46.5 Cd	30 to 100
Cu–Sn	15 Sn	– 120 to 30
Cu–Zn	38.5 Zn	– 180 to – 10
Ni–Ti	49 Ni	– 50 to 110
Fe–Pt	25 Pt	– 130 approx.

illustrated in terms of subtle molecular/atomic rearrangements within the rigid crystal lattice. However, in the present case, the stability of gels and polymers depends on soft interactions between the polymer chains and the entrapped solvent molecules. Hence it is interesting to envision reversible transformation between two phases with totally different properties, unlike the case of the austenite and martensite phases which have entirely different physical properties. Yet, to our amusement, smartness is not barred for this class of soft materials.

Gels are three-dimensional, water-swollen soft materials composed mainly of hydrophilic polymers cross linked at regular intervals by one or many of the following forces: hydrogen bonding, physical entanglements and van der Waals forces. The cross-links form a regular network structure trapping solvent molecules in the intermittent spaces and giving rise to a phenomenon called 'swelling'. The amount of fluid that a gel can incorporate within its 'pores' (the separation between successive cross-links) is given by the volume fraction of the polymer in the swollen gel,

$$Q = \frac{\text{Volume of the polymer}}{\text{Volume of the swollen gel}}$$

The gels could be made responsive by an appropriate choice of functional groups in the component polymer chains. For example, the swelling behaviour could become a function of pH, temperature, chemical/biochemical interactions with the environment.

pH-sensitive gels are especially attractive for applications in drug delivery wherein the drugs are to be released from the gels when they reach appropriate pH in physiological conditions. The basic principle behind such pH-dependent swelling behaviour is the protonation/deprotonation capabilities of the acidic/basic functional groups present either in the polymer backbones or in the pendant chains. The presence of such ionic groups in the constituent polymeric chains renders the swelling of such gels highly sensitive to minor changes in the pH and ionic strength of the surrounding medium. Many such examples are indicated in Table 5.3, where several such stimuli capable of creating a variety of plausible responses are listed from a general perspective, although the chemical processes responsible for these changes

Table 5.3 Examples of stimuli and specific type of response for tuning polymeric gels

Stimuli	Response
pH	Volume change
Temperature	Phase change
Ionic strength	Shape change
Electric field	Colour change
Magnetic field	Permeation rate
Light/UV	Viscosity change
Solvent	Refractive Index change

can be quite complex. For instance, specific pH sensitivity could arise from the presence of weak acid (acrylic, methacrylic acids, styrene sulphonate groups) or base (dimethylaminoethyl methacrylate), while thermo-responsiveness could be caused by *N*-substituted acrylamide derivatives like *N*-isopropyl acrylamide, *N*-cyclopropyl acrylamide, etc. Incorporation of ionic surfactants such as polyelectrolytes and azoaromatic compounds provide enough flexibility to tune their behaviour and smartness.

In another class of gels, the swelling behaviour is a strong function of temperature. This becomes possible due to the variation in phase equilibrium between the polymer and the swelling

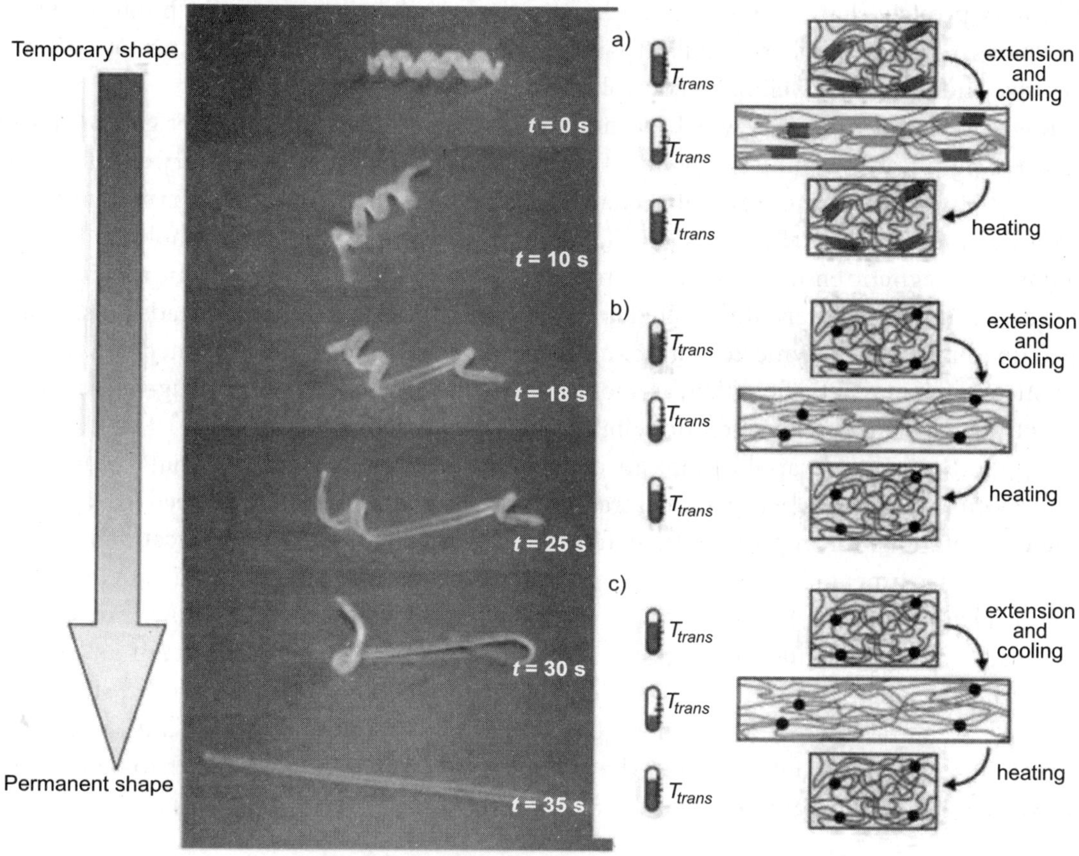

Fig. 5.5 *(see also Plate 4)* (a) Transition from the temporary shape (spiral) to the permanent shape (linear) of a network polymer synthesized from apoly(ε-caprolactone) dimethacrylate and butylacrylate. The switching temperature of the polymer is 45°C. (b) Schematic representation of the molecular mechanism of thermally induced shape memory effect in a) block copolymer with $T_{trans} = T_m$; b) covalently cross- linked polymer with $T_{trans} = T_m$; c) a polymer network with $T_{trans} = T_g$; T_{trans} is the temperature above which the chains are flexible; T_m is the melting point of the polymer and T_g is the glass transition temperature at which the polymer transforms to a rubbery/viscous state. [Reprinted with permission from John Wiley & Sons]

agent (i.e., the solvent) with temperature. For example, there could be a change in the miscibility/compatibility of the polymer and the swelling agent with a change in the temperature of the surroundings. More specifically, if a polymer with a lower critical solution temperature (LCST) is used to form the gel, it will become hydrophilic below the critical temperature, resulting in good swelling ratios, whereas above the CST, the polymer would be almost hydrophobic and may not swell in water to a significant extent. Such thermo-responsive gels are interesting candidates in a number of applications, including drug delivery and microreactors. Yet another type of responsive behaviour in gels could be achieved by complexing the constituent polymer with an oppositely charged polymer similar to polyelectrolyte complexes. Such interpolymer attractions result in excellent regularity in crosslinking, allowing the reduction of network pore size and degree of swelling to control the rate of drug release.

There are smart polymers which do not strictly fit into the class of smart gels owing to their less significant swelling behaviour. These systems exhibit a shape memory effect similar to that of alloys by virtue of reversible changes in chain conformation, local crystallinity and chain dynamics, also as illustrated in Fig. 5.5. On the other hand, hydrophobic polymers containing magnetic entities, called 'microbeads', are well known for prosthetic applications. In the presence of an externally applied magnetic field, the magnetic microbeads pulsate and open up pores in the polymeric matrix and release the drug molecules. The mechanism is so sensitive to the magnetic field that, as soon as the field is switched off, the drug-release stops abruptly, rendering excellent reproducibility to the drug delivery system.

Despite the valuable applications in drug delivery, prosthetic biomaterials, diagnostic applications, robotic grippers, smart extraction and separation systems, we need to overcome several limitations for improving their functional performance. Most applications require faster response time; the present set of hydrogels requires a few minutes for achieving about 50% of volume change. Some of the recently developed gels, however, show much faster response time—a few millisecond, especially with respect to the application of an electric field. Long-term application (e.g., prosthetic biomaterials) needs both improved structural rigidity and durability, in addition to biocompatibility, since many implants still elicit adverse effects inside a human body. The cost of many of these materials has to be lowered for widespread medical applications.

5.3.3 Electro/magnetorheological fluids

Imagine the superheroes (or villains as in the movie *Terminator-II*) depicted in science fiction movies and comics who can just flow through a small key hole and enter a closed room: this is exactly what electrorheological (ER) fluids are capable of doing. They are basically suspensions of fine particles in a liquid medium, in which the apparent viscosity changes enormously in a reversible manner with an applied electric field. For instance, a typical ER fluid can undergo a viscosity change of 5 orders of magnitude instantaneously with an applied electric field with

Mobile phones go rollable in the 'smart' way!

Motorola has created a breakthrough by solving problems with flexible mobile phone displays with the help of ER fluids. The idea is to use a reservoir of ER fluid beneath the foldable display or keypad, which can solidify when an electric current is applied to it and revert back to the fluid state when the electric current is removed. The result is you have a rolled-up mobile phone display, which springs open when you press a button to apply an electric current whenever you want to make or receive a call. Once the job is done, just push the button once again and off it folds like a candy roll!

a very short response time of a few milliseconds. The phenomenon was first discovered and published by an American scientist, Willis Winslow, and is sometimes called the 'Winslow effect' after its discoverer [4]. The simplest example of an ER fluid is a suspension of silica or zirconia particles in a highly viscous medium like silicone oil.

The significance of these smart fluids can be appreciated by looking at some of their interesting applications. The most striking future application for ER fluids is by the armed forces. Imagine a soldier wearing a bulletproof vest made of ER fluid—the vest can be made very light by applying an electric potential, turning it into a stiff and hard material only under dangerous circumstances. Another promising application is in the manufacture of flexible electronics. Although the concept of flexible electronic displays is not very novel, ER fluids are found to solve an important problem with these devices: flexible displays are by definition not rigid and you can imagine the degree of inconvenience you will face when your mobile phone flaps in the air like a flag! Recently, Motorola has filed a US patent for using ER fluid to achieve a rollable yet rigid cell phone display.

Physically speaking, these materials are typically fluids, pastes, gels or elastomers in the absence of an electric field. They transform into viscoelastic solids under a constant shear stress at sufficiently high electric fields (of the order of a few hundred volts/cm). The most interesting aspect of their behaviour is that the physical and mechanical changes are reversible with respect to the applied electric field. For instance, they can run like water under some conditions, ooze like honey in others and can even stick like gelatin depending on the strength of the electric field, temperature and composition. How does this happen? When the electric

Table 5.4 Classification of electrorheological fluids with specific examples

Class of ER fluid	Example
Dispersions	
Ionic conductors	Alumino silicates and zeolites
Semiconductors	Polyacrylonitrile, phenothiazines
Polyelectrolytes	Polylithium methacrylate
Solutions	Poly(hexyl isocyanate)
	Poly-γ-benzyl-L-glutamate

field is applied to a suspension of an ER fluid (microscopic silica particles suspended in an insulating liquid like corn oil), there is an instantaneous alignment of the particles into fibrillar structures. The alignment disappears when the electric field is removed, resulting in a reversible, reproducible response. Nevertheless, they have some limitations like poor stability of the suspensions, the high electric field, ~ 3 kV/mm, required for their operation and structural weakness. Hence such materials can be instantaneously switched between the solid and liquid states, just by turning the electric field on and off. Consequently, the most obvious applications of electrorheological fluids have been vibration damping, torque transmission and control. The electrorheological behaviour is exhibited by fluids with a variety of chemical compositions, which are summarized along with specific examples in Table 5.4.

Similarly, there are fluids which get strongly polarized in the presence of a magnetic field; they are called magnetorheological fluids or simply ferrofluids. These are also suspensions of very fine magnetic particles in a liquid medium. The particles are sometimes coated with a surfactant to avoid aggregation. Figure 5.6 shows a typical ferrofluid resting on a glass plate over a bar magnet. Although the terms magnetorheological fluids and ferrofluids are used interchangeably, it is customary to note that sometimes they are distinguished on the basis of particle size: while the latter represents nanoparticles held in the liquid medium by Brownian motion, the former essentially comprises micron-sized particles with lower dispersion stability. This class of materials has also influenced a wide number of fields right from modern electronics to defence applications. An interesting application of these materials is in the preparation of erasable magnetic inks used to make barcodes and pin numbers in credit cards.

Fig. 5.6 Magnetorheological behaviour: Picture of a ferrofluid resting on a glass plate over a bar magnet [Reproduced from http://en.wikipedia.org/wiki/File:Ferrofluid_Magnet_under_glass_edit,jpg under the terms of the GNU Free Documentation Licence]

5.3.4 Smart electroceramics

Thanks to the advent of smart windows, there is no need to draw the curtains—these windows consist of smart ceramics which can change their index of refraction of visible light in response to heat or an electric field when you need privacy. In general, electroceramics are ceramic materials with unique electric, optical and magnetic properties that make them multi-functional and ultimately endow smartness on the system containing them. The versatile combination of ruggedness and functional diversity of ceramics make this class of materials important in a number of fields. They can be classified on the basis of the nature of energy transduction—whether it is from electric to optical, mechanical to electrical, or any other—and summarized together with specific examples for each type, as in Table 5.5.

Let us consider here, three main classes of smart electroceramics as representative examples, namely thermistors, varistors and piezoelectric transducers, wherein temperature changes, electric potential and mechanical vibrations result in conductivity changes of the ceramic material respectively[5].

Varistors

The word 'varistor' is a combination of two words 'variable' and 'resistor'. These are non-Ohmic voltage-dependent resistors; their resistance decreases with increasing voltage in a nonlinear manner. They are often used in electrical circuits to gain protection from high-voltage pulsating noise, unlike a capacitor, which is used to bypass low-voltage, high-frequency alternating currents. The most common type of varistor is the metal oxide varistor (MOV) which consists of sintered particulates of a metal oxide like ZnO. The operating principle of an MOV is as follows. It consists of ZnO grains embedded in an insulating

Table 5.5 Classification of electroceramic materials based on their energy transduction mode along with specific examples of applications

Energy Transduction	Materials	Applications
Electrical → mechanical	$Pb(Zr_{1-x}Ti_x)O_3$ (PZT)	Positioner, optical tuner
Mechanical → electrical		Igniter
Electrical → chemical	$Zr_{1-x}Y_xO_{2-x/2}$ (YSZ),	Oxygen pump
Chemical → electrical	SnO_2	Gas sensor
Electrical → optical	$LiNbO_3$	Electrooptic modulator
Optical → electrical	GaN	Light detector
Electrical → magnetic	AB_2O_4 spinel: A, B = Mn, Zn	Write head
Magnetic → electrical	$La_{1-x}Ca_xMnO_3$	Read head
Electrical → thermal	SiC	Resistive heater
Thermal → electrical	AB_2O_4 spinel: A,B = Mn, Ni, Fe, Co, Cu $BaTiO_3$ perovskite	NTCR/PTCR thermistor

matrix with some additives like bismuth and manganese to form surface states at the grain boundaries. Each grain boundary forms a diode junction and the whole system becomes equivalent to a network of diode junctions. Thus, when a small voltage is applied, a small amount of current flows due to reverse leakage across the diode junctions. Subsequently, if the voltage is increased, the diode junctions break down and the matrix becomes conducting. This results in a highly non-Ohmic current–voltage behaviour, as depicted in Fig. 5.7. This is exactly the principle by which a varistor acts as a lightning arrestor: the sudden decrease in the electrical resistance of the material when struck by high-voltage lightning bypasses the current to the ground.

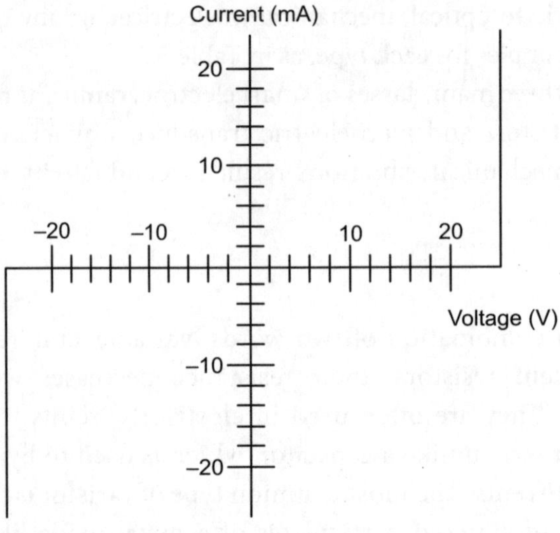

Fig. 5.7 Current–voltage characteristics of a varistor

Thermistors

Electroceramic materials have found application in temperature sensing and control. In the order of increasing level of smartness, they can be categorized as thermocouples, resistance temperature detectors (RTDs) and thermistors. Although all three classes of ceramics have temperature-dependent resistance, just like the voltage-dependent resistance observed in varistors, the level of smartness is defined by the temperature coefficient of resistance (TCR) and the response time, as compared in Fig. 5.8.

A typical example for an electroceramic material with thermistor properties is barium titanate ($BaTiO_3$). You can make this in the form of a small tablet with 10 ohm resistance at room temperature capable of passing say 5 A, but this current starts heating and once the temperature reaches about 110°C (Curie temperature), the resistance becomes equal to a few megaohms and the current stops to start cooling. The effect is reversible and, more importantly, both the resistance at room temperature and the Curie point can be controlled carefully using doping strategies (mainly cations) in the perovskite structure. These materials are extremely

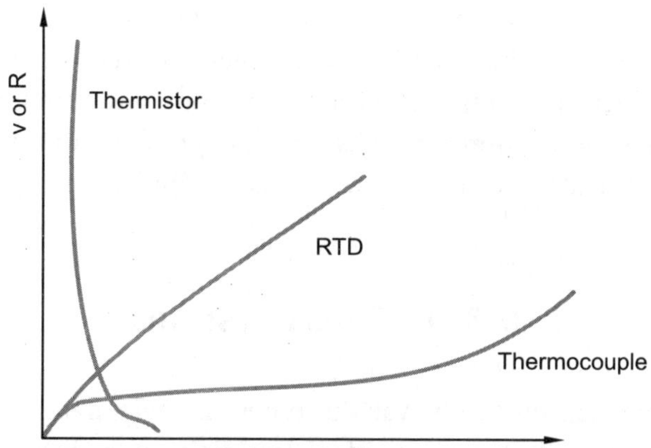

Fig. 5.8 Temperature-dependent voltage and resistance variation of a thermistor, resistance temperature detector (RTD) and a thermocouple

useful for interesting applications like self-regulating heaters for motor protection. The heating element fabricated from this material is made up of a number of holes through which air is blown to heat it up. When the temperature reaches a certain value characteristic of the material, it becomes resistive and current stops flowing.

Piezoelectric transducers

The piezoelectric effect is based on the dependence of electrical polarization on applied stress, in order to convert electrical to mechanical energy and vice versa. The word 'piezo' means 'to squeeze' (Greek). Lead zirconate titanate (PZT, $PbZr_xTi_{1-x}O_3$) is one of the most commonly used piezoelectric materials. The first practical application of piezoelectric materials was in SONAR, first developed during the First World War. The ultrasonic submarine detector developed in 1917 consisted of a piezoelectric transducer made of thin quartz crystals coupled with a hydrophone to detect the returning sound or echo, which helped to locate the distance from a particular object. Both low- (<500 Hz) and high-frequency vibrations (greater than a few kHz) can be easily created by modulating the ac voltage applied on these materials. Hence they are used for a variety of applications, ranging from marine farming and submarine detection to vibration suppression.

The working principle of a piezoelectric material is based on charge separation in the crystal lattice produced by a mechanical stress, unlike the charge separation in a dielectric capacitor produced by a potential difference. The effect has also been observed in bones [6]. Piezoelectricity in dry bones was first demonstrated by Fukada and Yasuda in 1957, who observed electrical polarization as a function of applied mechanical stress. Later, Becker and coworkers observed partial limb regeneration in rats stimulated by the application of weak electrical signals. Also, the ability of salamanders to regenerate lost limbs is believed to be due to axial electrical signals. Similar effects like electrostriction can also be used to make a ceramic smart as tunable transducers can be made. Electrostrictive materials and relaxor ferroelectrics (e.g., lead magnesium niobate) have several advantages over piezoelectric materials due to a large variation of the dielectric constant with composition and temperature. Many of these ferroic materials possess active domain walls (crystallographic boundaries which can move under external force or field) to cause visible change in dimensions (phase transformations) to be used as actuators.

5.3.5 Smart systems

So far we have had a virtual tour of the various types of smart materials and their principles of operation. Let us now see how the individual materials can be integrated to achieve smart 'systems'. We can try to envision smart systems corresponding to each type of smart material we have discussed. A smart shape memory material may lead to the design of aircraft wings which can change shape according to air pressure and flying speeds; a smart gel can act as insulin delivery pumps coupled with sugar sensors to form a smart diabetic kit; integration of smart chemical sensors and readout tools can provide smart toilets that can analyze urine, and provide warnings ahead of health problems; and smart electroceramic materials may provide smart rooms which will protect us from excess light, heat and even from noisy neighbours! We can envision more and more smart systems in future until limited by our own imagination. Recently, the applicability of smart systems and costumes in the Olympics has been analyzed [7].

Get Smarter and Run Faster

Athletes once used to compete with bare feet. The present trend is far different. There is a great demand for clothing and shoes which stick to the body and provide better fluidic motion with low resistance. Some of the shoes and clothes developed by Nike for the 2008 Beijing Olympics were composed of threads of Vectran, a super-strong liquid crystal polymer that withstands high temperatures. The resulting shoes were lighter and stiffer to offer very low drag. The clothes exhibited 7% lesser drag compared to the Nike outfits worn in the 2004 Games.

5.4 TECHNOLOGICAL LIMITATIONS AND CHALLENGES

Any emerging technology is accustomed to critical limitations that not only challenge its commercial success but also pave the way for further research and development to overcome them. Smart materials are not an exception to this law of nature. A major limitation for the commercial success of smart materials is the degradation of performance after cycles of operation, commonly denoted as 'functional fatigue'. This happens mainly due to some non-negligible irreversible changes in the structure of the smart material accompanying the major reversible phase change responsible for the smartness. There could also be secondary processes following one cycle of a reversible phase change. In the case of multi-component smart systems, the functional fatigue could be due to the gradual deterioration in communication between the individual components/constituents.

Another important limitation is their exorbitant cost which at present allows only limited strategic applications. In addition, many of the smart systems like spectacles, shoes and similar systems made for demonstration purposes are too heavy and efforts are on to make them volumetrically smaller and gravimetrically lighter. There are also many integration issues when such smart materials and systems are assembled into a smart room with the help of suitable software for voice and face recognition, in conjunction with unobtrusive processing systems, hidden cameras and other hardware for signal acquisition and processing [7]. Despite all these limitations, many strategic applications have been extensively developed.

5.5 CONCLUSIONS

Imparting anthropomorphic qualities like smartness, memory and trainability to materials is a fascinating objective and chemistry plays a critical role in designing these functional materials and the interactions of various constituents. The invasion of smart technologies have, no doubt, played an important role in revolutionizing various industries with their swiftness, better performance, multiplefunctions, miniaturization and cost-effectiveness. Yet, the technologies have to travel a long way to achieve considerable success in commercialization, which requires rigorous research to overcome the limitations mentioned in the previous section. For many engineering applications, structural materials are increasingly being replaced by smart functional materials, and wild predictions based on science fiction have aided the rapid and concerted development of this amazing class of materials. This is expected to have a tremendous economic impact although it is too early to think of societal aspects.

Further Reading

[1] Ball P, *Materials to Measure*, and Gandhi M V and Thompson B S, *Smart Materials and Structures*, Chapman & Hall, London,1992.

[2] Newnham R E and Ruschau G R, Smart electroceramics, *J. Am. Ceram. Soc.*, 74: 463, 1991.

[3] Tanaka T, Gels, *Sci. Am.*, 244: 124, 1981; Varghese S, Lele A K, Srinivas D, Sastry M and Mashelkar R A, Novel macroscopic self-organization in polymer gels, *Adv. Mater.*, 13: 1544–48, 2001; Varghese S, Lele A K and Mashelkar R A, Designing new thermoreversible gels by molecular tailoring of hydrophilic-hydrophobic interactions, *J. Chem. Phys.*, 112: 3063–70, 2000; Badiger M V, Lele A K, Balerao V S, Varghese S and Mashelkar R A, Molecular tailoring of thermo-reversible copolymer gels: Some new mechanistic insights, *J. Chem. Phys.* 109: 1175–84, 1998.

[4] Winslow W M, Induced fibration of suspensions, *J. Appl. Phys.*, 20: 1137, 1949.

[5] Teller H and Ayrahami Y, Electroceramics, in *Encyclopaedia of Smart Materials,* John Wiley & Sons, 2002.
[6] Reinish G, Piezoelectric properties of bones as functions of moisture content, *Nature,* 253: 626, 1975.
[7] Pentland A P, Smart rooms, *Sci. Am.,* April: 54, 1996; Science at the Olympics, *Science,* 321: 634, 2008.

EXERCISES

1. Using the simulation program given in the website http://www.smaterial.com/SMA/sma.html, simulate and interpret the stress–strain behaviour of a nickel–titanium alloy as a function of external temperature and experimental duration to observe its full range of behaviour from quasi-plasticity to pseudo-elasticity. (*Refer:* Nasser S-N, Choi Y J, W-G Guo, Isaacs J B, Taya M, High strain-rate small strain response of a NiTi shape-memory alloy, *J. Eng. Mater. Technol.,* 127: 83–89, 2005.)
2. Define the main characteristics of smartness in materials. How many of these can be defined quantitatively using degrees of intelligence?
3. Distinguish between passively smart, actively smart and very smart materials using suitable examples.
4. What are shape memory alloys? Why are they important? Mention their limitations.
5. Explain the limitation of the present generation of smart materials. How can these limitations be overcome?
6. How can a polymer gel be made sensitive to temperature changes or pH changes? What are the main limitations of smart gels?
7. Mention some important applications of electrorheological fluids.
8. Imagine that you have a pair of very smart shoes or spectacles. How useful would they be for your day-to-day functioning? What are their limitations?
9. Discuss the ethical issues involved in winning a sports medal using smart or intelligent materials with respect to the ban of performance enhancing steroid drugs.

6

Functional Materials for Sustainable Energy

This chapter introduces the environmental threats posed by many energy generation technologies and explains how the use of functional materials can provide possible remedies including the adoption of hydrogen economy and more use of renewable resources. A systematic description of specific energy conversion and storage systems, such as batteries, fuel cells, supercapacitors and hybrid power systems using a variety of functional materials, is given, along with recent advances. The broad impact of nanotechnology on future materials for energy technology is also discussed.

LEARNING OBJECTIVES

- To understand the energy scenario in developing and developed countries
- To appreciate the importance of sustainable energy conversion
- To become aware of the merits and demerits of different sustainable energy options
- To explore the role of functional materials in energy technology
- To feel the need for developing new functional materials for lithium ion batteries, fuel cells and ultracapacitors
- To appreciate the need for developing new functional materials for harnessing solar energy
- To visualize the future of energy technology with relevance to materials science

Fireflies

Fig. 6.1 *(see also Plate 5)* A photograph of a swarm of fireflies [Source: http://en.wikipedia.org/wiki/File:Leuchtk %C3%A4ref_-_Firefly.jpg; reproduced under the terms of the GNU free documentation licence]

If you have observed a firefly, you would have been stunned by the way it turns its lights on and of, i.e., the way it controls the intensity of its glow, depending on the purpose. We only know that this luminescence is of biochemical origin—the 'Luciferin Luciferase' interaction. There are many astonishing facts yet to be unravelled. A firefly is a perfectly reversible energy conversion system which can operate in cycles with 100% efficiency! Unbelievable as it may sound, 100% of its energy is given off as light with negligible heat loss. In comparison, an electric bulb gives off only 10% of its energy as light, 90% of which is wasted as heat!

In this chapter, we will see how the energy conversion efficiency of a firefly can be achieved with the help of functional materials.

6.1 INTRODUCTION

'Energy' provides a lifeline to humanity and is an inevitable topic in engineering and materials sciences. In the last chapter, we reviewed smart materials. Here, we are going to discuss their utility in energy technology: Are they smart enough to quench our ever-increasing thirst for energy? Do they offer better means of capturing energy from natural resources without creating problems for future generations?

Coal, oil, natural gas, nuclear, hydropower and biomass are some of the common energy resources. However, it is more convenient to interpret energy in terms of heat and electricity. The importance of the primary fuel resource is related to how efficiently it generates these secondary forms, viz., heat and electricity. Sometimes, heat is considered to be a sub-class of energy as it can also be generated from electricity. However, when we deal with efficient means of energy conversion, we should always remember that heating is not an efficient utilization of electricity. For example, heating water in a kettle using electricity consumes three to four times the amount of energy required when heating water directly over a flame. Hence, we discuss electricity generation and heat generation separately in this chapter.

It is interesting to have an overview of the history of energy resources in order to understand the current energy scenario. Until about 400 years ago, biomass (wood, crop residue and animal waste) was the primary source of energy. At that time, the population was much less, and the trees that were chopped down for heating and cooking were naturally replaced by new ones. This practice was environmentally benign since carbon dioxide released by burning wood was is absorbed by newly growing vegetation. Thus, biomass remained a dominant energy source until the beginning of the 19th century. With the advent of the Industrial Revolution, coal entered the fuel market first in Britain, followed by the United States, Germany and then Japan. Coal replaced charcoal for producing steel, and split wood for fuelling trains. The little energy demand that was not met by biomass and coal was fulfilled by oil and hydropower. Not being the age of automobiles, oil was mainly used for illumination and lubrication of machinery.

In the modern era of rapid technological development, and far higher population than before, we are growing incredibly hungrier for energy. Now we need more electricity to power our homes; more kinetic and heat energy to drive our automobiles and cook food; and enormous amounts of fuel for industrial production! In the United States, using the Internet alone accounts for 10% of energy consumption, which is expected to increase upto 60% in the next twenty years. As far as India is concerned, about 54% of the total commercial energy is obtained from coal while the remaining demand is met by oil and natural gas. Table 6.1 summarizes the electrical energy generation data in India from various sources in 2011/2012.

Table 6.1 Electrical energy generation data of India from various sources (Data Source CEA, as on 31/03/2011) (In MW)

	Coal	Gas	Diesel	Nuclear	Hydro	Res	Total	Percentage
State Sector	47257	4327	603	0	27257	3009	82453	47.5
Central Sector	34045	6702	0	4780	8885	0	54413	31.3
Private Sector	12616	6677	597	0	1425	15446	36761	21.2
Total	93918	17706	1200	4780	37567	18455	173626	100.0
Percentage	54.1	10.2	0.7	2.8	21.6	10.6	100.0	

Source: www.indianpowersector.com

The explicit dependence on fossil fuels as preprimary energy option poses two major questions: How long will the fossil fuel reserves last? How clean are the fossil fuel–based future energy conversion technologies going to be? While the first question is more than a matter of dispute, the second one requires serious attention in terms of impact on health and hygiene, and addition to cost and efficiency. Meeting energy demands, especially in developing countries like India and China, is the main source of air pollution, acid rain, toxic contamination of water bodies and release of radioactive waste. For instance, most of the components released from automobile exhausts, viz., carbon dioxide, methane, nitrous oxides, hydrofluorocarbons (HFCs) and perfluorocarbons (PFCs), are greenhouse gases (GHGs) and contribute to global warming (Table 6.2). In fact, a flippant classification of energy sources refers to energy from hell (coal, natural gas, etc.) and energy from heaven (solar, wind, etc.), and functional materials come under the second type.

Table 6.2 Composition of untreated automobile exhausts causing air pollution

Exhaust component	Four stroke spark-ignited Gasoline engine	Diesel engine
NO_x	100–400 ppm	350–1000 ppm
Hydrocarbons	500–5000 ppm C	50–330 ppm C
CO	0.1–6.0%	300–1200 ppm
O_2	0.2–2.0%	10%–15%
CO_2	10–13.5%	7%
SO_x	15–60 ppm	10–1000 ppm

The greenhouse effect and global warming

The accumulation of greenhouse gases in the atmosphere leads to an unpredictable increase in the global temperature (Fig. 6.2). 'Global warming' does not mean that the earth's surface will be set on fire by the greenhouse gases, but even an increase in global temperature by 1°C will have serious effects on climatic conditions, causing floods in the coastal regions and insufficient rainfall in other regions. Though some frigid northern countries may enjoy moderate weather due to global warming, the tropical regions, where the world's poorest live, will be badly affected. Unfortunately, people in these regions do not contribute to greenhouse gas emissions themselves. Many countries follow the regulation of the Kyoto Protocol laid down by the United Nations in 1997. It called for a reduction in greenhouse gas emission to an average of 5% below the 1990 levels to be achieved between 2008 and 2012 [1]. Unfortunately, this has not been realised and the subsequent Copenhagen Climate Summit in 2009, with about 8000 representatives from 192 countries, was also not a great success. Nevertheless, 55 countries which collectively emit 78% of the world's greenhouse gases have formally pledged to cut or limit their emissions. India is committed to reduce emissions by 25% by 2020, based on the 2005 reference level.

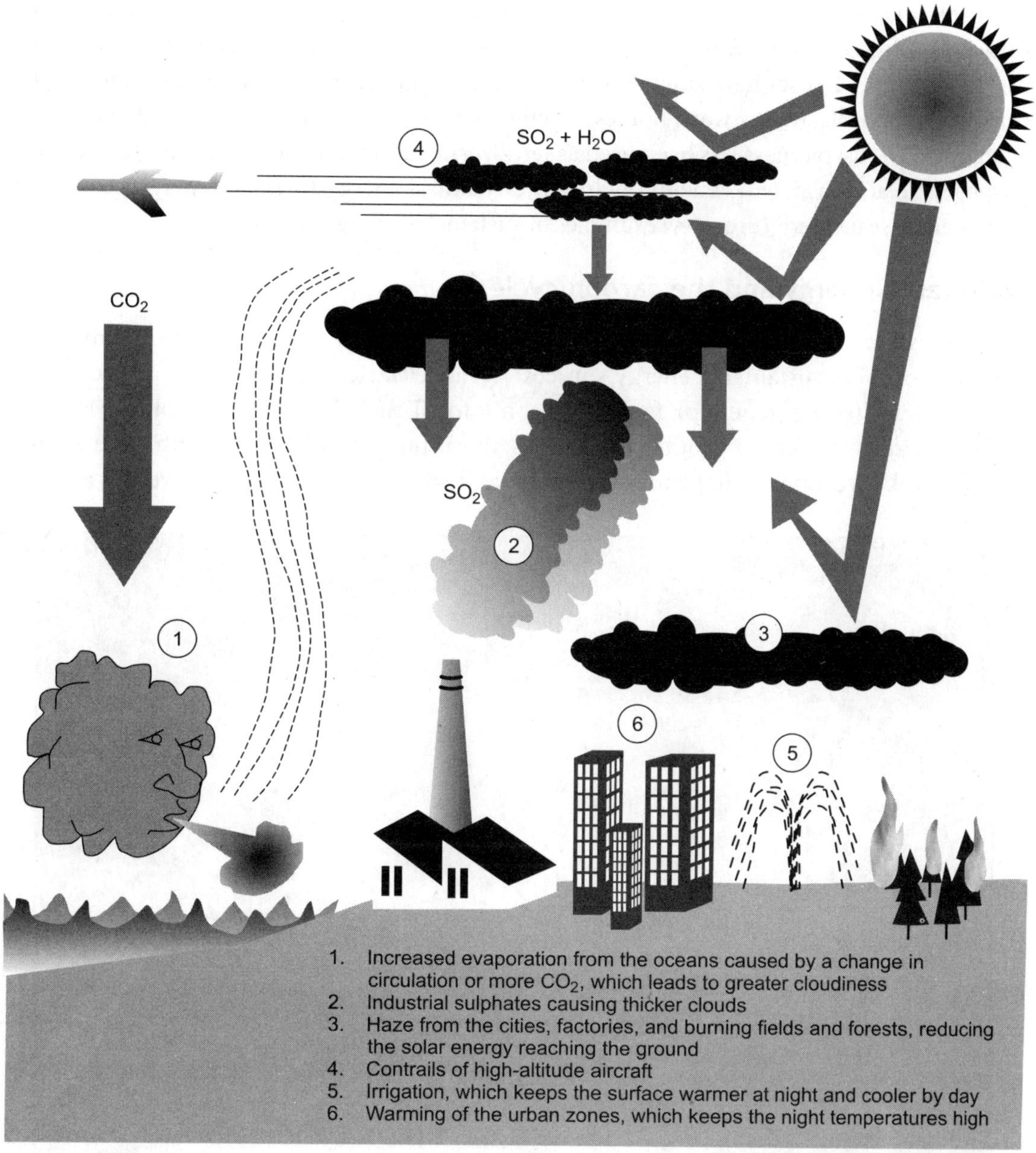

Fig. 6.2 Schematic representation of possible causes for the decreased diurnal temperature range [Reproduced with permission from American Chemical Society: Kukla G and Karl T R, Nighttime warming and the greenhouse effect, *Environ. Sci. Technol.*, 27: 1468, 1993]

An obvious solution to all these problems is to switch over from non-renewable energy sources like fossil fuels to renewable energy options. The idea of renewable energy is not new to us. For centuries, houses have been constructed to trap enough heat from the sun, and wind to ventilate without electricity; water bodies, together with wind power, have been used to transport people and goods; biomass has been used as fertilizers in agriculture as well as fuel for domestic purposes. Solar energy, wind energy, hydropower, biomass energy, hydrogen energy, geothermal energy and ocean energy are a few examples of sustainable energy sources.

Renewable energy and the carbon cycle

Some questions still remain: What is the efficiency of energy conversion? What about the reliability of these sustainable energy sources? While electricity can be generated to a rated plant capacity with a generator fuelled by some fossil fuels having Co_2 capture (Fig. 6.3) facility, biomass, nuclear or geothermal sources, this is not going to be easy with other sources like big mall. Hydropower depends on rainfall, and wind, solar and wave power on weather.

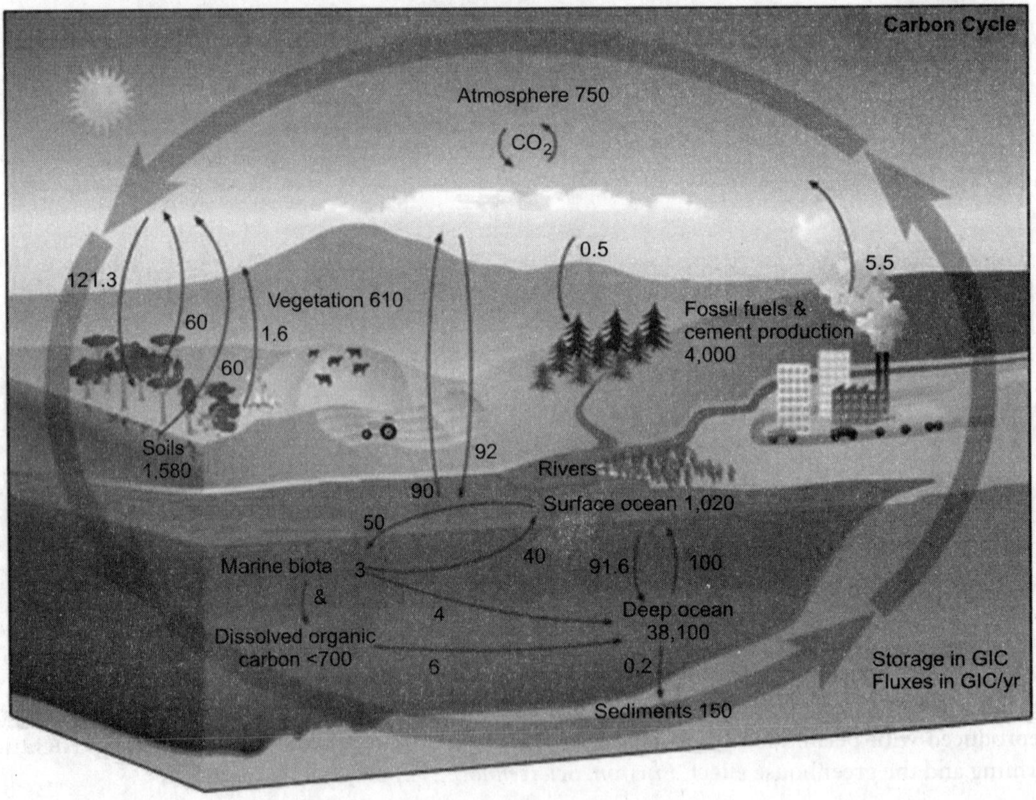

Fig. 6.3 *(see also Plate 5)* Storage and yearly changes of carbon content (expressed in gigatons of carbon) in the atmosphere, hydrosphere and geosphere [Adapted from http://en.wikipedia.org/wiki/File:Carbon_cycle-cute_diagram.svg under the terms of the GNU Free Documentation Licence]

While tidal power is predictable, there is no guarantee that peaks in electricity generation from changing tides will coincide with the peak in electricity demand! Thus, wind, solar, tidal and wave sources can only displace, not replace, conventional sources of energy at least.

Herein lies the importance of functional materials! We will discuss:

- What types of functional materials are suitable for different sources of renewable energy
- How the functional flexibility of a designer material improves the efficiency of harnessing energy from renewable sources
- How we can boost the overall performance of an energy conversion system by hybrid power options

However, the focus will be on solar energy conversion and electrochemical methods to achieve hydrogen economy and cleaner energy conversion, since these are the technologies which can be improved greatly using new materials science, unlike wind, hydro, geothermal and ocean energy which depend critically on weather changes.

6.2 MATERIALS FOR SOLAR ENERGY CONVERSION

The amount of solar energy striking the earth in one hour is almost equal (14 terawatt-years of energy) to the total amount of energy used by the world's population in one year! It is the cleanest form of energy available (truly widespread) in all continents. Even with so many advanced technologies available, we are unable to trap the entire energy effectively in terms of cost and efficiency. At present, only a tiny proportion (0.05%—this is changing very fast!) of the world's energy needs is supplemented by solar energy, though the annual growth of the market for solar cells is at about 40% per year. Look at the biological machinery in plants that enable them to trap solar energy by photosynthesis (Fig. 6.4). The biochemical pathways responsible for such high efficiency in plants are so complicated that we are still unable to understand them completely; mimicking photosynthesis at the labouretory is quite a farfetched goal. Some researchers, however, have been able to build successful photoconversion systems by immobilizing parts of biomolecules (viz., enzymes and photosensitizers) on artificial platforms.

There are, in general, three ways of trapping solar energy:

1. *Solar thermal:* trapping the heat energy of the sun's rays
2. *Photovoltaics:* solar photons produce electric current
3. *Photoelectrochemical:* solar energy is stored by electrochemical reactions

Though they appear different, a common aspect is that all of them require good sunlight. Hence they also share common limitations:

1. Solar power can be generated only during daylight, with peak output on clear days when the sun is directly overhead.
2. Solar output is markedly low on cloudy and rainy days.
3. The power output is also low at high altitudes where the sun does not rise high in the sky in winter.

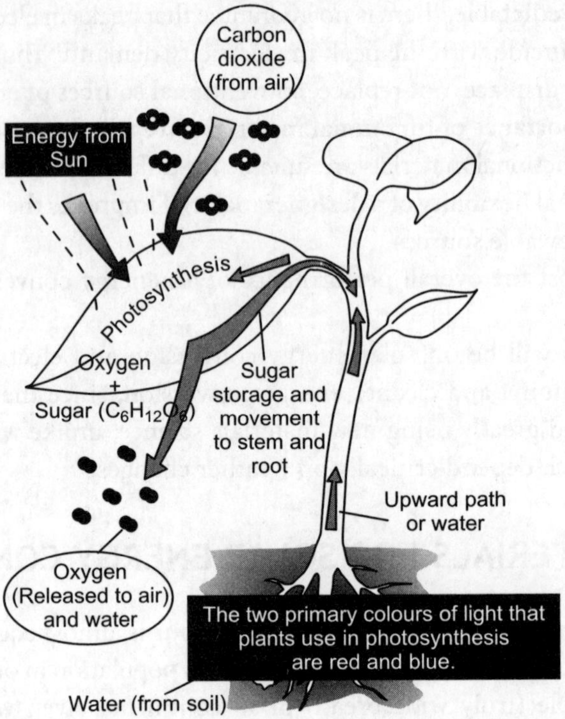

Fig. 6.4 Light harvesting mechanism of plants during photosynthesis [Adapted from http://www.nasa.gov]

However, solar power has an important advantage over its complementary wind power since it is produced during daylight hours when electricity demand is highest, reducing the need for peaking generators. Rapid strides in tapping wind energy have taken place during the last decade especially in developed countries like India and China. The potential of functional materials to facilitate the large-scale deployment of variable renewable (wind, solar) electricity generation, along with the option for reducing greenhouse gas emissions from the electric power sector, make them extremely attractive for improved grid reliability and stability.

Some of the most recent developments in materials for different energy technologies, except wind, are discussed in the following sections.

6.3.1 Solar thermal systems

In this method, the heat generated by sunlight is utilized to generate steam which in turn is used for electricity generation. When solar heat is utilized simply to make hot water, the system is called a 'passive solar thermal system'. A *solar thermal system* consists of a solar concentrator to focus sunlight which heats up a 'thermal fluid' followed by hot water/steam generation.

Thermal fluids are materials capable of storing and transferring heat in a sustainable manner. Many types of nanofluids are currently being emerged as efficient thermal fluids. A typical nanofluid consists of a carrier liquid, such as water or oil, dispersed with nanoparticles of cupric oxide (CuO), alumina (Al_2O_3), titanium dioxide (TiO_2), silica (SiO_2) or carbon nanotubes.

There are broadly two types of solar thermal systems: double tank and single tank. In the double-tank system, the heat transfer fluid is divided into two compartments: one kept at low temperature and the other at high temperature. Fluid from the low-temperature tank flows through the solar collector, gets heated and flows into the high-temperature tank where heat exchangers are kept. The heat trapped from the fluid using the heat exchangers is utilized in steam generation for electricity production. After losing heat to the heat exchanger, the fluid flows back into the low-temperature compartment and the cycle continues.

On the other hand, the single-tank system stores thermal energy over a solid (e.g., silica) while a heat transfer fluid flows through it. The solid material is packed with a temperature gradient in a single chamber. A heat transfer fluid near the solar collector cools down as it flows through the solid packing where the thermal energy is stored. For steam generation, a low-temperature thermal fluid is forced from the bottom of the solid packing to the top and then passed on to an adjacent heat exchanger where the heat is trapped.

Solar thermal conversion is the most efficient means of trapping solar energy. Natural solar power corresponds to 2.7 megawatts per square metre per year, which is actually a low rate. Hence, solar thermal systems require large land areas for placing mirrors to collect and concentrate solar energy. However, the land area is far less than that required for coal mines and plants. Deserts are often ideal locations for setting up solar thermal plants. The first solar thermal electricity generation plant was set up in the 1980s in the Mojave desert in California, considered to be the world's largest solar power installation with an output of 354 MW.

The solar thermal collectors are also classified as low-, medium- and high-temperature collectors for different applications, viz., for heating swimming pools, to provide hot water for houses and to generate electricity from heat by a so-called 'concentrated solar power' or 'captive solar power' (CSP) technology, respectively [2]. A typical solar water heater can reduce CO_2 emissions by 1 ton/year compared to water heating by natural gas and by 3 tons/year compared to electric water heating!

High-temperature solar collectors consist of an array of parabolic mirrors to focus solar radiation; the heat collected is used to drive any chemical process, an automotive tracking system for the sun's movement to increase the efficiency of heat engines or stored in a thermal mass and later converted to electricity. Figure 6.5 shows a flying solar farm developed by NASA.

The overall efficiency of a solar thermal collector is guided by the efficiencies of the individual steps, viz., heat gain, transfer, storage and transport. The first step is the effective accumulation of heat energy from the sun using suitable reflectors which can absorb short-wave radiation and reflect long-wave radiation. The accumulated heat is transferred using water present in the tubes arranged below the collector plates, which can be used as such for domestic purposes or stored for electricity generation in power plants. Media for heat storage include pressurized steam, concrete, a variety of phase change materials and molten salts such as sodium and potassium nitrate. However, the maximum efficiency achieved so far in converting solar energy to electricity using solar thermal power plants, has not been more than 30%. Recent efforts have been focussed on improving the efficiency of the various components in solar thermal systems. One important progress in heat gain is the use of solar concentrators to focus more and more solar radiation on the panels.

6.3.2 Solar photovoltaics

There are two ways of generating electricity from solar energy:

1. An indirect method called Captive Solar Power (CSP) using solar thermal collectors, which was discussed in the previous section.
2. A direct conversion method using devices called 'solar photovoltaics'.

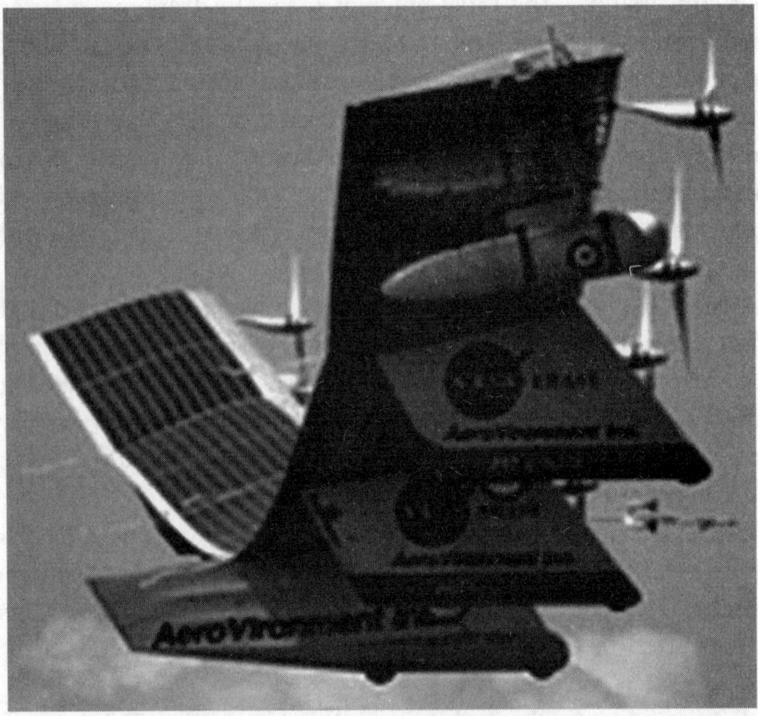

Fig. 6.5 Helios, the flying wing developed by NASA, powered by solar cells in the daytime and a hydrogen–air fuel cell at night for storage [Source: http://en.wikipedia.org/wiki/File:Pages_from_64317main_helios-1.jpg; reproduced under the terms of the GNU Free Documentation Licence]

Photovoltaic means electricity from light. Solar thermal systems utilize the heat energy of sunlight with a conversion efficiency of about 40%, whereas, photovoltaics do not deal with the heat content of sunlight but only with light energy which is directly converted into electricity, as shown in Fig. 6.6. The history of the photovoltaic effect dates back to the 19th century when Edmond Becquerel found an increase in the electrical current passing through two metal electrodes dipped in a conducting medium upon exposure to light. Followed by the discovery of photoconductivity in selenium in the 1870s, Charles Fritts invented the first photovoltaic solar cell made of selenium in 1883.

A photovoltaic solar cell consists of two layers of semiconductor material capable of converting sunlight to electricity. While one layer is made up of an electron-rich material, the other is essentially an electron-deficient one. When two such layers are sandwiched, an electric field is developed at the interface when exposed to sunlight. Thus the working principle basically involves the separation of electrons and holes at a p–n junction of a semiconductor. The output is a direct current, as in the case of a simple battery, which needs to be converted to alternating current for powering a house or connecting to an electricity grid. Most commercial photovoltaic solar cells are made of thin wafers (~200–300 microns thick) of crystalline silicon, usually between two and three square inches of area.

Photovoltaics can also be made up of polycrystalline materials, amorphous structures or thin films. There are also organic photovoltaics denoted commercially as 'plastic solar cells', which recently entered the renewable energy competition. Each of them has its own advantages and limitations and a characteristic trade-off between cost and performance. For instance, while SPVs based on single-crystalline silicon can offer conversion efficiencies of upto 15%, those made of cadmium telluride (CdTe) can reach 20%, which can be boosted to 40% by forming multilayer thin films with several layers capable of capturing light with a range of wavelengths. The cost factor of these systems is makes them unaffordable. Yet, scientists have not given up this area: more recently, researchers at 'Nanosolar' company have developed a unique technology that uses copper indium gallium selenide (CIGS) panels

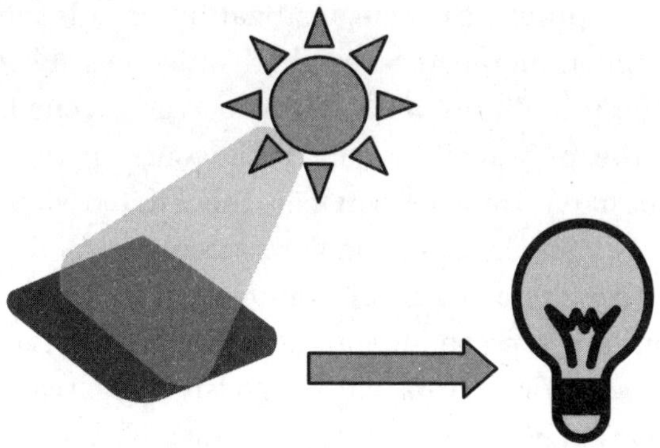

Fig. 6.6 Schematic of the principle of photovoltaic cells: sunlight falls on a silicon wafer and is directly converted into electricity

instead of silicon to manufacture solar cells using a process similar to newspaper printing! It involves coating metal sheets as thin aluminium foils with a layer of heat-absorbing nano-ink using printing press styling machines rather than mounting on glass as in traditional solar cells. With this process, the solar panels will be able to deliver energy for less than $1 per watt—far cheaper than that offered by coal-fired plants in future.

As in the case of the other upcoming renewable technologies, the solar photovoltaics (SPV) should also strike a balance between cost and efficiency to compete with the existing conventional energy technologies. For example, while SPVs can offer efficiencies upto 20%, their cost continues to be disheartening, which is on an average $0.25 per kilowatt-hour versus $0.05–$0.08 for various biomass-based fuels. The maximum theoretical efficiency of photovoltaics is explained by the Shockley–Queisser theory [3, 4].

Researchers found that photovoltaic systems which can overcome the constraints imposed by the above theory can have theoretical efficiencies upto 60%. Thus materials capable of producing multiple excitons from a single absorbed photon of energy higher than that of their band gap and those with intermediate bands are more promising for photovoltaic applications. This, in fact, has been proved recently with the help of lead selenide (PbSe) quantum dots which produce multiple excitons from a single absorbed photon with very high quantum yield. On the other hand, the emergence of organic photovoltaics is a significant leap in this area. Though their efficiencies are lower than inorganic competitors, their lower costs make them attractive. Quite a few years back, MIT developed plastic solar cells by using organic photovoltaics. Recent developments in organic photovoltaics include the incorporation of dyes (sensitizers), organic–inorganic composites and nanocomposites to increase the density and mobility of charge carriers. Despite all these impressive developments, lack of a suitable

Gratzel's dye-sensitized solar cell

The visible absorptivity and photoconversion efficiency of wide band gap semiconductors can be improved by dye-sensitization. In this method, dye molecules are adsorbed on the semiconductor surface, which enhances absorption of visible light for excitation. Thus, the initial photoexcitation does not occur in the semiconductor electrode working as the photovoltaic cell, but occurs in the light-absorbing dye. This is followed by a charge transfer between the excited state dye molecules and the semiconductor energy levels. Sustained conversion is facilitated by regeneration of the reduced dye either via a reversible redox couple, used as a mediator, or by electron donation from a p-type semiconductor. Electrodes for dye-sensitized solar cells are mesoporous semiconductors with high surface area capable of absorbing large amounts of solar radiation. Examples include TiO_2, ZnO and CdS sensitized with Rhodamine B.

energy storage system like an inexpensive rechargeable battery continues to act as a major impediment.

6.3.3 Photoelectrochemical devices

Unlike the solid state photovoltaics which operate based on charge separation at a p–n junction, photoelectrochemical devices are capable of storing solar energy by performing an electrochemical reaction. Long after the invention of the 'Becquerel effect' in 1839, the modern era of photoelectrochemistry began with the invention by Brattain and Garrett in 1954. They were the first to demonstrate how the reactivity of germanium electrodes can be controlled by varying their semiconducting properties and by optical illumination. This was the beginning of the idea of doping, i.e., the method of harnessing electrical and optical properties of semiconductors by the controlled introduction of impurities in their crystal lattice.

The overall efficiency of photoelectrochemical devices almost entirely depends on the semiconductor/electrolyte junction. When a semiconductor electrode is dipped in an electrolyte, the majority carriers (electrons in the case of n-type and holes in the case of p-type) in the semiconductor are transferred to the electrolyte in order to match their Fermi levels. The potential difference at the interface during this equilibration is responsible for the optoelectronic properties of the junction, such as rectification (diode characteristics) and photocurrent generation (i.e., generation of a voltage when the junction is illuminated). The mechanistic and kinetic aspects of the photoelectrochemical behaviour at semiconductor/electrolyte interfaces have been reviewed in detail [3–5]. These systems can be broadly classified into three types based on the final form in which they store energy and also how they harness solar energy:

1. photoelectrolysis cell
2. photoelectrochemical cell
3. photogalvanic cell

The *photoelectrolysis cell* stores solar energy as chemical energy in the form of products generated when the junction is illuminated. A good example for this type of cell is the photocatalytic splitting of water into hydrogen and oxygen. The second category, the *photoelectrochemical cell*, converts solar energy directly into electricity by giving a photovoltage when illuminated by sunlight. The third one, the *photogalvanic cell* or a *photosensitized solar cell*, involves a dye molecule in the electrolyte which primarily absorbs solar energy by undergoing charge transfer at the interface. A typical example is the Gratzel cell. Electrochemical photosystems offer several advantages over solid state photovoltaics such as [4, 5]:

- They are not very sensitive to defects in semiconductors.
- The solid/liquid interface is easy to produce and the production cost will be less.
- There are well-accepted methods of surface modification to create surface states and their effect on current–voltage characterestics/energetics can be accurately predicted.

Semiconductors commonly used in photoelectrochemical solar energy conversion include Si, CdS, ZnS, CdSe, ZnSe, ZnTe, GaAs, GaP, ZnO, $KTaO_3$, Ta_2O_5, $SrTiO_3$ and TiO_2. More specifically, for photocatalytic water splitting, metal oxide semiconductors like $SrTiO_3$, $KTaO_3$ and Ta_2O_5 are common anode materials and p-type non-oxide semiconductors such as p-Si and p-GaP are used commonly in the cathode. However, these cathode materials require more bias voltages as their Fermi level does not match with the energy level of the H_2O/O_2 system. To overcome this problem, thin films of semiconductors are coated on transparent supports to achieve H_2 evolution at low potentials of 0.2–0.3 V. On the other hand, for photoelectrochemical cells, CdSe, CdS and CdTe are commonly used in electrodes with the electrolytes being polychalcogenides, including sulphides and selenides. Also, the conversion efficiency of single crystalline electrodes is more than that of the polycrystalline analogues.

There have been many new approaches to improve photoconversion efficiency, electrode stability and reduce the bias voltage. For example, heterodiodes like *n*-CdS coated on *n*-GaAs, with the *n*-CdS side forming a junction with a liquid electrolyte, are attractive candidates. The photovoltage at the heterojunction adds in series to the photovoltage at the semiconductor/electrolyte interface, thereby increasing the open circuit potential under illumination. Interestingly, a heterojunction formed between a p- and a n-type semiconductor with sequential illumination of both the electrodes (with the wide band gap material illuminated first) is capable of offering better conversion efficiencies if their band gaps fall within the solar spectrum. Recently, an interesting means of improving the conversion efficiency of traditional n-Si photoelectrochemical cells has been achieved by making thicker films (>100 μm) to absorb 90% of the solar energy above its band gap (1.12 eV in the case of Si). This has been allows listed recently by orthogonalizing the absorbers by forming arrays of crystalline Si nanowires on an Au support which is inherently inactive towards photoelectrochemical energy conversion (Fig. 6. 7).

6.4 MATERIALS FOR ELECTROCHEMICAL POWER SOURCES

As worldwide concern about the use of fossil fuels is increasing with respect to resource depletion, pollution and global warming, there will be a progressive swing towards cleaner technologies for harnessing energy from renewable resources. In this context, electrochemical methods of generating and storing electricity are promising, especially for offering cleaner, noise-free and more efficient energy conversion.

Electrochemical power sources can be broadly classified into three types: batteries, fuel cells and electrochemical capacitors. Though the mechanisms of their operation are different, as shown in Fig. 6.8, all of them consist of two electrodes, a cathode and an anode dipped in an electrolyte. While batteries and fuel cells convert chemical energy directly into electrical energy by means of redox reactions at the cathode and anode, electrochemical capacitors are capable of storing energy by reversible adsorption/desorption of species at the electrode–electrolyte

(a) (b)

Fig. 6.7 Scanning electron micrographs of silicon nanowire arrays fabricated on an Si(111) wafer using a vapour–liquid–solid process with gold as the catalyst: (a) Cross-sectional view scale bar: 15 μm and (b) top view scale bar: 85.7 μm [Reproduced with permission from American Chemical Society: Maiolo J R, Kayes B M, Filler M A, Putnam M C, Kelzenberg M D, Atwater H A and Lewis N S, High aspect ratio silicon wire array photoelectrochemical cells, *J. Am. Chem. Soc.*, 129: 12346, 2007]

interface [6]. The difference between batteries and fuel cells is that the former is a closed system in which the capacity is limited by the amount of material stored in the container; while the latter is an open system which utilizes chemicals continuously supplied externally. Also, there are hybrid power systems which combine one or more of these systems.

6.4.1 Batteries

Batteries are further classified as primary and secondary, based on whether the chemical reactions are electrically reversible or not. In brief, a primary battery is a disposable battery, which is of no use once the initial supply of chemicals is exhausted (e.g., zinc–carbon and Li-MnO_2). On the other hand, a secondary battery can be 'recharged' electrically by reversing the polarity and driving the chemical reaction in the opposite direction, which results in the regeneration of the original reactants (e.g., lead-acid and lithium ion batteries). Batteries used in cars are basically of the lead-acid type and those used to power laptops and mobiles are lithium ion batteries. Figure 6.9 summarizes the electrochemical processes taking place during the charged–ischarge cycles in different types of rechargeable batteries. The performance of various types of secondary batteries and the issues associated with their development are compared in Table 6.3. Extensive details of materials are available on the history and development of lead-acid batteries [6] and excellent reviews on the choice of materials for currently used lithium ion batteries as well as their problems [7]. However, many advanced functional materials have been designed for a new generation of lithium rechargeable batteries with excellent safety,

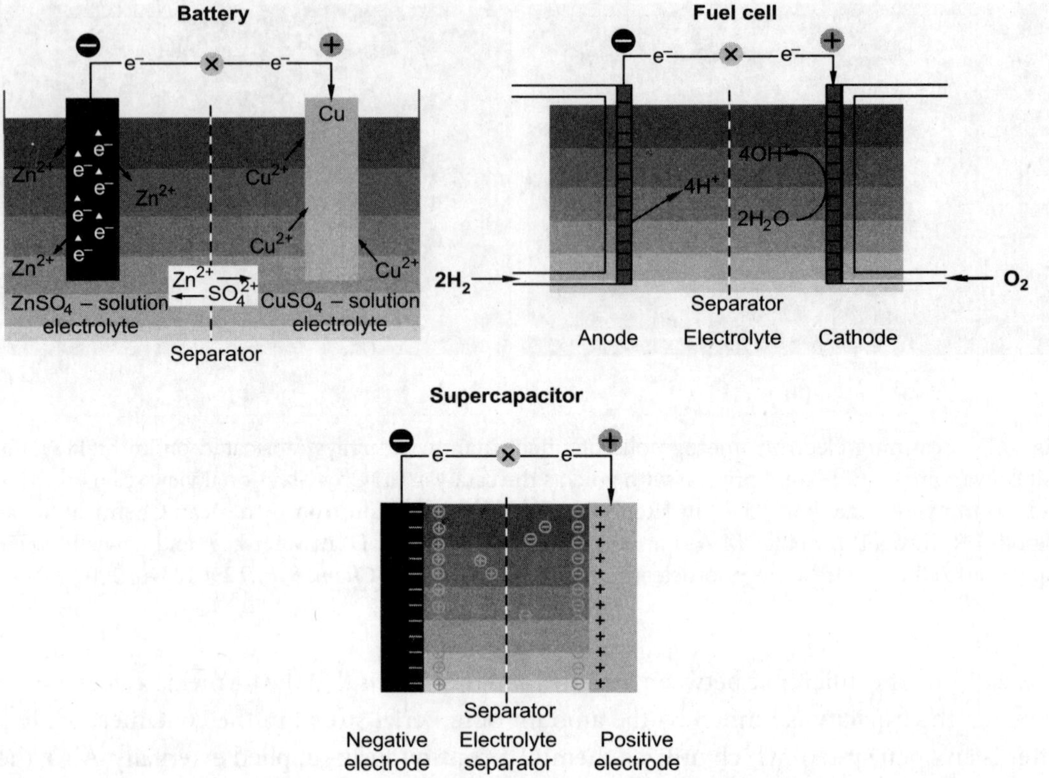

Fig. 6.8 Schematic representation of the working principles of a battery, fuel cell and supercapacitor [Reproduced with permission from American Chemical Society: Winter M and Brodd R J, What are batteries, fuel cells, and supercapacitors? *Chem. Rev,*. 104: 4245, 2004]

Table 6.3 Comparative performances and issues related to the development of common rechargeable batteries [6]

System	Capacity (Wh/kg)	Issues
Conventional types		
Nickel–zinc	66	Cost, life
Nickel–iron	44	Weight
Metal–gas		
Iron–air	88	Life
Zinc–air	88	Life, complexity
Zinc–oxygen	110	Life, cost
Nickel–hydrogen	66	Volume
Cadmium–oxygen	66	Life, cost
Alkali metal–high temperature		
Sodium–sulphur (β-alumina)	176	Life of separator
Lithium alloy–metal sulphide	165	Corrosion, materials
Lithium–chlorine	110	Cycle life

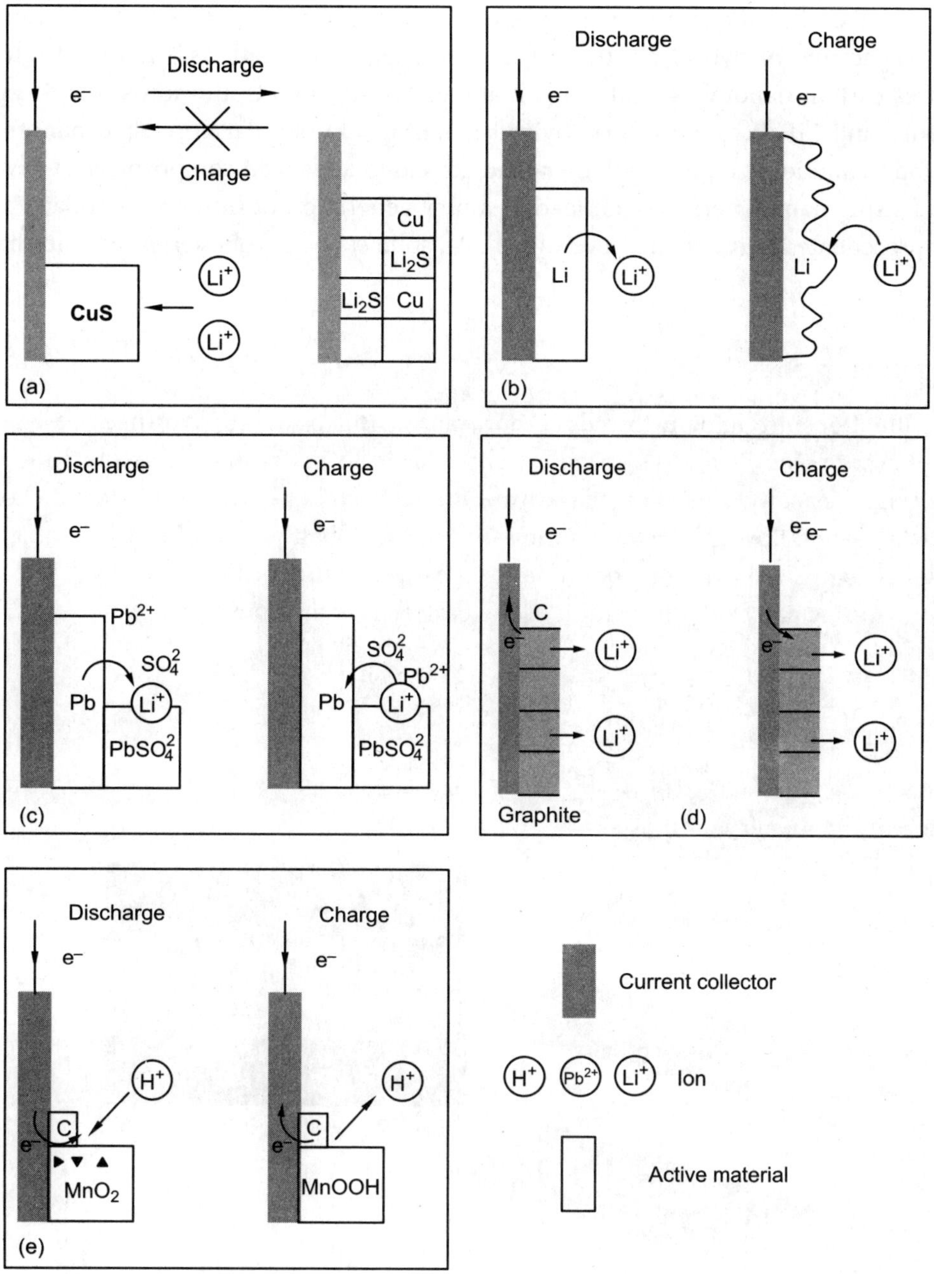

Fig. 6.9 Charge–discharge mechanisms of some of the most common secondary batteries [Reproduced with permission from American Chemical Society: Winter M and Brodd R J, What are batteries, fuel cells, and supercapacitors? *Chem. Rev.*, 104: 4245, 2004]

reliability and cycling life, both for applications in consumer electronics and for clean energy storage, especially for hybrid electric vehicles and space applications. Many of these like Si nanowires carbon nanotubes, and oxide matrices for storing lithium ion storage, especially for anodes and $LiFePO_4$, polymeric hybrid materials and similar core-shell nanomaterials for cathodes, and ionic liquid-, polymer- and gel-based advanced composite electrolytes—all designed using nanomaterials—can lead to a new generation of lithium secondary batteries with unprecedented performance levels [7, 8]. All solid state microbatteries for chips have also

Virus batteries

Viral infections are known to reduce our energy. But now they can help us generate energy! Very recently, an M13 virus has been used to pattern cobalt oxide nanowires. The design basically consists of patterning circular patches of the viruses over a layer of the electrolyte followed by dipping the assembly in cobalt oxide solution which results in a virus-templated assembly of the latter. This procedure is shown in the figure (left), and a scanning electron micrograph of the battery is also shown (right).

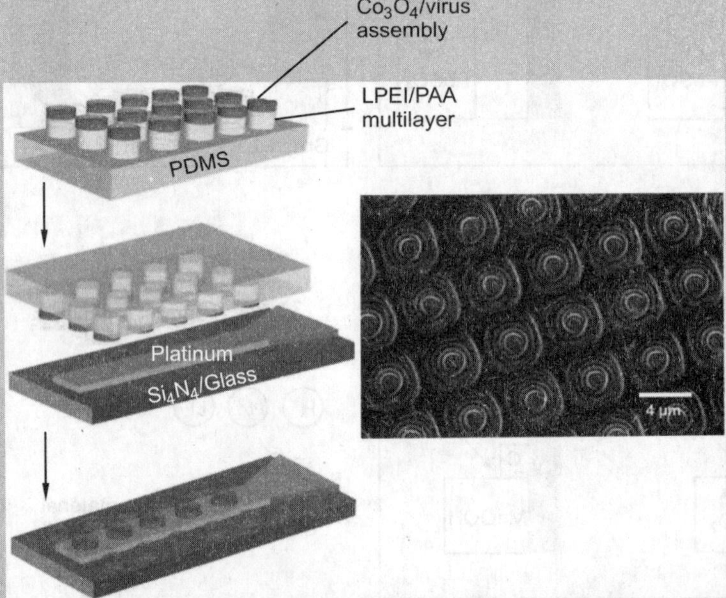

Fig. 6.10 *(see also Plate 6)* Cobalt oxide (CO_3O_4) nanowires assembled on a polyelectrolyte film using spiral M13 viruses are stamped on platinum microband electrodes to form a virus battery [Reproduced with permission from National Academy of Sciences, USA: Nama K T, Wartenaa R, Yoob P J, Liaua FW, Leea Y J, Chianga Y-M, Hammond P T and Belcher A M, Stamped microbattery electrodes based on self-assembled M13 viruses, *PNAS*, 105(45): 17227, 2008]

been found to be promising in addition to futuristic systems like Li-air and organic radical batteries.

6.4.2 Fuel cells

Fuel cells are also electrochemical energy conversion devices capable of converting chemical energy directly into electrical energy, similar to batteries. The basic difference between batteries and fuel cells is that the former works until the chemicals stored in the containers are exhausted, while in the latter, the reactants are fed continuously and hence it should work as long as the chemicals are supplied. In terms of power output, electrochemical energy conversion/storage systems are characterized by a typical plot known as the Ragonne plot (Fig. 6.11) which is a measure of energy and power normalized with respect to weight (or volume). The increasing research focus and technological interest in fuel cells as against batteries is due to their advantages of high efficiency, zero emission, fuel flexibility, zero noise and modularity.

A variety of reactants and electrolytes can be used in fuel cells, based on which they could be broadly classified into several categories, as described below in Table 6.4, along with cathode and anode reactions and the primary ion responsible for transport. However, only solid oxide fuel cells and polymer electrolyte fuel cells continue to receive strong attention, due to their rapid advancement and commercial promise, although other systems often receive sporadic research attention [9, 10].

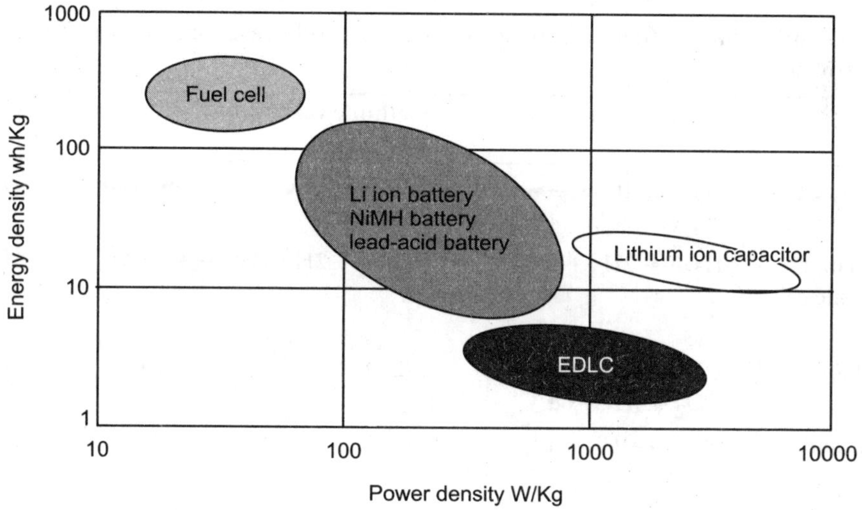

Fig. 6.11 Comparison of power output from different electrochemical energy conversion/storage systems (Ragonne plot) [Adapted from http://en.wikipedia.org/wiki/file:Lithium_Ion_Capacitor_Chart.png under the terms of the GNU Free Documentation Licence]

Hydrogen-based fuel cells are believed to provide clean power and heat and perform efficiently from a range of primary energy sources. While most of the common IC engines exhibit only about 15%–20% of the energy in gasoline, a fuel cell can convert 40%–65% of hydrogen's energy into electricity. On the other hand, the energy efficiency of an IC engine burning hydrogen fuel is only less than half that of a hydrogen-based fuel cell, though it does not pollute the atmosphere as much as IC engines based on fossil fuels. Solid oxide fuel cells (SOFC) offer very high efficiencies (>80%) in co-generation mode where both heat and electricity output can be tapped simultaneously for application. Thus, hydrogen-based fuel cells are gaining increased attention especially if hydrogen comes from renewable resources and the concept of hydrogen economy has both proponents and opponents [11].

The operation of a typical H_2/O_2 polymer electrolyte fuel cell briefly involves hydrogen as the fuel and oxygen as the oxidant. During the operation, hydrogen is oxidized to protons at the anode which move through the electrolyte to the cathode, while the electrons move to the cathode through an external circuit (Fig. 6.8). At the cathode, oxygen combines with protons and electrons to produce water. Thus, the overall process is the spontaneous reaction of hydrogen and oxygen to produce water which has a cell potential of 1.23 V. The efficiency of fuel cells is calculated using the ΔG or ΔH value of the overall cell reaction. However, there is an ambiguity in expressing the efficiency of H_2/O_2 fuel cells because the heat of the reaction will differ based on whether the product water is in the gas phase or the liquid phase. The ΔH value in the case of liquid water is around –286 kJ/mol and is called the higher heating value (HHV) while that in the case of water vapour is –242 kJ/mol and is called the lower heating

Table 6.4 Classification of fuel cells based on the electrode reactions and mobile ions present in their electrolyte

Fuel cell	Anode reaction	Cathode reaction	Conducting ion$^+$
Alkaline fuel cell (AFC)	$H_2 + 2(OH)+ \longrightarrow 2H_2O + 2e^+$	$1/2\ O_2 + H_2O + 2e^+ \longrightarrow 2(OH)^+$	$(OH)^+$
Proton exchange membrane fule cell (PEMFC)	$H_2 \longrightarrow 2H^+ + 2e^+$	$1/2\ O_2 + 2H^+ + 2e^+ \longrightarrow H_2O$	H^+
Direct methanol fuel cell (DMFC)	$CH_3OH + H_2O \longrightarrow CO_2 + 6H^+ + 6e^+$	$1/2\ O_2 + 2H^+\ 2e^+ \longrightarrow H_2O$	H^+
Phosphoric acid fuel cells	$H_2 \longrightarrow 2H^+ + 2e^+$	$1/2\ O_2 + 2H^+ + 2e^+ \longrightarrow H_2O$	H^+
Molten carbonate fuel cells	$H_2 + CO_3^{2-} \longrightarrow H_2O + CO_2 + 2e^-$	$1/2\ O_2 + CO_2 + 2e^- \longrightarrow CO_3^{2-}$	$(CO_3)^{2-}$
Solid oxide fuel cells	$H_2 + O_2 \longrightarrow H_2O + 2e^-$	$1/2\ O_2 + 2e^- \longrightarrow O_2$	O^{2-}

value (LHV). To avoid confusion, it is a common practice to express the theoretical efficiency with respect to the LHV, which is around 94.5% for a H_2/O_2 PEFC.

Before the fuel cells can be successfully commercialized, a number of barriers have to be overcome. Some of the most important issues in fuel cell technology include high cost, limited durability and low impurity tolerance by the noble metal catalyst. An extensive review of the challenges and approaches to commercialize fuel cells has been provided by Steele and coworkers [9]. More impressive is the development of microfuel cells where tiny fuel cell modules for applications ranging from sensors (0.1 W) and cell phones (1 W) to cameras (50 W), laptops (100 W) and power tools (200 W) could be designed using micro-moulding technologies, thus effectively utilizing the fuel cell's capability of providing 1000 Wh/kg instead of the normal 180 Wh/kg of lithium ion batteries. Micro-fuel cells offer a potentially disrupting technology with many functional materials, and many versions of MEMS-based fuel cells have been demonstrated on Si chips, both with methanol and hydrocarbons as feeds, using polymer electrolyte and solid oxide fuel cells respectively.

6.4.3 Supercapacitors

Supercapacitors or ultracapacitors have received considerable attention during the last three decades due to their unique capability of higher charge storage (i.e., several hundred times more than that of conventional capacitors), pulsatile delivery, opportunity charging and millions of cycles of life using a suitable electrode–electrolyte interface, as shown in Fig. 6.12.

These are different from both batteries and fuel cells since they can generate repeated bursts of power for certain types of applications [12]. The state-of-charge (which tells you how much energy is left in the device, irrespective of its nature as a battery or a capacitor) is a simple function of voltage and this coupled with high-power density and good cycle life enables them

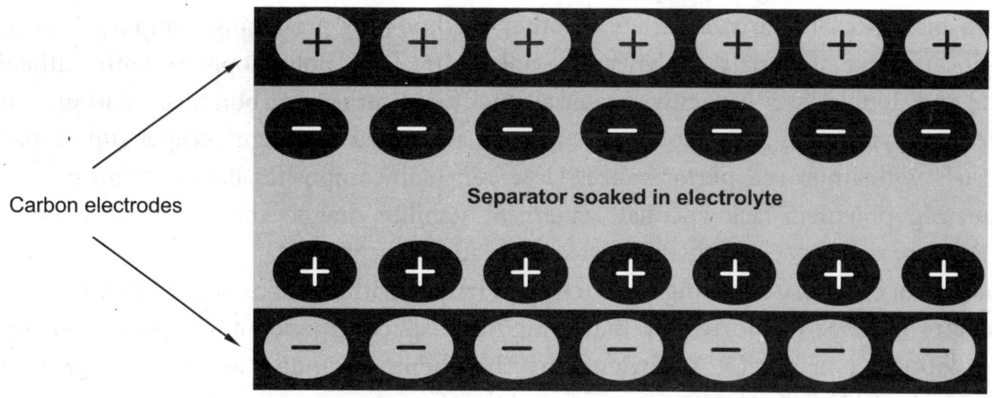

Fig. 6.12 Construction of a double-layer capacitor consisting of two electrodes separated by a membrane soaked in the electrolyte

to be useful in several applications ranging from light-weight electronic fuses, memory back-up power sources and surge protection devices to pulse power sources for smart weapons.

Electrochemical capacitors (ECCs) can also sometimes be classified as electric double-layer capacitors (EDLC) or pseudocapacitors (or redox capacitors) depending on the nature of interfacial processes [6]. The former has a capacitance associated with the non-Faradic charging and discharging of electrical double layers at the electrode–electrolyte interface and hence is called electrical double-layer capacitors (EDLCs), while the latter has Faradaic surface redox reactions or adsorption induced pseudocapacitance as the cause of origin. While EDLCs with capacities of many tens of farads per gram of the electrode material have been achieved employing high–surface area carbon powders or fibres, much higher capacitance values (even few hundreds of F/g) are accomplished with pseudocapacitors employing some high–surface area oxides or conducting polymers.

The large capacitance exhibited by some of these systems has been demonstrated to originate from a combination of double-layer capacitance and pseudocapacitance associated with the participation of adsorbed intermediates in the surface redox-type reactions. In recent years, the growing demand for miniaturized power sources of high power density has also stimulated great interest in electrochemical capacitors. For example, nanostructured carbon and conducting polymers possess large double-layer capacitance and (and also have high surface area) while oxides of multivalent metals such as ruthenium and iridium exhibit large Faradaic pseudocapacitance, and hence these two classes of materials find extensive applications as electrode materials in supercapacitors.

Several conducting polymers and transition metal oxides have been investigated as electrodes for supercapacitors. Among them, amorphous ruthenium oxide $RuO_2.xH_2O$ exhibits a high specific capacitance of 720 F/g. Unfortunately, ruthenium oxide is expensive and hence a considerable reduction in the cost of electrode material is needed to make the supercapacitor technology commercially viable. Several strategies have been pursued in this regard including the dispersion of ruthenium oxide in other less expensive oxide/carbon matrices. Similarly, a variety of other methods for producing composites of redox pseudocapacitive materials (polypyrrole, polyaniline and polythiophene with ruthenium oxide) and double-layer capacitive materials (activated carbon, carbon black, carbon aerogel and carbon nanotubes and graphene) have been attempted to design cheaper supercapacitor materials with improved performance. However, nanocomposites based on most of these conducting polymers lack adequate chemical stability due to their high propensity for degradation, and consequently their cycle life is adversely affected.

The use of composites having conducting polymers with metal oxides for electrochemical capacitors has been reported by many for ultracapacitors and more specifically, RuO_2, when deposited in poly(3, 4-ethylenedioxythiophene), is found to exhibit large specific capacitance of 420 F/g. Results using many of these nanocomposites suggest that when these organic–inorganic hybrids are combined at the nanoscale level, several new properties like enhanced electrochemical storage ability emerge due to synergistic effects. For example, a new and simple microwave assisted in *situ* intercalative polymerization reaction allows the intercalation of poly(3, 4-ethylenedioxythiophene) nanosheets into the van der Waals gap of MoO_3 to produce the nanocomposite [12]. This way of preparing a hybrid functional material has many advantages like high power density, simple charging methods, long cycle life (more than 500,000 cycles), very fast charge/discharge capability and finally no risk of over-charging, although there are disadvantages like linear discharge characteristics precluding the utilization of full energy in some applications, and that power is available only for a very short duration.

6.4.4 Hybrid power systems

Hybrid power systems are combinations of two or more energy conversion/storage systems that use the advantages of both and which are almost devoid of the limitations inherent in the individual systems. Such devices are also likely to help the global transition to a more energy-efficient society, since they can be coupled with both batteries and fuel cells to form hybrid power sources, especially suitable for electronic vehicle (EV) applications. Because of the synergistic benefits of the integrated system, the efficiency of a hybrid system is higher than that of the individual systems used separately. Examples of hybrid power systems include:

- Photovoltaics combined with battery storage or diesel power generation
- Fuel cells combined with microturbines, or wird energy
- H_2/O_2 fuel cells combined with water electrolyzers

Hybrid power technology is significant, especially for automobile applications. For example, when you apply a sudden brake in your fuel cell car, instant power could be supplied by a supercapacitor, a mechanism called 'regenerative braking'. Recently, another technology called 'plug-in hybrid' has been introduced in automobiles, in which a computer present on-board the vehicle can automatically choose between the available power systems based on the power requirements.

6.5 HYDROGEN ECONOMY—A MATERIAL CHALLENGE

Why are we so excited about hydrogen in these days? Is it because it is the first element in the Periodic Table? Let us review the reason behind this excitement and repeat the famous story of the hare and the tortoise: how hydrogen suddenly started winning over the sixth element in the periodic table 'carbon'.

In the earlier sections, we discussed the energy drive caused by the depleting supply of conventional fuels with increasing demands. However, there are expectations that go beyond supply versus demand concerns. We have started looking for convenience and cleanliness in energy systems. This section is aimed at providing a glimpse of how hydrogen holds the promise of providing an almost unlimited supply of non-polluting power.

When we carefully analyze the history of energy sources, during our transition from wood to coal to oil to natural gas, we have actually been following the trend of reducing the carbon and increasing hydrogen content in our fuels. So naturally, now we are stepping into the realm of 'hydrogen energy' to eliminate totally 'C' from 'HCs' (HC stands for hydrocarbon) [11]. The transition to the hydrogen economy is not because of the threat that we will run out of oil, as quoted by Sheik Zaki Yamani, *"The Stone Age did not end for lack of stone, and the Oil Age will end long before the world runs out of oil".*

Hydrogen: Quick facts

Hydrogen was first exploited for aviation in the 1920s and 1930s to control the buoyancy of aircrafts and as a booster fuel. During the 1950s, the US Air Force formed a secret multimillion dollar programme code-named 'Suntan' to develop hydrogen as a fuel for airplanes. As a result of immense research in high-pressure physics, solid crystalline hydrogen was first produced in the laboratory in 1979. This was followed by an interesting invention of semi-metallic solid hydrogen in 1989 using pressures more than 2.5 million times that of the earth's atmospheric pressure. A few years later, liquid metallic hydrogen was produced for less than a microsecond, using high temperatures and pressures. However, solid metallic hydrogen is still the dream of high-pressure physicists, which if achieved, could provide a zero-resistance electrical conductor and ultraenergetic fuel! Thus hydrogen is also a multi-functional material.

Here are some quick facts about the magical molecule:

- It has seven times more energy content (120.7 kJ/mol) compared to gasoline and three times that of coal (33 kJ/mol)
- When liquefied, it takes up just $1/700^{th}$ of the space it occupies in the gaseous form. So it is easy to store and transport!
- It provides clean energy: No harmful emissions!

Hydrogen is present everywhere in the universe; though not abundant in its free form, it is associated with other atoms to form molecules like water and methane. Unlike other energy sources, hydrogen is not a 'source' of energy: we need to spend energy to release hydrogen from its molecules. Instead, we can consider it an 'energy carrier' which will be useful to store and transport the energy generated from renewable sources like sunlight and wind. In other words, hydrogen complements electricity since it can be generated from electricity by electrolyzing water and in turn be used to generate electricity with the help of fuel cells (see section 6.4.2).

What are the chances that a 'hydrogen economy' will become a reality? Hydrogen energy can be discussed in three separate modules, namely, hydrogen generation, storage and conversion to electricity. The main drivers of the hydrogen economy are, in addition to the common merits of sustainability reduction of carbon emission and cleanliness, the high efficiency of the fuel cells used to convert hydrogen into electricity. However, most of the barriers in realizing hydrogen economy are with respect to its generation, though there are also issues in storing hydrogen. Another way of viewing this topic is with respect to the applications, which can be broadly classified as stationary and portable. For example, compact storage of hydrogen will be crucial for space and automobile applications and not for stationary power. On the other hand, the latter will be affected by issues related to installation of power plants and connection of individual units to the common electricity grid. Thus, the severity of the problem can vary with respect to the end-use of hydrogen. Let us review how the scenario shifted with the advent of novel functional materials and nanotechnology.

Hydrogen generation

We are aware that hydrogen is present in various forms everywhere in the universe. Now the question is: how do we release hydrogen from its molecules in an efficient, cost-effective and environment-friendly way? This is a major hurdle for the commercial realization of the hydrogen economy. Common ways of generating hydrogen are reforming of fossil fuels and electrolysis of water.

When we opt for fossil fuel reforming, we should be aware that we are going to pollute the atmosphere by releasing greenhouse gases and carbon when we burn the fossil fuels to generate the 'clean fuel', hydrogen. However, this is the only option of hydrogen generation we are left with until we are ready with efficient technologies to harness it from renewable sources. The details of various methods of reforming fossil fuels to generate hydrogen can be found in many textbooks. In brief, the first step involves the reaction of methane with steam at temperatures of about 800–900°C over a nickel catalyst. This process produces *syngas* or synthesis gas which is composed of hydrogen (70%), carbon monoxide (15%) and carbon dioxide (10%). The reaction mixture is further reacted with more steam to produce more hydrogen by converting carbon monoxide into carbon dioxide in a process called the *water gas-shift reaction*. Hydrogen is then separated from syngas and purified by removing carbon dioxide through an adsorption process.

Materials research plays a key role in reforming technologies too as there is a strong need to develop more and more efficient catalysts and this has been reviewed recently [13]. Although electrolysis of water is a greener way of producing hydrogen, it is energy intensive. The working principle of a water electrolyzer (using alkaline or nolymer electrolyter) is exactly the reverse of a H_2/O_2 fuel cell in which hydrogen and oxygen are 'combined' to form water. Ultimately, we end up using more electric power to electrolyze water than what will be obtained by using the hydrogen in a fuel cell. Hence this method of hydrogen generation is beneficial only in countries where electricity is cheap. Commerical water electrolyzers for hydrogen fuelling stations are available from Norsk Hydro, Stuart Energy, Teledyne, Proton Energy and Avalence technologies.

Nevertheless, if we are able to produce electricity from renewable sources like sunlight and wind, hydrogen generation from water electrolysis can become more cost effective. Hydrogen can be generated using solar energy in three broad ways (Section 6.3.2). One way is to convert sunlight directly into electricity using photovoltaic solar cells (Section 6.3.2). This method is limited by the cost of the solar modules currently available. Alternatively, the heat from solar radiation can be concentrated using big solar panels to reach a temperature of several thousands of degrees which can split steam into hydrogen and oxygen. The third option is *photolysis*, in which the sunlight can be directly used to electrolyze water. This can be done either by photoelectrochemical means or by the photobiological method.

A good example for a photelectrochemical water-splitting device is the Gratzel cell, which consists of a soluble metal complex catalyst to absorb solar energy and trigger water-splitting. On the other hand, a photobiological process deploys algae and bacteria for water electrolysis. Under specific conditions the pigments in these microorganisms can absorb solar energy and an enzyme in the algal cell can act as a catalyst to split the water molecule. This process can be repeated multiple times and is hence a cost-effective means to generate hydrogen from solar energy. The scientific challenge in this method is that due to the sensitivity of this enzyme to oxygen, it requires the production of oxygen-tolerant mutants to make this process more efficient.

Another cost-effective renewable source to produce hydrogen is wind. Electricity produced from wind turbines is much cheaper than solar power. In certain areas, wind-generated electricity is cost-competitive than fossil-fuelled plants. Thus, wind power will be a cost-effective way to produce pollution-free hydrogen in the future.

Hydrogen storage

If hydrogen is to be realized as a viable energy carrier, significant improvements over the hydrogen storage technologies currently available are required. Though the gravimetric energy density of hydrogen is higher than of any known fuel, it holds very little energy per unit volume, thus occupying more space than other fuels. Hence hydrogen is usually stored in a compressed or liquefied form. Most compressed hydrogen tanks operate at ambient temperatures at pressures of 350–700 bar which roughly consumes 10% of the gas's energy content. Alternatively, hydrogen can be liquefied at supercold temperatures (–253°C) which takes up only 1/700th as much volume as the gaseous form. Although liquid hydrogen has a higher energy density than the compressed form, liquefaction requires much more work than compression, consuming atleast 30%–35% of the gas's energy content. Another problem with liquid hydrogen is evaporation due to heat exchange between the cold tank and the warmer surroundings. It often happens when a hydrogen-powered vehicle is moving and using the fuel at a slow rate. Further, any accidental rupture of the container is always a concern, because of the wide range of compositions over which hydrogen–air mixtures are explosive. Hence there is increasing interest in using fundamentally different techniques for storage of gaseous hydrogen.

The favorable characteristics of a hydrogen storage material include:

- Rapid and reversible adsorption/desorption of hydrogen
- Large storage capacity (expressed in terms of gravimetric density) at ambient conditions
- Storage capacity at room temperature

Owing to the problems associated with physical methods of hydrogen storage, chemical methods of incorporating hydrogen atoms into the crystal lattice of materials are under investigation. Hydrogen is stored in these materials broadly by three mechanisms:

1. *Absorption* Metals absorb atomic hydrogen into their crystalline structure, e.g., MgH_2, AlH_3, intermetallics like $LaNi_5$ and metal-organic framework solids (MOFs) [14]
2. *Adsorption* Hydrogen is bonded into highly porous materials with a high surface area, e.g., carbon and porous polymer
3. *Chemical reaction* A reaction takes place between hydrogen and the storage medium. Hydrogen can be released from the medium by reversible chemical reactions under small changes in temperature or pressure, e.g., chemical hydrides like sodium borohydride.

However, most of these storage technologies apply only to small amounts of hydrogen, probably enough to serve a large fuelling station or a small distribution hub. However, in the 'hydrogen-powered' future, central hydrogen production plants may have to store much larger volumes of hydrogen with atleast a few days storage to accommodate fluctuating power demands and plant downtime. Hence further research is required to explore possible options such as underground salt caverns, depleted gas fields and empty mines.

6.6 IMPACT OF NANOTECHNOLOGY

In the early days, materials with low surface-to-volume ratio were preferred in order to reduce heat loss in thermal energy converters and to reduce friction in moving machinery parts. The principle is exactly reversed when it comes to catalysis for energy conversion, wherein the catalyst surface plays an active part in the reaction. Here we need catalysts with a high surface-to-volume ratio. This is easily achieved by bringing down the size of the catalyst materials to nanometre dimensions to benefit processes such as catalysis, electrocatalysis and electrochemical charge storage that are dependent on the surface area [15–18]. In the past few decades, nanotechnology has had a profound impact on emerging energy technologies, owing to the ease of tailoring their dimensions to facilitate a change in their fundamental properties, including redox potential, conductivity and charge storage, in comparison to those of their bulk counterparts. Several nanostructured materials like carbon nanotubes (single-walled as well as multiwalled nanotubes and more recently graphene), ruthenium oxide functionalized carbon nanotubes and conducting polymer-based nanocomposites have been used to prepare excellent electrodes for electrochemical power sources. On the other hand, nanomaterials have also been proved to be more efficient in solar energy conversion when compared to their bulk counterparts in many instances.

Carbon nanotubes are especially important for hydrogen storage[17]. Conventionally, alkali metal–aluminium hydrides have been widely studied for hydrogen storage. But there are many problems associated with these conventional materials, including irreversible thermodynamic behaviour and unfavourable hydrogen adsorption/desorption kinetics. Recently, single-walled carbon nanotubes have been found to catalyze the hydrogen adsorption/desorption reactions of sodium–aluminium metal hydrides. Specifically, the hydrogen storage capacity increases by about four times in the presence of carbon nanotubes. The enhancement in hydrogen storage capacity is attributed to the high diffusivity of hydrogen through the nanotube, which accelerates hydrogen transport. Carbon nanotubes also exhibit faster thermal energy transfer, which can improve the kinetics of hydrogen adsorption and desorption.

However, a significant concern for nanotechnology in fuel cell and energy applications is whether high-quality nanostructured materials of complex composition can be produced in high volume and low cost, and can be processed into useful products. This is especially significant for nanostructured hybrid materials as they are often prepared using a combination of standard processes used for organic materials and also for ceramic oxides with sometimes conflicting requirements of calcination, annealing and separation methods. Some of these materials have not been tested rigorously to establish their long-term stability (both thermal and oxidative stability) and this could be exacerbated by applications like rechargeable batteries where continuous application of electric field during charging can cause damage.

6.7 CONCLUSIONS

Availability of affordable energy is essential for continued human development and many parts of the world have difficulty in providing minimum comfortable living standards to the people by and large. A reliable supply of energy lies at the heart of our mobility and lifestyle and if we want to accomplish sustainable energy without compromising environmental quality and global carbon emission standards, many key materials need to be developed urgently for clean energy generation and efficient storage. Although fuel cells offer a clean energy generation pathway, the use of platinum in the electrodes of many fuel cells makes this an expensive solution and we need to replace them soon with nitrogen-doped carbon nanotubes or conducting polymer hybrids. Similarly, we need to make more durable lithium batteries using hybrid electrodes from recyclable biomass-based materials. Paper batteries and microfuel cells, nanogenerators from body heat, piezogenerators from tactile generators, etc., are expected soon due to the availability of an astonishing variety of functional materials. Chemistry has played an important role in developing many nanostructured functional materials for overcoming some of the barriers with respect to generation and storage of energy using fuel cells, batteries, supercapacitors and harvesting solar energy; a fascinating variety of materials are expected to be available in the coming decade, eventually facilitating the possibility of energy sticks just like the sticks we commonly use for laptops.

Further reading

1. Nersesian R L, *Energy for the 21st Century: A comprehensive guide to conventional and alternative sources,* M. E. Sharpe Inc., USA, 2007.
2. Roeb M and Müller-Steinhagen H, Concentrating on Solar Electricity and Fuels, *Science,* 329: 773, 2010.
3. Nozik A J, Beard M C, Luther J M, Law M, Ellingson R J and Johnson J C, Semiconductor quantum dots and quantum dot arrays and applications of multiple excitation generation to third generation photovoltaic solar cells, *Chem. Rev.,* 10.1021, 2010.
4. Meyer G J, The 2010 millennium technology grand prize: dye sensitized solar cells, *ACS Nano,* 4: 4337, 2010.
5. Lewis N S, Toward cost effective solar energy use, *Science,* 315: 798, 2007.
6. Brodd R J and Winter M, What are batteries, fuel cells, and supercapacitors, *Chem. Rev.,* 104: 245, 2004.
7. Tarascon J M.and Armand M, Issues and challenges facing rechargeable lithium batteries, *Nature,* 414: 359, 2001.
8. Nystrom G, Razaq A, Stromme M, Nyholm L and Mihranyan A, Ultrafast all-polymer paper-based batteries, *Nano Lett.* 9: 3635–39, 2009.
9. Brandon N P, Skinner S and Steele B C H, Recent advances in materials for fuel cells, *Annu. Rev. Mater. Res.,* 33: 183, 2003.
10. Busby R L, *Hydrogen and Fuel Cells: A Comprehensive Guide,* Penwell Publishing.
11. Wald M L, Questions about a hydrogen economy, *Sci. Amer.,* 290: 66, 2004.
12. Murugan A V and Pillai V K in Cheetham A K and Rao C N R, (Eds), *Nanomaterials Chemistry,* 1st Edn, Wiley, New York, 2007.
13. Farrauto R J, Liu Y, Ruettinger W, Ilinich O, Shore L and Giroux T, Precious metal catalysts supported on ceramic and metal monolithic structures for the hydrogen economy, *Catalysis Reviews,* 49: 141, 2007.
14. Gratez J, New approaches to hydrogen storage, *Chem. Soc. Rev.,* 38: 73, 2009.
15. Subhramannia M and Pillai V K, *Shape dependant electrocatalytic activity of platinum nanostructures, J. Mator. Chem.* 18 (2009) 5858–70.
16. Raimondi F, Scherer G G, Kotz R and Wokaun A, Nanoparticles in energy technology: Examples from electrochemistry and catalysis, *Angew Chem. Int. Ed.,* 44: 2190, 2005.
17. Dresselhaus M S and Thomas I L, Alternative Energy Technologies, *Nature,* 414: 332, 2001.
18. Bard A J, Inner-Sphere Heterogenous Electrode Reactions, Electrocatalysis and Photocatalysis: The Challenge, *J. Am. Chem. Soc.,* 132: 7559, 2010.

EXERCISES

1. Mention the important advantages of designing lithium battery cathodes like cobalt oxide in the form of nanowires using viruses as the templates?

2. What is 'super' about supercapacitors? How are they different from conventional capacitors on the one hand and storage devices like batteries and fuel cells on the other?
3. Mention the advantages and disadvantages of hydrogen economy. Why are we not adopting it, despite our imminent environmental quality degradation and climate change problem?
4. Why are polymer electrolyte fuel cells considered to be the more realistic option among all fuel cells?
5. Using Faraday's law, illustrate how the energy density and power density of a typical rechargeable battery can be calculated when there is a balanced cell reaction with well-defined anodic and cathodic electrode reactions. Consider lithium ion or lead acid battery as an example.
6. What is an electric vehicle? What are the major problems preventing their large-scale commercialization? How are they distance to from hybrid vehicles?
7. What are micro-fuel cells? Why are they important? Explain the advantages of micro-fuel cells fabricated using MEMS techniques.
8. Can we design rechargeable batteries from biomass? Discuss the implications if functional anodes and cathodes could be obtained from biomass.
9. Are critical material-related issues preventing large-scale power generation using solid oxide fuel cells? Discuss.
10. It is often said that the progress of solar energy is limited by lack of a suitable storage medium. Discuss the pros and cons of this debate using lead acid and lithium-ion rechargeable batteries as examples.

7

Materials for Polymer Electronics

This chapter displays a variety of soft, yet flexible functional polymers for diverse applications in solid state electronic devices, including organic light emitting diodes, photovoltaic devices, field effect transistors, liquid crystal displays and memory devices. The basic principles for the rational design of materials for organic electronics (printed electronics) are illustrated, emphasizing the important role of molecular structure, crystallinity, microstructure, molecular packing and alignment. It further identifies important challenges as well as limitations from the synthetic level up to the implementation of these materials in real devices, thus integrating polymers into nanoscale heterostructures.

LEARNING OBJECTIVES

- To understand the importance of polymer electronics as an emerging theme of application of functional materials
- To investigate the charge conduction mechanism in polymer electrodes and junctions
- To illustrate the working principles of basic polymer electronic devices with respect to tenability of functions
- To understand the limitations of polymer electronics and to suggest new challenges in fabricating polymer-based electronic circuits
- To explain the rationale behind selecting polymers for LEDs, FETs and solar cells
- To list the advantages of polymer-based electronic circuits and prospective developments

7.1 INTRODUCTION

In the early 1900s, vacuum tubes were used for various electronic applications like radio broadcasting, television, radar, sound reproduction, large telephone networks and devices. Later, the vacuum tubes were replaced by transistors. A major leap in the electronics industry was marked by the invention of integrated chips (IC) technology in the mid-20th century, following the pioneering efforts of Jack Kilby of Texas instruments and Robert Noyce of Fairchild Semiconductor in 1958. ICs are more advantageous than discrete circuits, both in terms of cost and performance. They are cheaper because they can be printed as single units comprising all the circuit components, simply by photolithography instead of building one transistor at a time. Their performance is superior because the components can switch quickly by consuming less power, as they are arranged close to each other. Other advantages such as mass production capability, quality control and reliability are also important and have helped in making this technology a great success.

Owing to its significance and relevance to the development of the electronics industry, IC technology has been improved at several stages. ICs developed in the early 1950s contained only a few tens of transistors and were called small-scale integrated circuits (SSI). These were followed by medium-scale integrated circuits (MSI) which contained a few hundreds, and then by large-scale integrated circuits (LSI), with the cost per chip dropping from \$1,000 per SSI chip to about \$25 per MSI chip. Currently, we are in the age of very large-scale integrated (VLSI) and ultralarge-scale integrated (ULSI) chips, with about 1 million transistors per chip (integration density of 10^8), wafer scale integration (WSI) and system on a chip [1]. An interesting comparison of the IC originally developed by Jack Kilby with that developed recently by Intel is shown in Fig. 7.1.

(a) (b)

Fig. 7.1 Photograph of (a) modern integrated circuit and (b) IC originally developed by Jack Kilby [Reproduced from (a) http://publicdomainpictures.net and (b) http://nl.wikipedia.org/wiki/Bestand:Integrated-circuit-open.jpg under the terms of the GNU Free Documentation Licence]

The trend in miniaturization in IC technology was first generalized by Gordon E Moore, co-founder of Intel, in 1965, which later became popular as *Moore's law* (Fig. 3.11). The law is capable of explaining almost every characteristic of digital electronic devices such as processing speed, memory capacity and even the number and size of pixels in a digital camera. The most important feature in this figure is how the integration density increases with every year. The number of transistors per chip actually depends on various factors:

- size of the smallest transistor that can be etched by lithographic techniques
- size of the wafer
- average number of defects per square inch
- costs associated with producing multiple components (including package costs)

Since Moore's law predicts a dramatic increase in processing speed of computers with time, it was assumed that it should not take too long for the computer to become infinitely fast—an extrapolation from Moore's law. However, physicists have recently found that computers do have a speed limit, just like the speed of light; if electronic components continue to shrink with time, we should eventually code bits of information on atomic clusters and molecules, and ironically, smaller means faster in the microelectronic world for approaching a speed limit on computing.

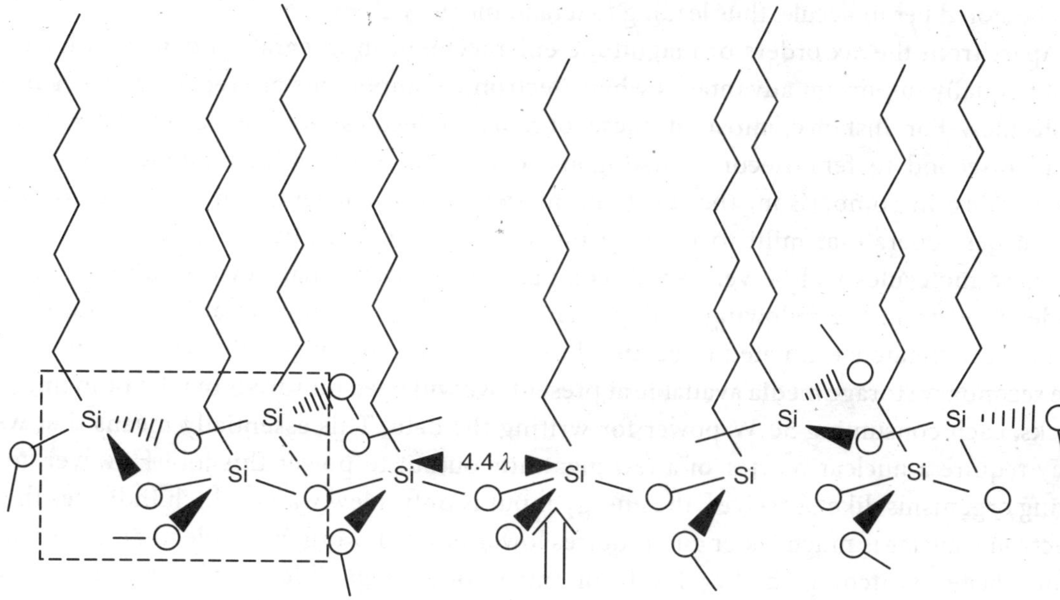

Fig. 7.2 Designing molecule electronic components on conventional semiconductors like silicon is shown as a schematic description of a polysiloxane bonding on the Si substrate surface, where the arrow points to an equatorial Si-O bond that can be connected either to another polysiloxane chain or to the surface. The terminal hydrocarbon chain can have an azo group, capable of showing reversible cis-trans isomerism upon photon impingement, thus acting as a molecular switch (adapted from the PhD thesis of Sneha Kulkarni, University of Pune, 2006)

Four decades of Moore's law

Moore's first law states that the number of transistors per chip doubles every 16 months and the second law states that the cost quadruples every 16 months. In the 1950s, transistor production was in the millions, which later became a quintillion in 2003, with cost following the opposite trend, exactly as predicted by Moore's law. It has been estimated that a transistor now costs the same as one printed newspaper character. Also *the size of each transistor has reduced so drastically that about 200 million could fit on the head of a pin.*

Now we have almost reached the end of Moore's law with the integration density (number of transistors per unit area of the chip) typically achieved in the order of 10^8. In order to make electronic devices even smaller, faster and cheaper, we need to design radical strategies for accomplishing a higher degree of integration. Imagine we have electronically conducting 'molecules' which can be assembled on a chip. For example, 10^{14} molecules could be packed in 1 cm^2 and hence 5 to 6 orders of magnitude more integration is possible, if each molecule can act like an electronic circuit (Fig. 7.2). Owing to the limits of lithographic techniques in etching the smallest transistor on a chip, inorganic semiconductors are being gradually replaced by organic materials. There are several organic molecules, such as azo compounds, which undergo cis–trans isomerization on photon impingement, where one bit of information can be stored per molecule, thus leading to terabit memory chips.

Apart from the six orders of magnitude enhancement in integration density, we have other equally important advantages when electronic components are replaced by organic molecules. For instance, most of these organic molecules undergo electron transfer in nanosecond to femtosecond (analogous to electron transfer in biological systems) time scales; in comparison, the most recent switches in conventional microelectronics can at best operate at milli to microseconds. More significantly, the power consumed by these molecules will be very small compared to conventional devices, which can be understood from the following analogy. The information content in an adult brain has been approximately estimated to be 10^{15} bits. If we want to transfer the whole content to the secondary storage media available at present, we will need hundreds of CDs or memory sticks, each consuming 50 W power for writing the data. This essentially means that we may require a nuclear reactor of a few gigawatts output to power this job! However, for living organisms, like ourselves, the energy input is only a few watts, which indicates that electron transfer is much faster and requires lower power for organic molecular materials. Thus, faster switching, higher levels of integration, negligible power and flexibility for manufacturing are the driving forces for seeking organic molecules and polymers as electronics components to facilitate one of the most revolutionary technologies, affectionately known as *printed* or *plastic electronics* [2].

In the early days, organic molecules were thought to be insulators at room temperature until Akamatu and Inokuchi studied the conducting behaviour of two polycyclic fused-ring systems with quinonoid structures [3], viz., violanthrone and pyranthrone. They found that the temperature dependence of the conductivity was similar to that of semiconductors with band gap between 0.75 and 1 eV, although the resistivity was too high (10^9 Ωcm) at room temperature. Later, Akamatu discovered a molecule, a perylene–bromine complex, with much higher conductivity of the order of 1 S/cm, followed by the most recent, widely employed organic conductor *pentacene*, which is basically a polycyclic aromatic hydrocarbon. A major breakthrough in the field of organic conductors was the discovery of salts of the radical anion of tetracyanoquinodimethane (TCNQ) by Kepler et al. in 1960, which had an activation energy for electronic conduction of less than 0.01 eV with a room temperature conductivity of 100 S/cm. Subsequent synthesis of tetrathiofulvalene (TTF) by Wudl et al. led to the discovery of metallic conduction in TTF-TCNQ complexes down to 59 K, with a maximum conductivity of 8000 S/cm. The field of organic conductors witnessed another major breakthrough with the advent of 'superconductivity' in salts of fullerenes, C_{60}, with transition temperatures ranging from 18 to 45 K. Many of these experiments have demonstrated that organic semiconductors hold great promise, since their long-range order provides the performance limit enabling tuning of their intrinsic transport properties. However, molecular conductors are also flanked by instabilities, such as *Peierls instability** and other electronic instabilities, leading to a metal–insulator transition, which may also originate due to disorder and compositional changes.

7.2 FROM MOLECULAR ELECTRONICS TO POLYMER ELECTRONICS

Despite the spectacular success in reducing the cost per chip by increasing device density and achieving unprecedented speeds (10 million transistors/cm^2 can perform about 1000 billion operations in one second), microelectronics is currently being replaced by macroelectronics (also called polymer electronics or plastic electronics), where macromolecules act as electronic components. The most attractive characteristic of macroelectronics is its uncanny ability to have roll-to-roll processing with hundreds of metres on flexible supports (like newsprint) in large volumes at low cost per unit area enabling printed flexible electronics. In this chapter, we will stick to electrically conducting 'macromolecules' (polymers) and devices fabricated with them, and will not include small molecular conductors which are suitable for a topic on 'molecular electronics'.

The field of 'conducting polymers' began with the mind-blowing research of three scientists, Alan J Heeger, Alan G MacDiarmid and Hideki Shirakawa, who won the Nobel Prize for chemistry in the year 2000, when they found that 'the conductivity of polyacetylene increases by a billion times when oxidized with iodine vapour'. The story dates back to the early 1970s when Shirakawa synthesized a polyacetylene film having a metallic lusture by accidental addition of more catalyst to the reaction vessel. At the same time, MacDiarmid and Heeger were involved in examining an inorganic polymer film (made of sulphur nitride) with a metallic lustre. Fortunately, both the groups met in a conference and their collaboration was responsible for the emergence of polymer electronics.

A fundamental difference between a conjugated polymer and a simple conjugated molecule is its electronic band structure. Figure 7.3 shows how energy bands develop from a singly unsaturated organic molecule to a long-chain molecule to a polymer with an unsaturated backbone. Thus, conducting polymers are long-chain molecules with conjugation of π bonds extending almost throughout the chains.

The advantages of polymeric conductors over simple molecules are:

- The highly anisotropic and quasi one-dimensional nature of these macromolecules results in very strong electron–phonon interactions, leading to strong relaxation effects and large Peierls gap*.
- These are mostly semiconductors and the band gap can be easily tuned by the process of doping. In some of these materials, the band gap can also be tuned by quantum size effects, thanks to nanotechnology.
- The ease of processing them in the form of thin films and the added flexibility make conducting polymers promising candidates for a variety of applications, both as interconnects and as packaging materials, ranging from consumer electronics to

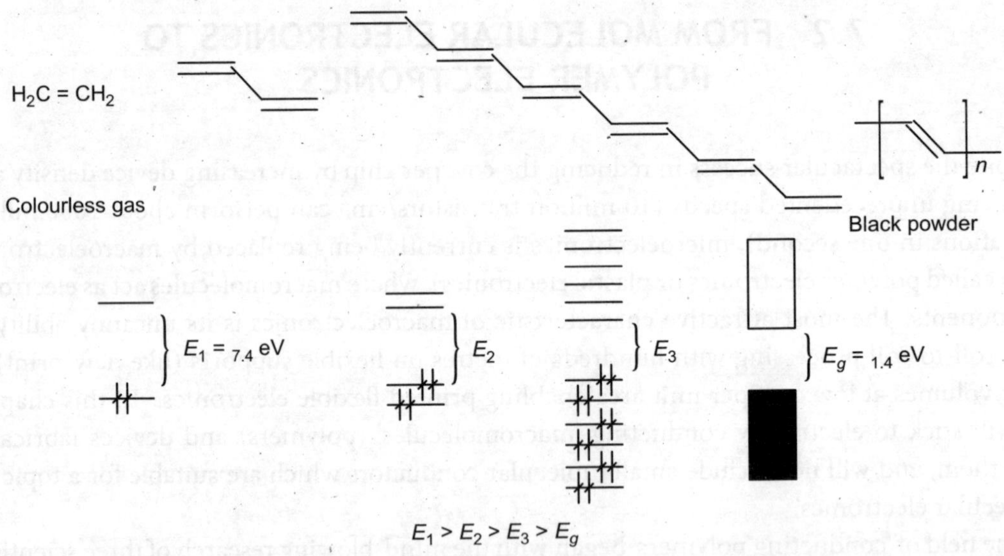

Fig. 7.3 Effect of conjugation on the electronic band structure of unsaturated molecules to polymers with unsaturated backbone [Adapted with permission from John Wiley & Sons: *Encyclopaedia of Polymer Science and Technology*, Vol. 6, 2002]

*Peierls distortion is a mechanism that allows a one-dimensional metallic chain to spontaneously become an insulator by doubling its periodicity.

power electronics. Thus, printing of 'electronic circuits' using organic molecules on transparent substrates like polyethylene terephthalate (PET) and polycarbonate is possible, saving space, enhancing speed and increasing reliability and also enabling easier transportation.

How does a plastic material 'conduct' electricity? In other words, what are the criteria for a polymer to conduct electricity? It is not very different from the universal criterion for electrical conductivity: *the presence of mobile electrons*. Now the question should be reframed as 'What is the source of mobile electrons in an organic polymer?' If we observe the molecular structure of polymers, we can easily find that the insulating ones have a saturated backbone with σ bonds or non-alternating π bonds, whereas those with conjugated π bonds conduct electricity. Thus, the presence of alternating single and double bonds in a conjugated polymer makes it conduct electricity by lowering the electronic excitation energy to 1.5–4 eV (values typical of semiconductors) compared to that of their saturated counterparts (above 7 eV). All conjugated polymers have a σ bond backbone of overlapping sp^2 hybrid orbitals, while the remaining out-of-plane *pz* orbitals overlap with those of the neighbouring carbon or nitrogen atoms, resulting in π bonds. Although the molecular structure of conjugated polymers is represented as alternating single and double bonds, the π electrons are delocalized throughout the molecule, which is mainly responsible for their electrical conductivity.

It has been shown, however, that a fully conjugated metallic polymer system is unstable due to Peierls distortion. In addition, there are two other important criteria for a polymer to act as a semiconductor. First, the σ bonds constituting the backbone should be strong enough to prevent the macromolecule from splitting apart in the excited state consisting of electrons and holes. Second, the π molecular orbitals in the neighbouring polymer chains should overlap with each other to provide electrical conductivity in three dimensions.

Another interesting question that comes to our attention regarding the electronic conduction mechanism of polymers is 'Despite the lack of crystallinity, how does a polymer form energy bands like an inorganic semiconducting crystal?' In conducting polymers, the band gap across which the electrons are excited is the energy difference between the bonding and antibonding levels (HOMO–LUMO gaps) formed during the quantum mechanical overlap of the π 'molecular orbitals'. Hence, there are a number of differences between inorganic semiconductors and conducting polymers, in the charge conduction mechanisms and lattice relaxation phenomena associated with them, which differentiate their application domains. For example, in a conducting polymer, electronic excitation is often associated with lattice reorganization, which results in broadening of its spectral bandwidth (Fig. 7.5).

This feature of conducting polymers, although problematic for applications like optical displays, is actually favourable for lasing and amplification. Some of the features of charge conduction in inorganic and polymeric semiconductors are compared in Table 7.1.

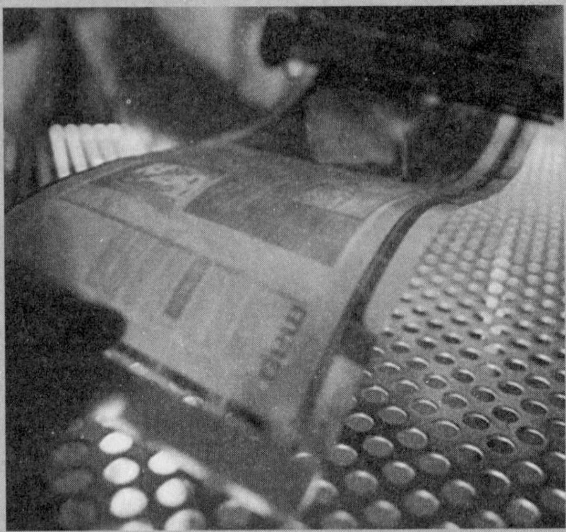

Fig. 7.4 Photograph of a flexible display made of polymer [Reproduced from http://en.wikipedia.org/wiki/File:Flexible_display.jpg under the terms of the GNU free documentation licence]

Plastics

The word 'plastic' immediately brings to mind ideas like flexibility, light weight, elegant design and compactness. If we are under the impression that plastics are just insulators which can prevent an electric shock, we need to devise our opinion. Materials scientists have now made it clear that certain types of plastic can actually 'conduct' electricity! This field of research and its major spin-off—collectively called 'polymer electronics'—is expected to make an enormous impact on the future of the electronics industry and our quality of our life. For example, a traditional factory would require an investment of about \$1.3 billion and 5,000 employees to manufacture 40,000 m^2 of silicon chips, while it is expected to cost only \$10 million and 50 employees to manufacture an organic semiconductor of the same area using roll-to-roll and lamination techniques!

Although the performance of single crystals (have perfect order) can never be achieved, polymeric semiconductors offer many advantages in comparison to inorganic semiconductors. For instance, the work function of conducting polymers can be easily tuned by doping them with oxidants or reductants or even electrochemically. Doping a polymer is quite different from doping an inorganic semiconductor. In the latter, doping involves substituting an atom/ion with another having a higher/lower valence to introduce extra electrons/holes. In the case of polymers, doping is usually a redox reaction in which the dopant provides or extracts electrons from the π electron cloud of the polymer, giving rise to *polarons*. One of the greatest advantages in terms of manufacturing is processing, where flexible roll-to-roll thin films can

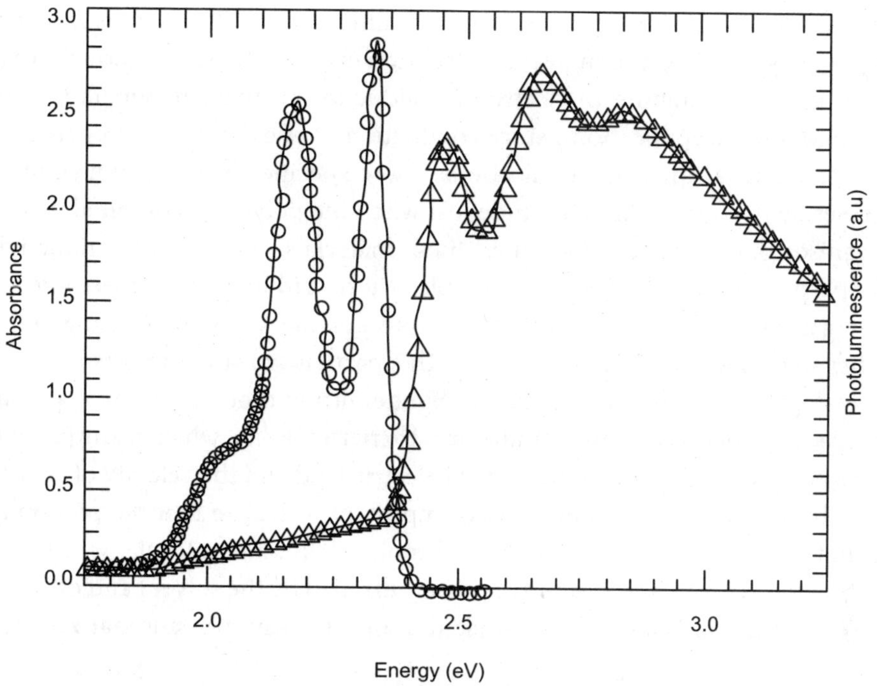

Fig. 7.5 Absorption (open triangles) and photoluminescence emission (open circles) spectra for poly (*p*-phenylenevinylene) film at low temperature (75 K). The broad bandwidth ranging from 1.5 to 3.1 eV can be observed [Adapted with permission from Royal Society of Chemistry: Bradley D D C, in Ryan A J, (Ed.), *Emerging themes in polymer science*, Chap. 3, 2001]

Table 7.1 Comparison of polymeric and inorganic semiconductors

No.	Polymeric semiconductors	Inorganic semiconductors
1.	The electronic wave functions are localized in the subunits containing conjugation.	Delocalized electronic wave functions
2.	Broad spectral bandwidths resulting from strong coupling between the lattice vibrations and electronic states, which is disadvantageous for applications like optical displays.	The added charge often goes to the pre-existing valence or conduction band states without causing significant lattice reorganization.
3.	Low dielectric constant (3–4) and strong electronic interactions arising from localized wave functions, resulting in very high exciton binding energy (~0.5 eV).	The best value of exciton binding energy is for ZnO (~ 0.06 eV). Normally it is of the order of 0.005 eV only.
4.	Inter-chain interactions are weaker than intra-chain interactions in conjugated polymers. This leads to non-linear optical properties.	Mostly isotropic in nature
5.	Band gap can be tuned by appropriate functionalization	Band gap can be tuned by exploiting quantum size effects (nanotechnology)

be fabricated for large-area applications. Another dimension of flexibility is the tunability of their energy gap by tailoring the molecular structure of the polymer, as shown in Fig. 7.6. In addition, the anisotropic nature of electronic conduction in these polymers has interesting consequences for device applications, since conduction in one direction gives rise to vectorial electron transfer crucial in many applications. More specifically, the conductivity, in some cases, increases by two orders of magnitude just when the polymer is oriented by mechanical stretching (anisotropic conductivity). In all these materials, the ratio of conductivity in the parallel and perpendicular directions is a reliable criterion to investigate these effects.

The band gap of most of the useful conducting polymers lies in the range of 1.5–3 eV, which implies that they can emit visible light. This particular feature makes them promising candidates for optoelectronic devices such as light emitting diodes, photovoltaics and liquid crystal displays. Another important parameter is carrier mobility, which is the proportionality constant between the magnitude of the applied electric field and the velocity of charges, which can be tuned by structure. At this point, it is important to realize that the photophysics of a polymer is not as simple as that of an isolated molecule/macromolecule, which is routinely explained in textbooks. The processibility is also controlled by the solvent and other important parameters. The photophysics of an isolated molecule can be summarized as follows.

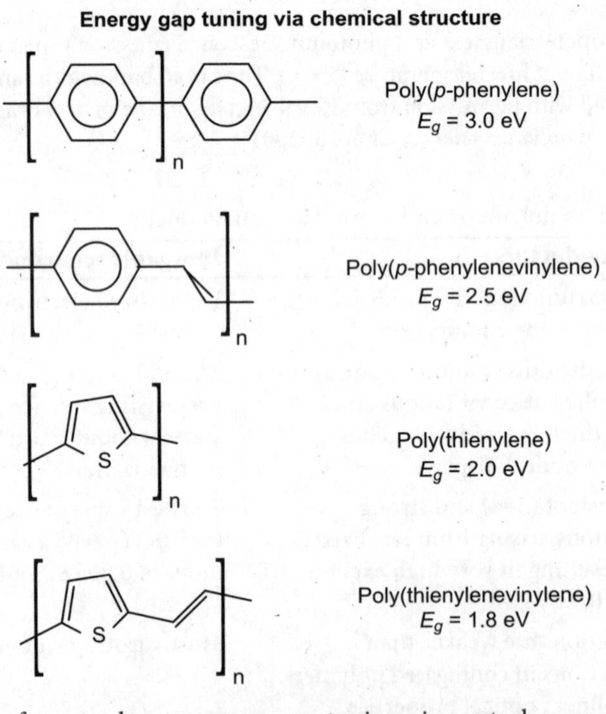

Fig. 7.6 Illustration of approaches to energy gap tuning via control over chemical structure. The corresponding energy gaps of the polymer are also shown [Adapted with permission from Royal Society of Chemistry, Bradley D D C, in Ryan A J, (Ed.), *Emerging Themes in Polymer Science*, Chap. 3, 2001]

Photoexcitation initially populates the excited singlet state, which deactivates subsequently into a lower lying singlet state radiatively (fluorescence), non-radiatively or by vibrational relaxation (VR), internal conversion (IC) or intersystem crossing (ISC) to a triplet state (phosphorescence). Photophysics in the condensed phase is much more complicated due to contributions from several other factors such as intermolecular relaxation phenomena or short life time of the excited state due to intermediate charge states, Further, parameters like π electron delocalization, inter-chain interaction, band gap, carrier density, extent of disorder, morphology and processing of materials determine the final electrical and optical properties. There are several mechanism of photoluminescence quenching, the most common of which is the Forster-type energy transfer. It briefly involves non-radiative energy transfer from a donor to an acceptor molecule.

Most of the challenges in polymer electronics are linked with the design of new monomers, oligomers and polymers, where chemistry has a pre-eminent role. If we have the right type of materials which are stable with excellent device characteristics, new mass markets could open up for low-cost, thin and flexible electronics which can be integrated into almost anything like clothes, spectacles, toys, etc., to facilitate innovative products including RFID tags, RAM protection, electronic ticketing, automation and smart or intelligent electronics. In order to illustrate the common materials-related challenges, we will turn our attention to some specific examples in the following sections.

7.3 POLYMERIC SEMICONDUCTORS IN LIGHT EMITTING DIODES

A light emitting diode (LED) is a device that can generate visible light when an electric field is applied. Although conventional LEDs are made up of inorganic semiconductors which have band gap in the range of visible light energy, they have several disadvantages in terms of cost and miniaturization, especially due to the brittle nature of the inorganic solid. Conjugated polymers have been identified as better candidates for diode applications in view of the following advantages [4]:

- Excellent mechanical stability
- Ease of processing into thin films
- Flexibility, light weight and compactness
- Ease of functionalization to tune their colour
- Solubility in organic solvents which allows solution processing

The first visible light emitting diode was made in 1962 by Nick Holonyak Jr, General Electric Company, who came to be known as 'the father of light emitting diodes'. This was followed by several improvements including organic LEDs (OLEDs) consisting of specially designed polymers and oligomers capable of emitting light in an external electric field by a phenomenon called 'electroluminescence' and polymer LEDs consisting of polymer molecules instead of simple organic molecules.

7.3.1 Organic light emitting diodes

The basic organization of an LED is shown in Fig. 7.7. In brief, it consists of a transparent conducting oxide as anode (e.g., indium tin oxide), a hole transport layer, an emissive layer, an electron transport layer (ETL) and a metallic low-work function electrode as cathode. Originally, only inorganic semiconductors were considered as photoactive materials for LEDs. However, in 1990, Richard Friend and Jeremy Burroughes demonstrated how a thin layer of polymer, sandwiched between two electrodes, could act as an LED. Following this invention, there have been numerous efforts in the field of polymer LEDs, which are summarized along with a comparison of light emitting efficiencies of various types of LEDs in Fig. 7.8.

The basic construction of a polymer LED involves two electrodes, one to inject electrons (cathode) and one to inject holes (anode), sandwiching a conducting polymer film in which the electrons and holes combine to form excitons. The excitons are excited state entities which decay to emit visible photons, which means that the polymer diode is functioning!

What are the criteria for the individual components in a polymer LED? The cathode is usually a low-work function material like calcium ($\varphi = 2.8$ eV) which can release electrons easily, and the anode or the positive electrode is a high-work function material like Indium-doped tin oxide (ITO, $\varphi = 4.5$ eV) that can 'suck' the electrons injected by the cathode. Typical examples for materials used in organic LEDs are shown in Fig. 7.9.

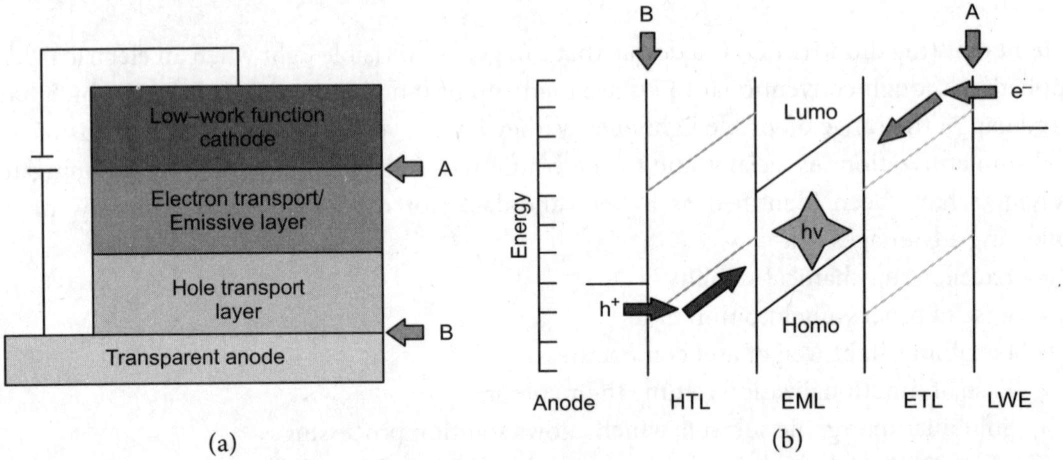

Fig. 7.7 Schematic of (a) typical OLED heterostructure and (b) the corresponding energy level diagram where HTL is the hole transport layer, EML/ETL is the electron transport/emissive layer and LWE is the low work function cathode [Adapted with permission from American Chemical Society: Veinot J G C et al., *Acc. Chem. Res.*, 38: 632, 2005]

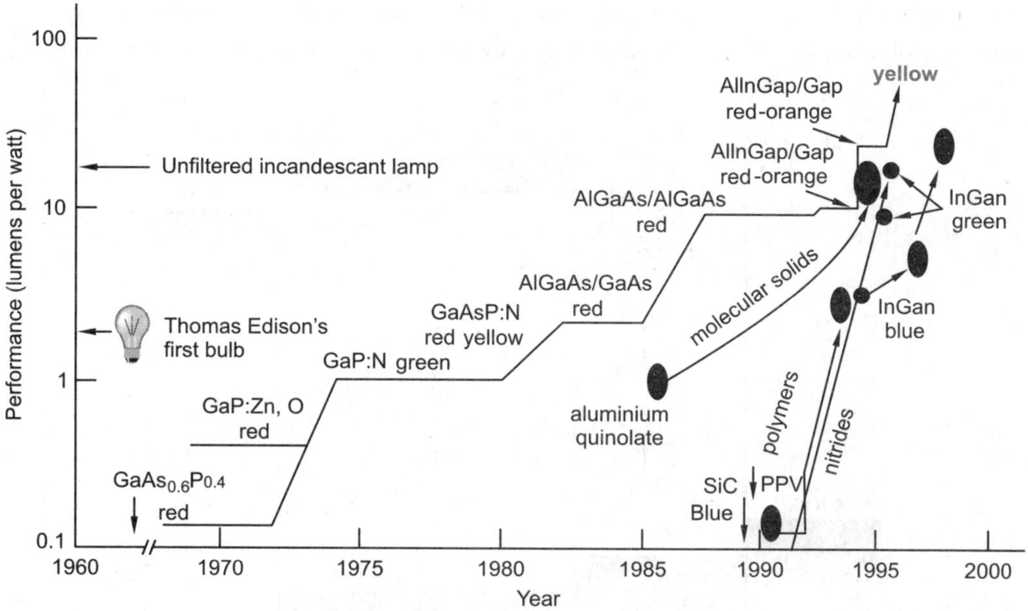

Fig. 7.8 *(see also Plate 6)* A comparison of the 'luminous efficiency' of inorganic and organic light emitting diodes. The semiconducting material in organic LEDs can either be a polymer or a sublimed film of small molecules [Adapted with permission from Institute of Physics Publishing: Friend R, Burroughes J and Shimoda T, Polymer diodes, *Physics World*, June 1999]

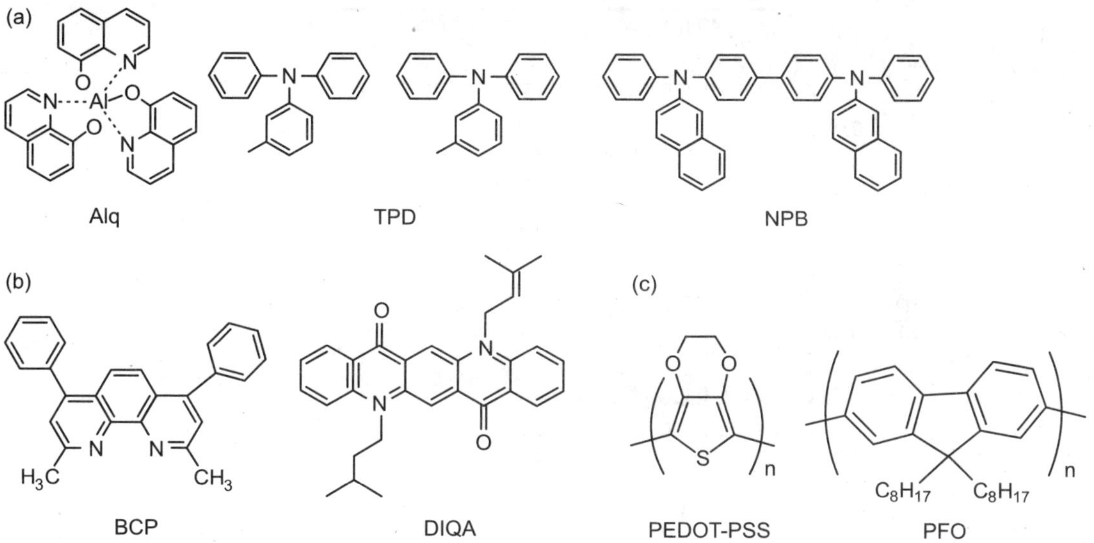

Fig. 7.9 Structural formulae of (a) typical electron transport (Alq) and hole transport materials (TPD and NPB); (b) exciton/hole blocking material (BCP) and emissive dopant (DIQA); (c) hole transport (PEDOT-PSS) and emissive (PFO) polymers [Adapted with permission from American Chemical Society: Veinot J G C et al., Towards the Ideal, Organic, Light Emitting Diode. The Versatility and Utility of Interfacial Tailoring by Cross-linked Siloxane Interlayers. *Acc. Chem. Res.*, 38: 632, 2005]

Figure 7.10 illustrates a simple polymer LED consisting of an additional layer of a conducting polymer, PEDOT, to bridge the wide energy gap between the semiconducting

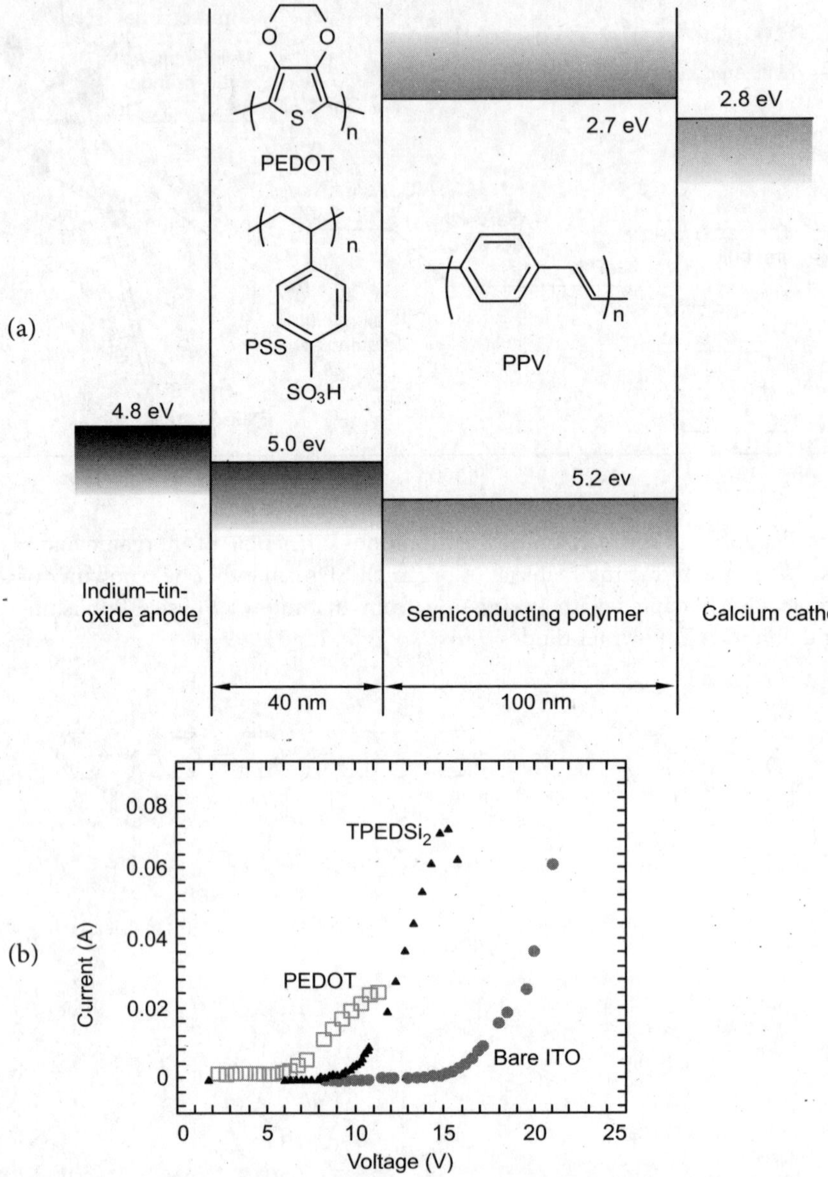

Fig. 7.10 A polymer LED made with PPV [poly(phenylene vinylene)] sandwiched between a calcium cathode and an anode made of a conducting polymer on indium–tin oxide (ITO): (a) Current–voltage characteristics of a polymer LED made of poly-3, 4-ethylenedioxythiophene-polystyrene sulphonate (PEDOT), 1, 4-bis(phenyl-m-tolylamino)biphenyl (TPD) compared with bare indium-doped tin oxide [Adapted with permission from Institute of Physics Publishing: Friend R, Burroughes J and Shimoda T, Polymer diodes, *Physics World,* June 1999]

polymer and the anode material, along with the current–voltage characteristics of a polymer LED with PEDOT-PSS and TPD [1, 4-bis(phenyl *m*-tolylamino)biphenyl] as the hole transport layer and PFO [poly(9, 9-dioctylfluorene)] as the electron transport layer. Though polymer LEDs sound simple as per the above description, their real picture is somewhat critical when we look for devices with better efficiency and lifetime. The challenges can be categorized as those pertaining to the improvement of the properties of the respective electrodes, electrode/polymer interfaces and polymer interlayers, each of which will be discussed in brief in the next few paragraphs.

The importance of multi-functional materials, which we have been discussing thus far from different perspectives, becomes obvious when we analyze the materials issues in a polymer LED. For example, ITO is not the best anode material as its work function is a strong function of its composition and surface morphology, and hence its history of preparation. In addition, there is a difference of at least 0.4 eV between ITO and most of the semiconducting polymers, which is overcome by an additional layer of a conducting polymer with an intermittent band gap. Still, we have to understand the nature of the interfaces formed between each of these layers. On the other hand, the efficiency of electron injection from the cathode material largely depends on the interfacial chemistry consisting of the cathode material and the semiconducting polymer.

Similarly, there are a number of experimental as well as theoretical modelling challenges in understanding electrical transport in semiconducting polymers. A good polymer material for LED applications is expected to have the following characteristics:

- Ability to process and deposit at low temperature
- Offer good mobility for electrons and holes
- Allow exciton formation
- Allow excitons to decay and emit photons

A good LED uses hundreds of layers of different materials with specific functions like a hole-inducing layer, although the overall quantum efficiency of a polymer LED depends on the individual efficiencies of each of these steps. Simple statistical calculations assuming that the number of triplet states is three times that of singlet states, predicts a maximum quantum efficiency of 25%. But the maximum experimental quantum efficiencies obtained with polymer LEDs are not greater than 10%, because the efficiencies of steps 2 and 3 are not 100%. But tunability is the advantage, as for example, carrier mobility in poly(3-hexyl) thiophene is observed to increase by three orders of magnitude when the molecular weight increases by one order of magnitude. Other than such issues related to materials, general challenges in polymer LEDs include how to enhance power efficiency, viz., linking morphology and electrical properties, good brightness (~ 100 cd/m^2) at a low voltage, low mechanical stability of doped polymers and good colour definition to enable colour mixing to facilitate displays in the whole range.

7.4 POLYMER PHOTOVOLTAICS

Solar photovoltaics as a clean energy option was mentioned briefly in the previous chapter (section 6.4.2). Here, we will provide more details of the progress in the field of polymer-based photovoltaic devices. The working principle of a photovoltaic device is just the opposite of that of an LED: while the latter emits light in response to an applied electric field, the former absorbs light of energy higher than its band gap and generates a potential difference. This happens when the electron–hole pairs (excitons) formed by the absorption of photons disintegrate and redistribute their charges. In simple terms, a layer of a semiconducting polymer sandwiched between two appropriate electrodes will act as an LED under forward bias, and as a photovoltaic cell if light is shone on it in reverse bias. Nevertheless, splitting a bound electron–hole pair in a polymer, whether it is formed by photoexcitation or an electric field, is never an easy task. To achieve this, we often need two polymer layers with different electron affinities back to back, so that excitons will split by transferring electrons from one to the other in a process called 'photoexcited electron transfer'. Figure 7.11 shows an illustration of a simple photovoltaic device.

As in the case of polymeric LEDs, here also the major challenges are due to materials-related issues and limitations in photoconversion efficiencies. What are the criteria for a good photovoltaic material?

- Fast and efficient photoexcited electron transfer between the donor and the acceptor molecules
- Good carrier mobilities
- Selectivity of the electrodes to the direction of carrier drift in the case of photovoltaic devices involving bulk hetero junctions

For example, fullerene (C_{60}) has been shown to be the best electron acceptor that could be coupled with many semiconducting electron donating polymers, as it forms a stable radical anion and the kinetics is very fast. Similarly, there have been many advances in electron donating polymers with which efficiency of up to 5% has been achieved.

Many of the recent developments in Gratzel cells [5] (dye-sensitized solar cell), rainbow solar cells (cells which can catch the rainbow! i.e., they can absorb a wide range of visible wavelengths), etc., indicate that high-efficiency, low-price organic solar cells would be available in the near future, although impurities and disorder-induced defects might limit the performance.

The major limitations affecting the efficiency of photovoltaic devices are due to the following factors:

- Limitations in the thickness of the photoactive material imposed by the low charge carrier mobilities (~ 10^{-4} cm^2/Vs), which increases the resistance with increasing film thickness
- Sensitivity of carrier mobility to the nanoscale morphology of the polymer films

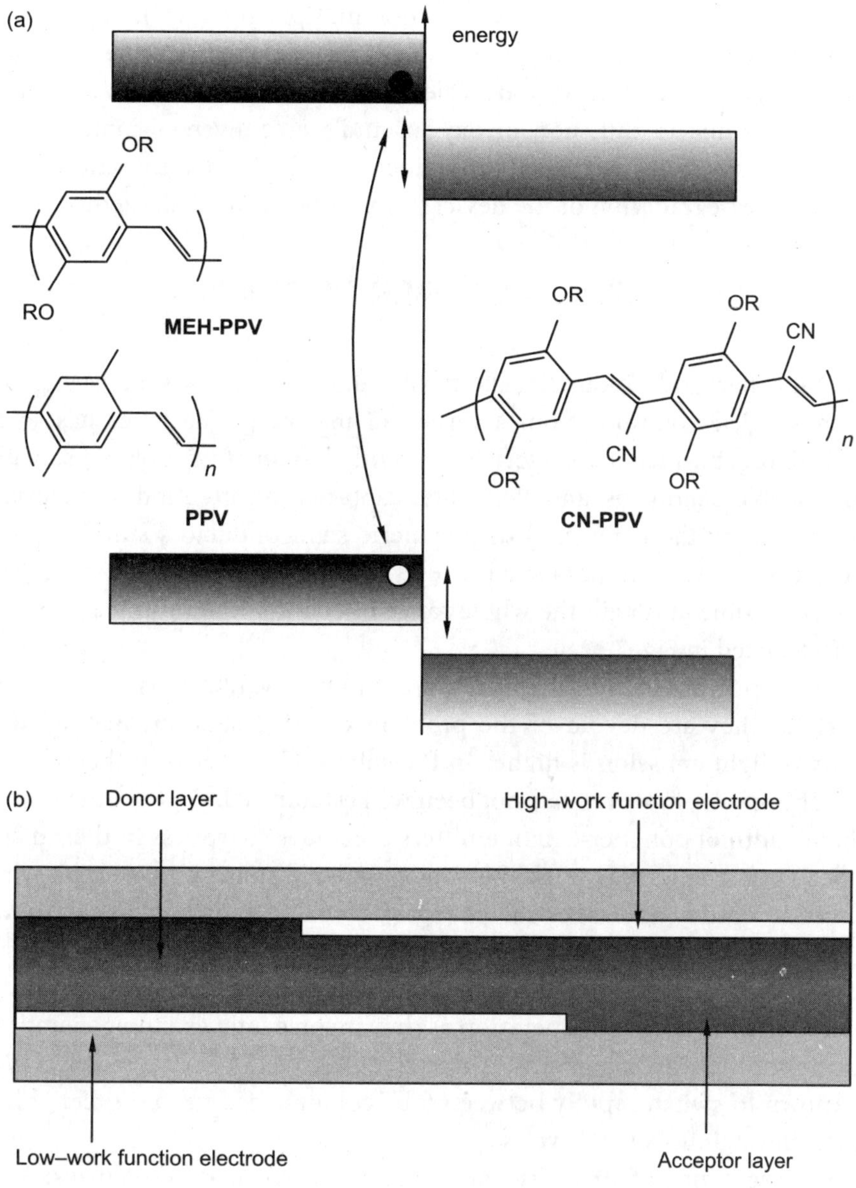

Fig. 7.11 (a) Energetics of transport phenomena at the donor and acceptor layers in a polymer-based photovoltaic device; (b) Optimum design of a device for obtaining the best performance. [Adapted with permission from Institute of Physics Publishing: Friend R, Burroughes J and Shimoda T, Polymer diodes, *Physics World*, June 1999]

- Short life time of carriers; typical life time of organic and polymeric solar cells without the use of encapsulation is about one day, while with different encapsulation strategies and barrier layers, it could be extended to a few weeks under full solar illumination

- Complex performance degradation (with multiple proceses), especially if exposed to oxygen or water. For example, a single layer of polyphenylene vinylene-derivative sandwiched between the ITO and Al electrodes undergoes degradation in photovoltaic performance due to diffusion of oxygen and water. Even if complex encapsulation schemes such as sealed glass containers or high-vacuum chambers are used, performance degradation of the devices cannot be avoided altogether.

7.5 POLYMER DISPLAYS

The demand for sharp, full colour, flat and flexible display systems is increasing exponentially, forcing technological solutions from a variety of materials. The focus has so far been on inorganic and organo-metallic materials. Recently, conducting polymers, with their key features of 'tunable band gaps' and 'flexibility', captured the attention of materials scientists. It is possible to tune the band gaps of polymeric semiconductors simply by changing the molecular structure of the monomer, a processs commonly known as 'band gap engineering' [6]. It is even possible to obtain the whole range of colours from a single polymer simply by doping it as depicted in Fig. 7.12.

In addition, polymeric light emitters are more advantageous than their inorganic counterparts as they are devoid of the problem of 'solid state quenching', due to which the intensity of light emission is higher in the solution state than in the solid state for dye molecules. The reason, however, has not been well established. On the other hand, the broad spectral bandwidth of polymeric light emitters precludes sharpness in their displays.

How does a polymer display work? Polymers used in displays are materials which undergo reversible and reproducible spectral changes, associated with changes in conjugation, induced by electrochemical redox reactions. Although the device configuration looks similar, consisting of a conducting polymer sandwiched between two electrodes, polymer LEDs differ in their principle of operation as they involve only exciton generation and decay without any bonding rearrangements. A classical example for such a material is polyaniline, which is known to switch rapidly between four colours, viz., yellow, green, blue and black with a switching stability of 10^6 cycles.

There are two types of displays—active and passive matrix displays. While *passive matrix displays* require current to externally control the brightness of the individual pixels, *active matrix displays* have transistors which can control the current passing through the pixels.

Polymer displays are found to be superior to cathode-ray tube and liquid crystal due to.

- Sharp images
- High brightness
- Improved contrast

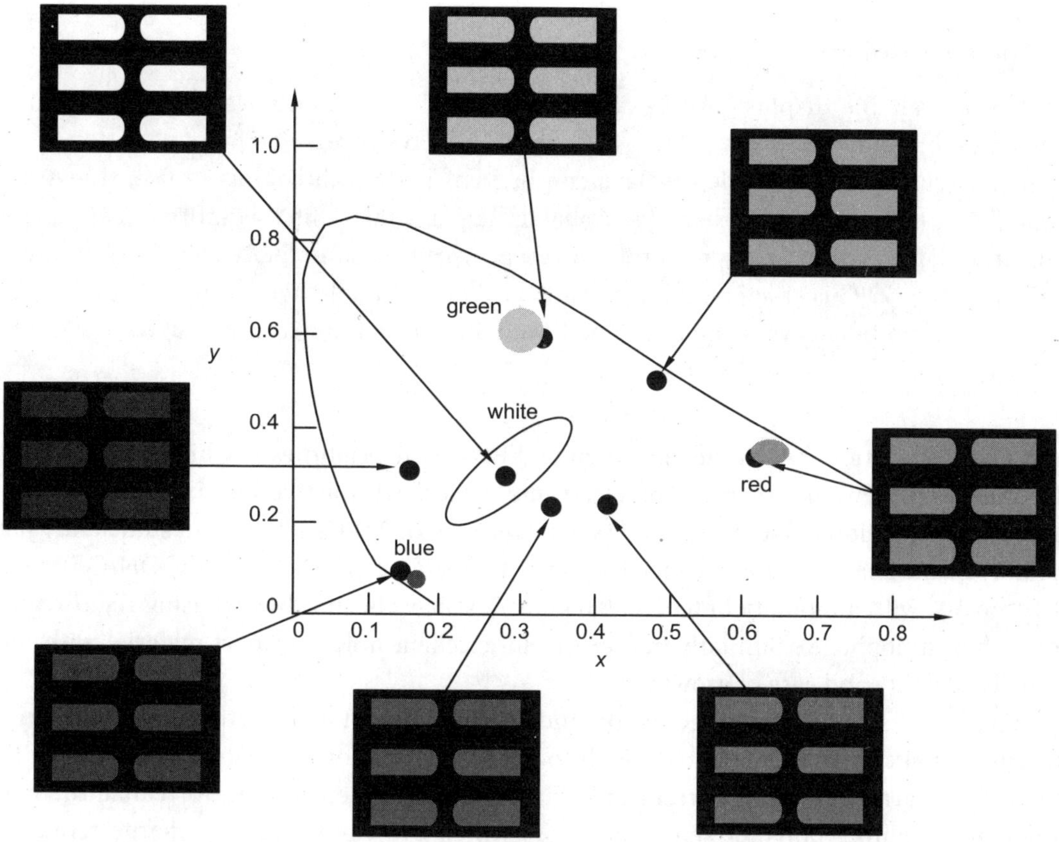

Fig. 7.12 *(see also Plate 7)* Polymers based on poly(fluorene) emit light over a wide range of colours [Adapted with permission from Institute of Physics Publishing: Friend R, Burroughes J and Shimoda T, Polymer diodes, *Physics World*, June 1999]

- Wide viewing angle
- Low power consumption

7.6 FIELD EFFECT TRANSISTORS

A transistor is a device used to amplify or switch electronic signals in circuits. It basically consists of a semiconducting material connected to three terminals: the current passing through one pair of these terminals changes the current flowing through the other pair. With increasing demands for miniaturization of electronic devices, fabrication of electronic components like transistors on flexible plastic substrates using solution-processable semiconducting polymers has captured global attention.

Rollable Displays

While all rollable displays are flexible, not all flexible displays are rollable. Flexible displays, although not yet available in the market, have received a lot of attention over the past years. Such flexible displays can be bent without breaking—a useful feature compared to conventional displays. Rollable displays take this flexibility a major step further. Being as thin as paper, a rollable display can be completely rolled up into the size of a finger. This creates unique advantages for mobile devices, where displays can be large when in use, yet rolled or folded away into a small area when not in use.

In the last section, we discussed polymer LEDs with brightness as high as 10^5 cd/m^2. However, to achieve all-polymer optoelectronic devices with active matrix technology, it is important to develop polymer transistors with very good ON/OFF ratio and sufficiently high mobility of the charge carriers, which can drive the polymer LEDs. Recently, ON/OFF ratios of 10^2 to 10^4 with a mobility of 0.01 to 0.04 cm^2/Vs^1 have been achieved using regio-regular poly(3-hexylthiophene). Similarly, *rubrene* is an excellent hole transport material with high mobility, stability and ease of growth.

Organic FETs can be classified as top and bottom contact architectures. However, rigid structures make them fragile and difficult to handle. An important feature of polymer FETs is that they carry electronic current only via positive charge carriers. To realize their full potential, designing polymer semiconductors which can carry negative charge remains a challenge.

7.7 INTELLIGENT POLYMERS FOR DATA STORAGE

One of the interesting advances in the wake of polymer electronics is the deployment of conducting polymers for memory applications. Although progress in data storage systems has proceeded with exponential increase in hard disk capacity, as predicted by the famous Moore's law, it is now time to realize the theoretical limits in patterning the drives with lithography. Parallel to Moore's law, Gerald Butter of Bell Labs formulated a law called *Butter's law of photonics*. It states that the amount of data coming out of an optical fibre doubles every nine months, and hence the cost of transmitting a bit of information over an optical network decreases by half every nine months. Similarly, the value of a digital camera is estimated using the 'pixel per dollar' plot developed by Barry Hendy of Kodak Australia.

Hence, the trend is quickly switching to semiconducting polymers which can self-assemble into regular patterns. A polymeric data storage device consists generally of three layers. The middle layer is a copolymer film with thickness of a few nanometers, sandwiched between a layer of conducting polymer (50 μm thick) and a metal film like Au (0.5 μm thick). Recently, a company called Plastic Logic was spun out of Cavendish Laboratory to sell polymer logic gates, and another start-up called Polymer Vision is planning to expand in a big manner. Fraunhofer has many plastic chips capable of monitoring body functions and is eventually planning to commercialize a small blood lab that fits into the pocket of a jacket. Compact, ready-to-install electronic modules requiring minimum space and compatible with printing on polycarbonate films is the key feature enabling 'printed electronics'.

What is the mechanism of binary data storage in a polymer? In conventional data storage devices, Si stores information in bits of information as '0' for fully discharged, and '1' for fully charged state. In the case of polymers, data is stored as the change in conductivity as a function of applied voltage. In certain voltage ranges, the current will be too low; when a certain voltage is reached, there is a sudden increase in the resulting current by almost 100 times, defining the '1' state of data storage.

Self-assembling polymers for data storage

Researchers from the University of Wisconsin-Madison and Hitachi Global Storage Technologies have reported a way to improve the quality and resolution of patterned templates such as those used to manufacture hard drives and other data storage devices. When added to lithographically patterned surfaces specially designed materials called block copolymers self-assemble into structures with improved quality and resolution over the original patterns. These structures can be used to make templates with nanoscale elements like silicon pillars which may be useful for manufacturing higher capacity hard disk drives.

The specific advantages of polymeric data storage systems over conventional ones include light weight and use of low-cost equipment such as ink-jet printers which provide tremendous flexibility for assembly and manufacture. It is easy to control the regularity of patterns and the possibility of fast reading and writing offers excellent performance coupled with low manufacturing costs and low device failure. Laminar electronics with transparent packaging is another attractive feature, which with 3D assembly can bring revolutionary technological gadgets. However, many long-term stability and durability issues plague the commercial prospects of these promising devices.

7.8 CONCLUSIONS

Though we have discussed only some specific cases of electronically conducting and semiconducting polymers in the above sections, there are many more applications. However, many common issues and challenges need to be overcome to realize the full potential of polymer electronics, some of which are given below.

- In most cases, the conductivity of the polymers is highly sensitive to the environment. For example, doped polyacetylene, while highly conductive in an inert environment, loses its conductivity when exposed to air. Similarly, polythiophenes also exhibit intermediate stability, necessitating encapsulation.
- Conducting polymers have poor mechanical stability which is exacerbated with doping. Hence they are often incorporated into matrices of non-conducting polymers like poly(vinyl chloride) to achieve better processability.
- Most of them are hole conductors and achieving electronic conduction is still a challenge. The mobilities are still very poor in comparison with that of inorganic semiconductors.

Nevertheless, advantages like cheap solution processing, especially on flexible plastic substrates, tuning functions and the possibility of patterning far outweigh these limitations. Several systems like rubrene and pentacene have surpassed amorphous Si in performance for transistors despite durability issues, and breakthroughs in single crystal FET fabrication will enable more widespread use of conducting polymers in the near future.

Further reading

[1] Haddon R C and Lamola A A, The molecular electronic device and the biochip computer: Present status, *Proc. Natl. Acad. Sci.*, USA, 82: 1874–1878, 1985.
[2] Feldheim D L and Keating C D, *Chem. Soc. Rev.*, 27: 1–12, 1998.
[3] Akamatu H and Inokuchi H, On the electrical conductivity of violanthrone, iso-violanthrone and pyranthrone, *J. Chem. Phys.* 18: 810, 1950.
[4] Schwartz B N, Conjugated polymers as molecular materials: How chain conformation and film morphology influence energy transfer and interchain interactions, *Annu. Rev. Phys. Chem.*, 54: 141, 2003.
[5] Hagfeldt A and Gratzel M, Molecular photovoltaics, *Acc. Chem. Res.*, 33: 269, 2000.
[6] Sariciftsi N S, Plastic photovoltaics, *Materials Today,* Sept. 2004.

Exercises

1. What are the major advantages if we replace all the incandescent lamps in our country with compact fluorescent lamps (CFLs) or LEDs? What prevents this type of replacement?
2. Explain the similarities between the manufacture of newsprint and polymer electronic displays.
3. What parameters limit the performance of organic electronic devices, and how can we overcome these challenges ?
4. Name three polymer electronic devices nearing commercialization or which are already available.
5. What are the essential differences in designing a molecule for OLED, OFET or organic solar cells?
6. Mention three important advantages of using a molecule as an electronic component in a circuit. What are the possible limitations?

7. Discuss the advantages and problems of polymer photovoltaics compared to devices based on silicon (both amorphous and single crystal).
8. Why are quantum dots attractive for designing solar cells? How is this concept useful in preparing 'rainbow' solar cells?
9. What are Gratzel cells? Why are they important?
10. Using a search engine such as Google or Yahoo, find recent start-up companies like Konarca, Helios, Plastic Logic, Solar Vision, etc., in the area of polymer electronics and compare the materials being developed by them.

8

Functional Nanocomposites

This chapter shows how synergistic functions can be gained by combining two or more functional components. It demonstrates how a performance better than that of the individual components could be achieved, especially when one of the components is nanostructured. The important interfacial phenomena that control the properties of these nanocomposites are explained using appropriate theoretical models, ending with typical illustrations using carbon nanotubes, metal nanowires and other dimensionally confined structures. Although there are many open questions, research is continuing to strive for more efficient nanocomposites for fulfilling global challenges.

LEARNING OBJECTIVES

- To define nanocomposites and to understand their classification
- To recognize how nanocomposites are different from conventional composites
- To suggest some examples of nanocomposites, highlighting their unusual properties with respect to carbon nanotube–based polymeric composites.
- To describe important applications of nanocomposites in the civil and aerospace industries
- To explain the advantages of designing nanocomposites based on natural composites like wood and bone
- To predict the revolutionary changes expected in the area of polymer-based nanocomposites

The nano-effect

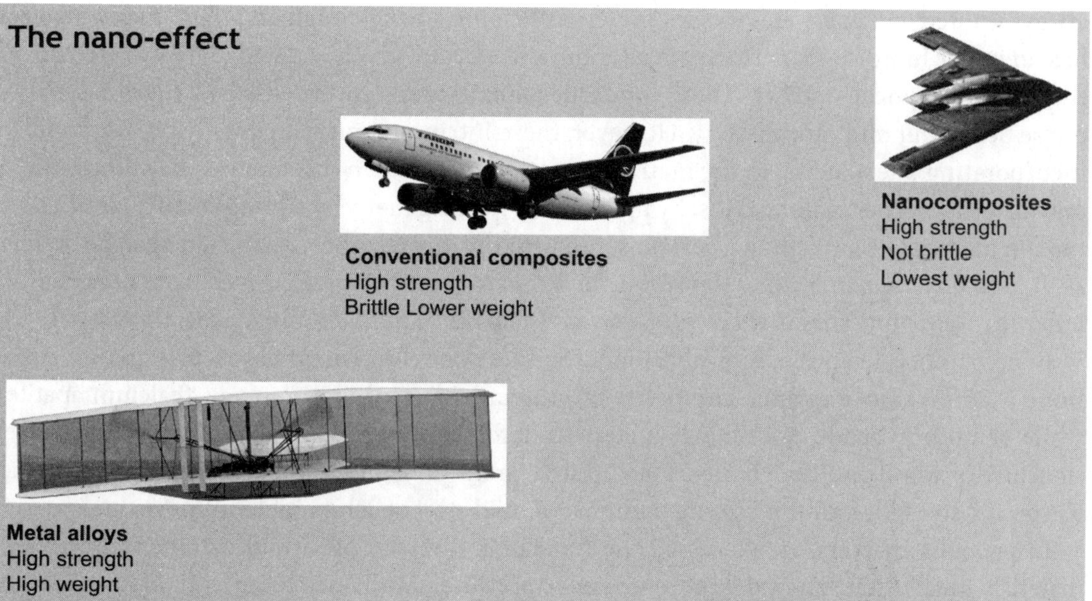

Fig. 8.1 Comparison of properties between alloys, bulk composites and nanocomposites

Most materials begin to display exotic properties when they are reduced to nano (10^{-9} m) dimensions. The 'nano-effect' arises when the dimensions become comparable to a critical length scale, at least in one dimension. For instance, while zinc oxide can exhibit nano-effects even at 200 nm, gold does not when the particles are bigger than about 10 nm. The length-scale that distinguishes these two materials is the electron mean free path, or more accurately, the *phase coherence length*. Thus, if we are looking for the nano-effect in electronic/electrical properties, the reference length-scale is the electron's mean free path or the de Broglie wavelength of that material. Similarly, in the case of magnetic applications, the size of the magnetic domains should be considered as the reference to nano-behaviour. Now, the question is: Can nanomaterials complement macro materials when they are interfaced together? The objective of this chapter is to take the reader on an exciting journey to appreciate the transition from traditional to alloys through innovative bulk composites to game changing nanocomposites!

8.1 WHY 'NANO'COMPOSITES?

Everything in this world, including our body, is made up of materials, which in turn are made of atoms and molecules. Materials can be homogeneous, heterogeneous, biological or synthetic and are widely used for providing shelter, food, energy and other forms of comfort. Society has always wanted and continues to seek materials that are strong, tough and light. Every material has an upper limit for its performance (endurance level), which is decided by its mechanical, thermal and optical stability. These properties are, in turn, governed by its thermodynamic phase behaviour and morphology. However, these intrinsic limits can greatly be overcome by incorporating one material in the matrix of another material. In this manner, key properties of one material can be reinforced just by introducing heterogeneity by adding small quantities of a foreign material, compliant in a certain sense with the former. Thus, composites can be defined as: '*...multi-phase materials obtained by the artificial combination of two or more materials, in order to attain properties that cannot be acheived by the individual components themselves*'.

Bone, bamboo, feather, natural fibres and wood are examples of naturally occurring composites. Bone is an organic–inorganic composite of protein (collagen) and minerals (calcium apatite), while bamboo is made of cellulose material reinforced by silica. Similarly, the cellulosic cell structure of wood and fibre bound together by lignin—a natural polymeric substance—makes its specific strength four times more than that of mild steel of comparable stiffness.

In previous chapters, we discussed the functional diversity of several natural and synthetic materials and illustrated how they become much more useful with increasing levels of functionality. This chapter will demonstrate another interesting dimension of functional materials; that materials can 'communicate' with each other to bring synergy within a composite system! A minute quantity of carbon nanotube (CNT) powder sprinkled in your bicycle might win you a gold medal in the Olympics! This is not a far-fetched assumption: a CNT-reinforced plastic bicycle designed by Lotus Engineering won Chris Boardman a gold medal in the 1992 Barcelona Olympics. Combining the elegant flexibility and light weight of polymers with the unique mechanical behaviour of CNTs, this example illustrates the importance of composite materials.

The question that automatically springs to mind is: (Why carbon 'nanotubes'? Why not a bicycle with graphite powder?) The answer is, while CNTs can help win medals, a bicycle with a graphite powder composite will not bear your weight! While both graphite and CNT are allotropic forms of carbon, the former can yield a very strong composite while the latter cannot. The difference is in their size. Nanosize carbon, in the form of long wires, fibres or tubes, has far different properties from simple graphite powder. The essentials of nanoscience, how the properties change and exotic properties appear when a material reaches nano-dimension, have been discussed in *Chapter 6*. For instance, ceramics, which are normally brittle can be deformed easily when their grain size is in the nanoscale. Here we will try and understand how these nanoscale compositions affect the macroscopic properties of a composite material.

As mentioned in the National Nanotechnology Initiative [1],

> *The advances at the nanoscale will be meaningless if they cannot be interfaced well with the technology at larger material components, systems and architectures to produce usable devices.*

The utility and processibility of a composite depends on the aggregate properties of the filling material, and the nature and strength of interaction between the phases. When metallic nanoparticles, carbon nanofibres or nanometre-thick filaments or sheets of a ceramic are introduced into a matrix of another material, for example, a polymer, the enormous surface area of the nano-sized filler can create significantly large interfaces with the polymer matrix. The nanomaterials also contain a large number of defects which help to strengthen their interface with the matrix material. As a result, nanocomposites are exceptionally strong, hard and ductile at high temperatures, wear resistant, and corrosion resistant. For example, recently it was found that epoxy matrices modified with nanoclays were stronger than those modified with conventional nylon fibres [2]; unlike bulk composites, they can be engineered at the molecular or atomic level.

Nanocomposites offer several advantages over pure materials:

- Design flexibility
- High stiffness and strength
- Light weight
- Rapid processability
- Less corrosion and degradation problems
- Enhanced durability
- Low cost

Thus, nanotechnology holds promise to revolutionize the world of structural materials using nanocomposites of unparalleled combinations of strength and lightness. Some of these composites endow extraordinary strength of about 100–200 GPa compared to normally used Kevlar and carbon fibres which have strengths of about 3–6 GPa.

'The Last Judgment' rejuvenated by nanocomposites

The Last Judgment, a mosaic on the exterior of St Vitus cathedral in the heart of Prague Castle is a masterpiece made of a million multicoloured glasses, embedded in mortar. The glass has high potassium content. Owing to corrosion due to harsh weather conditions (acid rains with high SO_2 levels, temperatures varying between –30 and 65°C), the salt deposits that formed over a period of several decades blurred and corroded the painting. Previous attempts to stop corrosion using organic polymers were unsuccessful because of their poor durability, poor adhesion to the glass and large diffusion coefficient of SO_2 and water. The problem was finally solved by coating it with a fluoropolymer nanocomposite.

Having understood the importance and relevance of nanoscience in the synthesis and processing of composite materials, we will see in the following sections, how nanocomposites are classified, and how to model and engineer the interactions at their interface, enabling remarkable predictive ability. Let us first look at some of the general aspects of multi-functional composites. One of the outstanding examples for multi-functionality is provided by the type of material used for building aircrafts: a given material is tailored to perform differently for different parts (materials with functional gradients), as discussed earlier.

Figure 8.2 shows a Boeing aircraft and its various parts made by different composites or composite variations of the same material with different properties. What an amazing combination of structural engineering materials are used! Consider a composite of strong ceramic fibres in a metal matrix (e.g., SiC fibres in an Al matrix). This would be a strong, rigid composite, which can be used in airframe material where moderate loads are encountered, such as in the skin of the fuselage. On the contrary, if metal fibres are embedded in a ceramic matrix, composites of excellent toughness and strength are obtained, as the strength of the ceramic matrix combines with the ability of the metal fibres to deform and deflect cracks. When a crack is deflected, more load is required to continue its propagation, thereby making the material tougher. Thus, such composites can aid in reducing the weight and increasing the payload of domestic aircrafts. High-temperature ceramic metal matrix composites can increase the operating temperature of engines. For example, rocket nozzles used currently are made with a unique combination of tungsten, silver, carbon, ceramic and steel, each to satisfy

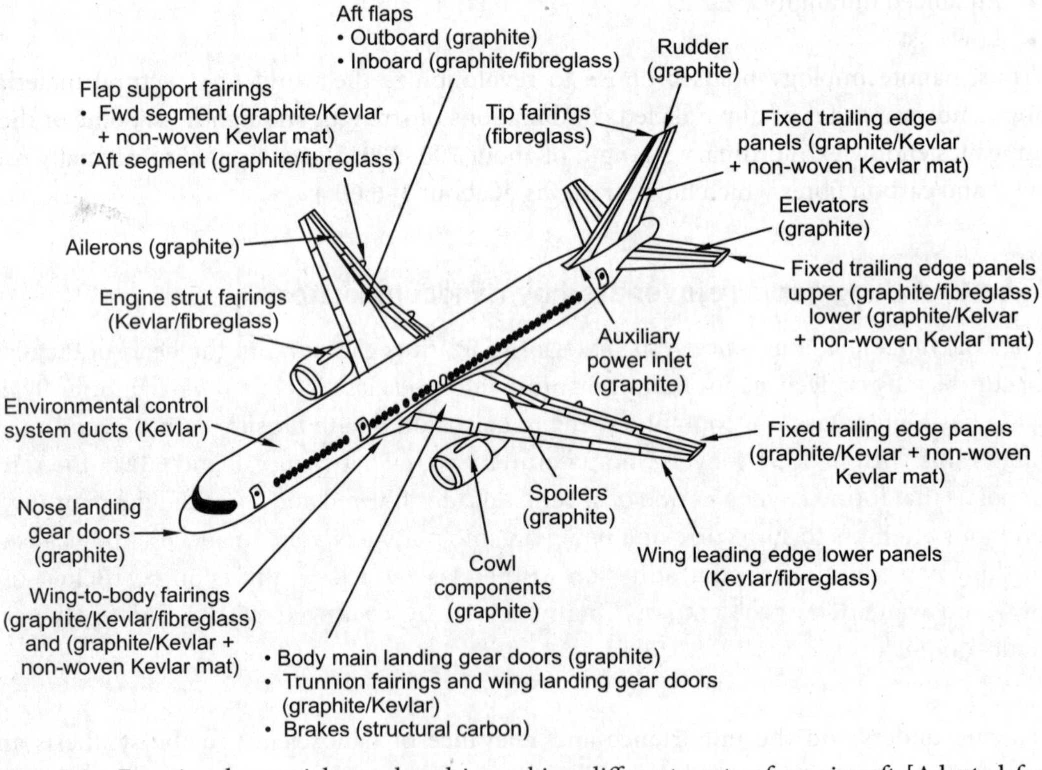

Figure 8.2 Functional materials employed in making different parts of an aircraft [Adapted from http://www.mrl.columbia.edu/ntm/images/composite5.jpg]

several conflicting requirements of critical dimensional, mechanical, corrosion and thermal tolerances.

Composites exhibit many properties which are either absent or negligible in either of the components, thereby introducing multi-functionality. Let us consider polymer/carbon fibre composites. Carbon fibres are known for their strength and rigidity, but they have very low ductility, which limits their direct application in fabricating parts of a device or a machine. Epoxy resins, on the other hand, though not inherently strong, can form composites with carbon fibres to efficiently transfer load to the fibres and the fibre/epoxy interface can deflect and stop small cracks. More recent composites include functionalized graphene/polymer nanocomposites, where the one-dimensional filler, like carbon nanotube, is completely replaced by two-dimensional nanomaterials, such as graphene with suitable functional groups to make use of its parallel physical properties and cheaper processing techniques [3]. The classification based on, grouping common characteristics and properties, will aid further understanding of nanocomposites along with enhanced durability and performance.

8.2 CLASSIFICATION OF NANOCOMPOSITES

Composites are classified into three major types: fibrous, laminar and particulate.

Fibrous composites are composed of reinforced fibres in a matrix. During the 1970s, 'high-strength composites' and 'advanced composites' were spoken of in the reinforced plastics industry. These terms have been generally associated with reinforcements that offer stiffer, stronger composites, in comparison to the traditional composite of glass fibres in a polyester matrix.

Laminar composites are composed of two or more layers of materials held together by the matrix binder. Examples are automobile parts such as windshields and laminated glass, where isotropic layers of materials are bonded together to form inhomogeneous composite laminates.

Particulate composites consist of particles dispersed in a matrix. These particulates may be powdered, crystalline or amorphous, or they may be metallic- or ceramic-containing natural or artificially prepared materials. The matrix must be capable of being forced around the reinforcement during some stage in the manufacturing of the composite. There are a number of matrix materials, including carbon, ceramic, glass and polymers. Concrete and solid rocket propellants are other familiar examples of particulate composites.

However, the above method of classification of conventional composites needs modification when one of the constituents is nanostructured. This is especially significant when the aspect ratio is very high for the dispersed phase (e.g., while using one-dimensional materials, such as nanorods and nanowires, or two-dimensional materials, such as nanoclays or graphene, since the percolation threshold for electrical, thermal or mechanical properties can come down significantly. For example, a rheological study of polycarbonate/multiwalled carbon nanotube composites indicated an unusual increase in the viscosity above a percolation limit of 2% with a concomitant increase in the storage modulus explained on the basis of a very high aspect ratio of the carbon nanotubes. More recently, a remarkable *in situ* preparation of Nylon–CNT composites showed that the morphology and properties can be modulated by tailoring the CNT–polymer interfacial interaction [4].

Abalone shell—a natural nanocomposite

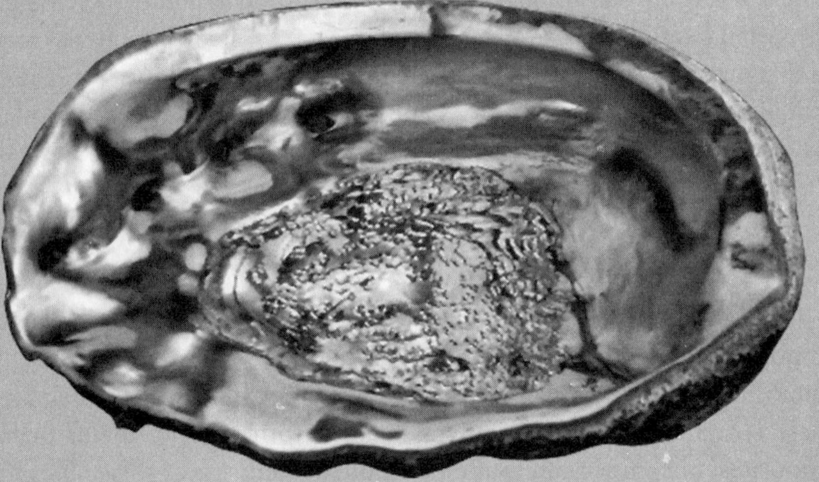

Fig. 8.3 *(see also Plate 7)* An iridescent abalone shell with all the colours of the ocean [Reproduced from http://en.wikipedia.org/wiki/File:AbaloneInside.jpg under the terms of the GNU Free Documentation Licence]

Abalone is an edible sea snail belonging to the family of molluscs. The shell is known for its exceptional strength, as it slides its tiles without shattering when struck. The composition of the abalone shell has been a matter of debate for materials scientists, which if revealed could result in the design of bio-mimetic tough materials for applications like body armour. The abalone shell is basically a nanocomposite of calcium carbonate tiles stacked together with the help of a sticky protein substance (glycoproteins); it stretches in response to applied stress, preventing the shell from shattering.

A convenient and simple way of classifying nanocomposites is based on the type of matrix or the dispersion medium (Table 8.1).

When the dispersed phase is a high–aspect ratio structure like carbon nanotubes, the percolation threshold for mechanical, electrical or thermal behaviour comes down

Table 8.1 Classification of nanocomposites based on the type of matrix and their sub-classes

Matrix	Sub-classes	Example
Polymer	Ionic conductor	Nafion
	Electronic conductor	Polyaniline
	Thermoplastic	Polyimide
	Thermoset	Epoxy resin
Metal		Tungsten in copper matrix
Cement		Concrete, carbon fibre/cement composite
Carbon	Amorphous	
	Graphitic	Carbon–carbon composites
Ceramic	Inter-granular	
	Intra-granular	Borosilicate glass (Pyrex)

significantly, and accordingly many of these nanocomposites find important applications as structural and heat dissipating elements. Many thermal barrier coatings available today make use of nanocomposites of yttria-stabilized zirconia in its metastable, tetragonal form along with (cubic) to withstand the thermal expansion stresses associated with heating and cooling during operation. The ability of these nanocomposite coatings to manage large strains without failure enables them to operate at high temperatures for applications like gas turbines. Similarly, several nano-coolants are designed based on the fluid suspension of nanometre-sized particles and tubes/wires/fibres for extraordinary heat transfer capabilities. For example, a single-walled carbon nanotube–polymer epoxy composite has shown a 125% increase in thermal conductivity with a meagre 1 wt% nanotube loading at room temperature, thus demonstrating how nanofluids can be manipulated to obtain enhanced thermal transport and faster heat dissipation [5].

8.3 SYNTHETIC STRATEGIES

The method of synthesis depends on the type and chemical composition of the constituents of a nanocomposite. As it is difficult to describe all the methods in this text, the reader is referred to review articles on specific types of nanocomposites [1–3]. This section will discuss the preparation of the most common types, namely, polymer, ceramic and carbon nanocomposites.

Ceramic nanocomposites

Mechanical alloying or ball milling is the most conventional method of preparing nanocomposites, especially if one of the constituents is a ceramic material, or is difficult to dissolve in common solvents. In this process, alloying occurs as a result of repeated breaking up of the component particles. Increasing the energy of the milling process can even result in chemical reactions. For example, magnetic oxide/metal nanocomposites can be prepared by a mechanically induced displacement reaction between a metal oxide and a more reactive metal. This process is called 'high-energy ball milling'.

The next common method is *sol-gel processing*, which enables the synthesis of nanocomposites at low temperatures (<100°C). It briefly involves the incorporation of a second phase into a porous aerogel prepared by the polymerization of silica, alumina or resorcinol–formaldehyde monomers in solution. As the pore size of the aerogels is in the range of nanometres, it is easier to get the second phase in the nanosize, and the process is reproducible.

Another class of ceramic nanocomposites can be prepared by intercalating layered ceramic crystals with organic or inorganic species. The layered ceramic matrix may be either neutral, like graphite, or charged, like montmorillonite clays. In the case of neutral layered crystals, small ions of size appropriate to the interlayer separation can be included simply by equilibrating them in the corresponding solution. On the other hand, charged layer intercalates are prepared by exchanging the counter-ions associated with the charged matrix with structured ionic polymer molecules.

Polymer nanocomposites

Polymer nanocomposites are one of the most widely commercialized classes of nanocomposites owing to the versatility in the range of polymer matrices suitable for a variety of applications. The polymer matrix can be electrically conducting, ionically conducting or insulating, depending on the applications. Common methods of preparing these nanocomposites are solvent casting and melt mixing, although *in situ* methods after attaching the monomer on the dispersed phase are often more interesting. Solvent casting involves two steps:

1. Initial dispersion of the nanoparticles in a polymer solution
2. Evaporation of the solvent to prepare the final polymer nanocomposite

This method is commonly applicable to all the three types of polymer matrices. For example, it has been adopted for preparing carbon nanotube composites of electronically conducting, ionically conducting and thermoplastic insulating polymers [4, 5]. On the other hand, melt mixing involves elevated temperatures and high shear forces to disperse the nanomaterial, unlike solvent casting which uses sonication for preparing the dispersion. Sometimes, both the methods are used in conjunction to obtain uniformity in the composites. High–aspect ratio nanomaterial ingredients are further aligned by mechanical stretching or spin casting of the polymer.

Electrospinning has been used extensively in the preparation of CNT composites for polyethylene and polysulphones. A Nylon–CNT composite showed that by tailoring the CNT–polymer interfacial interaction the morphology and properties can be altered. Thus, the preparation and characterization of these polymer matrix composites offer unprecedented opportunity to create new hybrid functional materials.

Maya blue—a nanocomposite from the pre-classic period

Mayan art is considered to be the most sophisticated and beautiful of the ancient cultures that belongs to the pre-classic period (1500 BC to AD 250, influenced by Mesoamerican civilizations including the Olmec, Teotihuacan and the Toltecs. What puzzles researchers till date is the astonishing blue colour used in these paintings (see Plate 7, Fig. 8.4), which is resistant to dilute mineral acids, alkalis, solvents, oxidants, reductants, moderate heat and even microbes, preventing biocorrosion. This blue colour is not based on copper or ground lapis lazuli or lazurite, commonly found in European and Asian paintings. It has been recently discovered that Maya blue is actually a nanocomposite of indigo molecules and iron—Fe_2O_3 nanoparticles encapsulated in amorphous silica substrate entrapped in structured clay matrices of palygorskite mixed with small amounts of sepiolite and montmorillonite [b].

Lessons from functional group chemistry

Apart from the strategies of physical inclusion and entrapment, nanocomposites can also be prepared taking lessons from the nature of interactions of functional groups used in organic synthesis. Non-covalent interactions between functional groups of nanocomposite components greatly determine the nature of the interface, and hence the function of the resulting material. Some of the important types of interactions include hydrogen bonding, van der Waals forces, metal coordination, electrostatics, dipolar and hydrophobic interactions. For example, Fig. 8.5 shows a nanocomposite formed by hydrogen bonding between various functional groups, which suggests the possibility of designing reconfigurable nanocomposites in future.

Usually, it is difficult to predict whether a certain synthetic protocol will be suitable for a given class of nanocomposites, because conventional phase diagrams hardly hold when materials scroll down to the nanoscale. Many of them are metastable in the nano-regime and undergo phase segregation, which in turn is difficult to be quantified as it is a strong function of shape anisotropy and interfacial interactions. For example, high–aspect ratio (ratio of length to diameter) nanomaterials like wires, rods, tubes and fibres are known to percolate a given polymer matrix more efficiently than those with spherical or cubical symmetry. Nevertheless, whatever be the type of nanocomposite, common considerations in the choice of the components are,

- Phase boundary and ability to control interfacial composition
- Compliance between the major and minor phases
- Stability of the individual phases during and after preparation
- Definition stability of the nanocomposite material under processing conditions and finally
- Tunability of interfacial composition to get adhesion

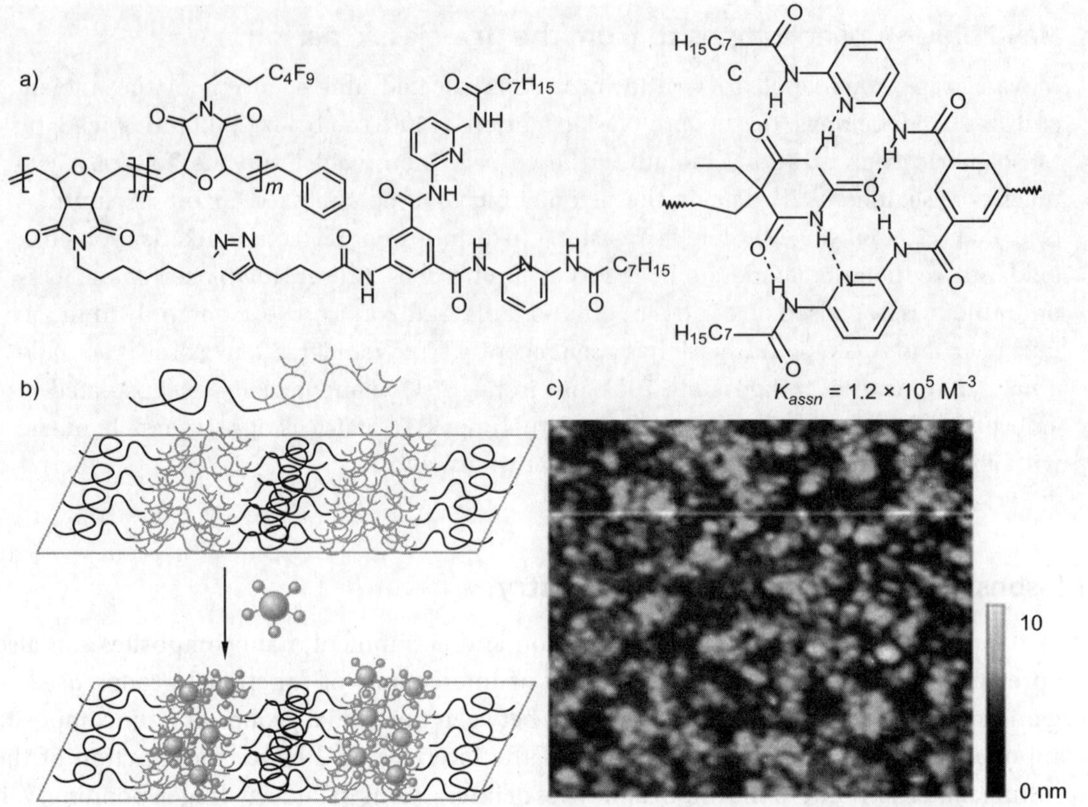

Fig. 8.5 Polymer nanocomposites based on hydrogen bonding interactions: (a) a diblock copolymer with six-point hydrogen bonding; (b) Selective deposition of nanoparticles on phase-separated block copolymer films; (c) AFM image of the polymer nanocomposite showing the organization of nanoparticles in the polymer film. [Reprinted with permission from the American Chemical Society: Binder W H, Kluger C, Josipovic M, Straif C J and Friedbacher G, Directed Nanoparticle Binding onto Microphase-Separated Block Copolymer Thin Films, *Macromolecules*, 38(23): 8092, 2005]

Bio-mimetic methods, as explained in *Chapter 4*, are an important strategy for making nanocomposites. For example, many stimuli responsive polymer nanocomposites have been prepared using valuable lessons learnt from natural nanocomposites such as spider silk, bone and mollusc shell. However, the design based on the skin of the sea cucumber is truly magnificent, as it has an uncanny ability to rapidly and reversibly alter stiffness. Artificial nanocomposites have been similarly prepared using rigid cellulose nanofibres—instead of collagen fibrils as in the sea cucumber—in a rubbery host polymer to mimic the chemo-responsive mechanic adaptability.

8.4 HOW TO MAKE NANOCOMPOSITES 'FUNCTIONAL'?

With rapid development in nanotechnology and the emergence of new form of faster and better performing devices and systems, modernization, the demand for multi-functional materials and devices is increasing exponentially. The best way to invoke multiple functions into a system is to combine two or more materials with different functions to form a composite using an appropriate chemical strategy. Interestingly, almost all the biological systems capable of performing multiple and flexible functions consist of composites of two or more materials. More specifically, nanocomposites can be tweaked to achieve multi-functionality mainly by two means:

- One approach is to introduce nanomaterials or nanodomains into intrinsically smart or functional matrices like smart electroceramics for applications such as self-healing architectures and smart windows, as discussed in *Chapter 5*. Thus it is possible to improve the performance of functional ceramics such as ferroelectric, piezoelectric, varistor and ion-conducting materials by incorporating a small amount of ceramic or metallic nanoparticles.
- The other way is to choose the components in such a way that they develop multi-functionality by synergetic interactions. For example, a composite material capable of conducting ions at one end, electrons at the other end and mixed conduction in the middle can be fabricated by forming concentration gradients of an ionically conducting (e.g., ZrO_2) and an electronically conducting (e.g., In_2O_3) oxide. This type of a functional nanocomposite is pretty useful in improving the electrode–electrolyte interface of electrochemical devices. An interesting example is provided in Fig. 8.6 (see Plate 8), where filter papers soaked with a solution of polydiacetylene–silica nanocomposite exhibit temperature-dependent colour changes 'thermochromic shift'. The preparation procedure involves the self-assembly (refer to *Chapter 3*) of diacetylene surfactants on silica particles followed by polymerization using ultraviolet radiation.

Though we have mentioned only a few examples for making nanocomposites functional, logically there can be many ways of achieving multi-functionality by exploiting synergetic interactions between a wide range of materials.

8.5 INTERFACIAL ENGINEERING—HARVESTING MAXIMUM PERFORMANCE

The performance and durability of a composite material depends on three important factors:

- Nature of the fillers (both amount and shape)
- Nature of the matrix, especially its morphology and composition
- The efficiency of interactions between the matrix and the filler materials

While the first two parameters can be controlled at will by the choice of materials, it is the third parameter that is the most important and difficult to control. In the case of nanocomposites also, it is the interface between the nano-ingredients and the macroscopic matrix that determines their overall performance. For instance, let us analyze the effect of interfacial interaction on the mechanical properties of a nanocomposite, such as carbon nanofibres incorporated in different matrices like polymer, metal and ceramic.

Though the fibres are intrinsically brittle, they can provide good reinforcement to improve the mechanical properties of the matrix depending on the nature of interaction between the fibre and the matrix. However, the bonding between the fibre and the matrix should neither be too strong nor too weak. Specifically, in the case of a brittle matrix like ceramic, excessive fibre-matrix bonding can result in cracks propagating in a direction perpendicular to the interface and reduce the mechanical strength of the composite. On the other hand, in the case of ductile matrices like polymers and metals, any crack initiated in the fibre will be terminated at the matrix, even if the fibre—matrix bonding is strong [7]. Figure 8.7 accordingly demonstrates a method of tuning the distances between nanoparticles incorporated in a polymer and a dendrimer (a class of hyper-branched surfactant molecules) medium, respectively.

The interaction between major and the minor phases can be due to simple chemical bonding, inter-diffusion, van der Waals forces or mechanical interlocking. The strength of the interaction depends on the nature of bonding existing at the interface of the nanomaterial and the matrix. For instance, chemical bonding requires the density of functional groups to be high on the surface of the nanomaterial, which can be achieved by exploiting our knowledge of functional group chemistry, discussed in the previous section; inter-diffusion requires the interface to

Carbon that cuts! The Damascus sword

The Damascus swords, once famous in the Middle East, were very sharp, strong and flexible. Examination of one of them under an electron microscope reveals that the secret behind their properties is nanotechnology [8], inadvertently used by blacksmiths centuries ago. Damascus blades were forged from steel obtained from India called Wootz, which is supposed to be brittle due to its high carbon content (1.5%). Although carbon nanotubes are very strong (their Young's modulus being 6–10 times that of steel and tensile strength about 20 times higher than that of steel) and light, they can buckle and a composite can have all the benefits of both steel and carbon nanotubes with unmatched performance. Amazingly, the incorporation of carbon nanotubes of diameter less than a nanometre has rendered interesting properties to this steel, which is otherwise useless for sword making! Tipu's sword has also been found to contain a similar type of engineered steel.

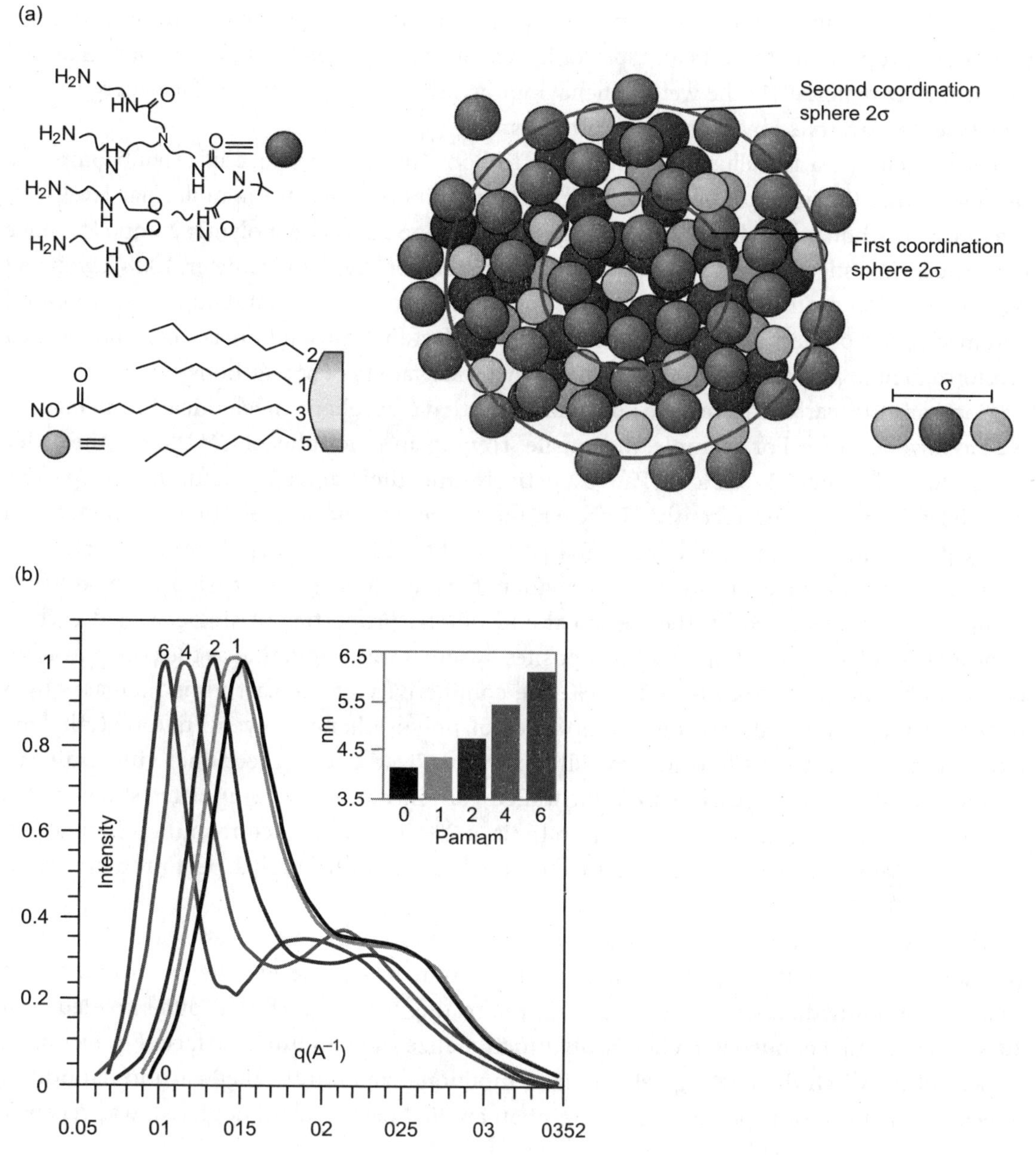

Fig. 8.7 *(see also Plate 8)* Assembly of nanoparticles using poly(amido amine) (PAMAM) dendrimers and control of inter-particle spacing using dendrimer molecules with increasing levels of branching [Reprinted with permission from the American Chemical Society: Frankamp B L, Boal A K and Rotello V M, Controlled interparticle spacing through self-assembly of Au nanoparticles and poly(amidoamine) dendrimers, 124(51): 15146, 2002]

be very clean and mechanical interlocking depends on the roughness of the surface. Another important property that affects all types of interactions is the wettability of the nanomaterial by the matrix material. As the wetting behaviour greatly depends on the surface energy, it can be efficiently controlled by chemical treatments.

Let us examine a few illustrations on how to boost the performance of a nanocomposite by engineering the interface between the major and minor phases at the molecular level with reference to carbon nanotube–polymer composites. Carbon nanotube–polymer composites have been widely investigated due to the large aspect ratio (ratio of length to diameter: 1000) favouring good orientation control, excellent electrical and thermal conductivity, and improved structural and mechanical properties, perhaps motivated by the fact that carbon fibre is a commonly used reinforcement in polymers and other matrices in a wide variety of applications.

Compared to carbon fibres, carbon nanotubes have excellent mechanical properties as well as lower density. For example, the tensile strength and modulus of CNT are of the order of 11–200 GPa and 270 GPa–1TPa, respectively, and their amazing actuation properties have been demonstrated recently. However, they have only limited elastic compliance and hence processing them in a polymeric matrix would facilitate their application as actuators over large areas. Consequently, many polymers have been extensively tried to make CNT composites, as illustrated by the electrical and optical properties of single-walled carbon nanotubes–poly(3-octylthiophene) composites, where it was found that as the concentration of nanotube increases from 0 to 20 wt%, the conductivity of the cast films increases by 5 orders of magnitude. Electrospun composites of polyurethane, polyaniline/poly(ethylene oxide) and polyvinylidene fluoride have all shown improved electrical conductivity. Similarly, rheological study of polycarbonate multiwalled carbon nanotube composites showed that the viscosity increases above a percolation limit of 2% along with a concomitant increase in the storage modulus, which was explained on the basis of a very high aspect ratio of carbon nanotubes.

The interface of these composites is normally tailored in two broad ways. One is to provide good mechanical alignment and orientation by choosing long macromolecules to wrap the individual nanotubes. Another interesting way is to exploit our knowledge of functional group chemistry to chemically functionalize the nanotube surface. For example, a method to switch the wetting behaviour of functionalized multiwalled carbon nanotubes woven in the form of paper, as a function of an applied electric field depicted, was recently demonstrated (Fig. 8.8) [9].

While one could tune the wettability of hydrophobic carbon nanotubes as a function of applied electric field, in another instance, hydrophilically functionalized carbon nanotubes were found to boost the performance of proton exchange membranes used in fuel cells. More specifically, composites of carbon nanotubes functionalized with sulphonic acid groups with Nafion-H^+, a proton conducting polymer, were found to increase the proton conductivity of the polymer electrolyte as well as the overall

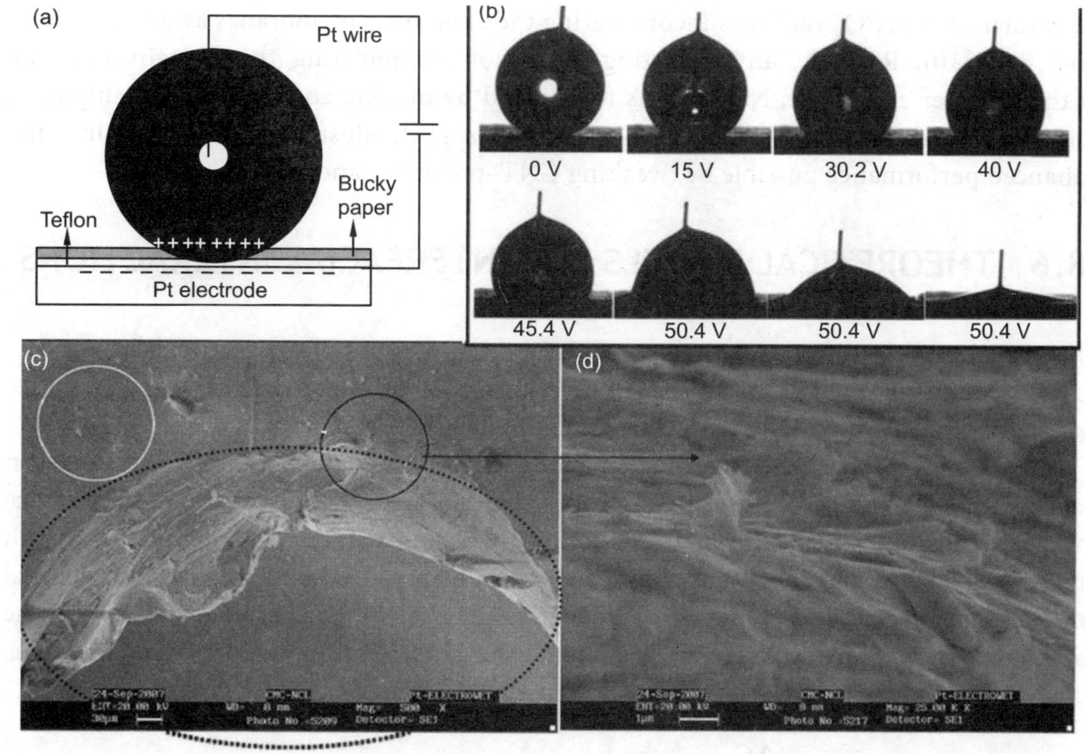

Fig. 8.8 (a) Schematic of electrowetting experiments in which a drop of water is placed on a hydrophobic paper made of multiwalled carbon nanotubes functionalized using ozonolysis subjected to an external electric field; (b) Changing the wettability of the nanotube paper as a function of applied potential; (c) and (d) Scanning electron micrographs of the carbon nanotube paper at different magnifications. [Reprinted with permission from the American Chemical Society: Kakade B, Mehta R, Durge A and Pillai V K, Electric field induced switching of superhydrophobic to superhydrophilic surfaces in multiwalled carbon nanotube papers, *Nano Lett.*, 8: 2693, 2008]

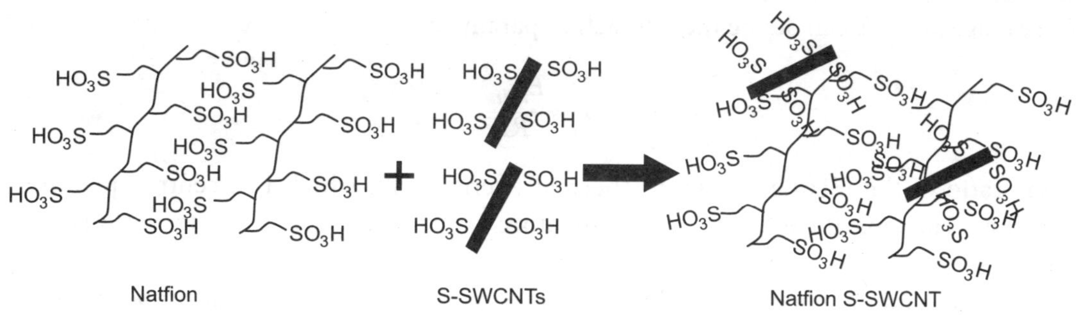

Fig. 8.9 Schematic representation of nanocomposite formation using chemically functionalized carbon nanotubes (-SWCNT) with Nafions to form a nanocomposite membrane by mixing solutions of the components in *N, N*-dimethylacetamide (DMAc)

performance of H_2/O_2 fuel cells incorporating the composite membranes as the electrolyte (Fig. 8.9) [10]. Recently, an interesting means of manipulating the domain structure of the polymer electrolyte, Nafion, was formulated by making composites with sulphonic acid functionalized multiwalled carbon nanotubes [11], illustrating the flexibility and enhanced performance possible by tweaking CNT–polymer nanocomposites.

8.6 THEORETICAL MODELS FOR INTERFACIAL INTERACTIONS

Theoretical models are important for predicting the properties of existing materials and to custom-design new materials with desired functions. They can be broadly classified into three types: thermodynamic, micromechanical and molecular modelling.

First, let us discuss the thermodynamic background for interfacial interactions in nanocomposites. The properties of composites critically depend on several parameters like miscibility, mixing, compatibility and adhesion. The thermodynamics of mixing a polymer with an inorganic nanomaterial like carbon nanotubes can be predicted directly from the chemical structures and a force field of the two components. The simplest and best known theory of the thermodynamics of mixing and phase separation in binary systems is the Flory–Huggins model. The general expression for calculating the free energy of mixing of a binary system is:

$$\frac{\Delta G}{RT} = \frac{\phi_b}{n_b} \ ln\, \phi_b + \frac{\phi_s}{n_s} \ ln\, \varphi_s + \chi\, \phi_b \phi_s$$

where ΔG is the free energy of mixing (per mole), ϕ_i is the volume fraction of component *i*, n_i is the degree of polymerization of component *i*, χ is the interaction parameter, *T* is the absolute temperature, and *R* is the gas constant. The first two terms are due to combinatorial entropy, which is always negative, favouring a mixed state over the pure components, while the last term represents the free energy of interaction. If the interaction parameter, χ, is positive, this term disfavours a mixed state. The balance between the two contributions gives rise to various phase diagrams. We can define the interaction parameter,

$$\chi = \frac{E_{min}}{RT}$$

as the ratio of the mixing energy to thermal energy (*RT*), which is a central quantity in the Flory–Huggins theory, and its temperature dependence gives rise to various phase diagrams.

Micromechanical modelling deals with understanding the mechanical properties of the composite like elastic modulus, flexural strength, resonant frequencies and vibration modes and can be done numerically as well as analytically. Numerical simulations involve describing a system with a set of mathematical equations and solving them using mathematical formulae.

When the system becomes more complicated, the mathematical expressions become complex and numerical methods like finite element and finite difference are used. On the other hand, if we know the behaviour of the system in a given set of conditions, we can predict the solution analytically and this method is called *analytical simulation*. However, for simple systems, numerical methods provide a more accurate estimate of bulk properties compared to the analytical simulations.

While the micromechanical models assume a continuum, molecular modelling considers elements in the nanometre scale without any continuum-based assumptions and is hence more realistic in predicting the properties. However, only small volumes of atoms can be considered while analyzing a material which otherwise will become cumbersome and time consuming. Molecular modelling can be further classified as *ab initio* and molecular dynamics. Ab initio simulations are performed by making an approximation to the solution of the Schrodinger equation. The ab initio simulations are usually performed by three procedures, namely, single point calculations, geometry optimizations and frequency calculations.

In *single point calculations*, the energy and wave function are calculated for a fixed geometry, whereas in *geometry optimizations*, the energy is calculated for a number of possible geometries and the most stable geometry is arrived at by minimizing the energy values. Geometry optimizations are normally carried out in an iterative manner, just like a conditional loop in a computer program, until the lowest energy configuration is reached. This can in turn be done in a number of ways which will not be discussed here. Similarly, *frequency calculations* deal with predicting the frequencies and intensities of infrared and Raman excitations of a composite material.

Supplementary to the *ab initio* calculations, which can yield absolute energy values and geometries, *molecular dynamics* (commonly denoted as MD simulations) can predict the temporal evolution or the time-dependence of interatomic distances by integrating the equations of motions of a set of atoms. Finally, the arithmetic average of the instantaneous values gives the physical quantity which is correlated with the macroscopic property of the composite using statistical mechanics. Though we have provided only a very short note about the various theoretical treatments for a beginner, there have been many more advances in this area, such as *multiscale modelling approaches*.

8.7 APPLICATIONS OF NANOCOMPOSITES

Nanocomposites span the entire applications ranging from biomedical and soft photovoltaic functional paints to high-strength aerospace coatings, due to an amazing combination of synergetic properties arising from the interaction between both the phases. Although most nanocomposites are designed for enhanced durability, especially keeping their high specific strength and modulus in mind, they are critical for a variety of structural applications in the aerospace, automotive and building industries. Non-degradable polymeric resins are used as the matrix to make consumer products, facilitating improved performance coupled, with reduced weight and cost [12]. A few typical examples are illustrated here.

8.7.1 Electronic and optoelectronic devices

Nanometre-size particles with hybrid molecular and bulk behaviour define a new class of materials with several interesting optical and electronic applications. For example, light emitting diodes based on new materials such as porous silicon and other quantum dots embedded in soft processable polymers have been developed recently. By taking advantage of developments in the preparation and characterization of direct-gap semiconductor nanocrystals and electroluminescent polymers, hybrid inorganic–organic electroluminescent devices have been constructed. Light emission arises from the recombination of holes injected into a layer of p-type semiconducting poly *p*-phenylene vinylene (PPV) with electrons injected from *n*-type cadmium selenide nanocrystals. Using the quantum size effect, the colour of the emission can be tuned from red to yellow by changing the size of the nanocrystal.

8.7.2 Electrochemical energy storage

Recently, Yoneyama et al. [13] successfully attached oxide particles with very low isoelectric points, such as WO_3, SiO_2 and Ta_2O_5 into polypyrrole film by electrochemical oxidation of pyrrole in the presence of oxide suspensions at a pH higher than the isoelectric point of the oxide. These composites have been found to be useful as electrode materials for batteries and also for electrochromic applications. Oxide particles which do not belong to this class, such as TiO_2, can also be incorporated into polypyrrole if a small amount of electrolyte anions with specific adsorption to the oxide, for example, SO_4^{2-}, are added to the deposition baths containing oxide suspensions. As polypyrrole is one of the most popular conducting polymers, its technological application as cathode material for rechargeable lithium batteries has been widely studied.

The same research group also incorporated TiO_2 particles inside polyaniline films and demonstrated photo-induced electrochromism. Surprisingly, these modified polyaniline films can be used as a letter pad for writing with laser beams to aid image storage [13]. However, even with the use of highly porous polypyrrole, the volumetric energy density is not very high, because the amount of electrolyte anions involved in the redox reaction is limited. This limitation can be improved by incorporating electrochemically active anion-adsorbed MnO_2 as a dopant. Although manganese dioxide is one of the promising materials for use as cathode material for Li-batteries, it has extremely low conductivity, and it is essential to have a conducting network for complete utilization of the active material and also for accomplishing high power density. Usually, some conducting form of carbon, such as acetylene black or graphite powder (more recently, carbon nanotubes, carbon nanofibres or graphene), is mixed with MnO_2 particles. If polypyrrole films containing MnO_2 particles could be used as cathode materials, it could form PPy–MnO_2.

8.7.3 Application in electro-catalysis

Another important application of these hybrid nanostructured composite materials is in electrocatalysis. For example, many fuel cell reactions like the electro-oxidation of methanol in principle, require an efficient reversible redox process where the catalysts need sustained stability. Since some of the important fuel cells operate in an acid medium, which requires both the catalyst and support to be highly stable, the building of an efficient nanocomposite electrode is very important. This principle has been followed by several researchers, describing the preparation of nanocomposites in which nanoparticles of Pt, Pd, Cu, etc., are combined with polypyrrole, polyaniline, polythiophene etc., to form efficient electrocatalytic electrodes.

8.7.4 Magnetic applications

Several nanostructured materials show interesting size-dependent magnetic properties like superparamagnetism and quantum tunnelling of magnetization. Hence, some of these unique nanostructured magnetic materials have been used to form composites with promising applications in diverse areas. A versatile process for the preparation of maghaemite/polyaniline (γ-Fe_2O_3/PAni) nanocomposite was first reported and casting of the homogeneous solutions gives free-standing nanocomposite films with good electrical conductivity (σ = 82–237 Scm^{-1}), much higher than that of the iron oxide/conducting polymer system prepared by mixing. The nanocomposite films were superparamagnetic and did not show hysteresis at 300 K.

8.8 CONCLUSIONS

Availability of functional nanocomposites, irrespective of their use in organic electronics or for making Formula One racing car tyres, has changed our life enormously in recent times. The ultimate impact of nanocomposites will surely cover a huge range of engineering disciplines, including civil, mechanical and biomedical applications, offering new solutions to key problems such as lightweight and durable structures, more efficient management of energy, environment and recyclability issues. Many nanocomposites prepared by blending selected polymers such as Nylon or vinylidene fluoride, with a very small amount of nanostructured materials like carbon nanotubes, graphene, clay particles and silver nanowires, show enhanced thermal stability along with a more than 100% increase in bulk modulus above the glass transition temperature. For example, the addition of a small amount of nanomaterials, much less than the percolation threshold, dramatically alters the structural, mechanical and electronic properties by modifying the polymer interface.

Continued efforts to design and build a range of nanocomposites in which both the soft medium as well as the hard or hybrid dispersed phase would actively interact and communicate seamlessly in response to external stimuli, or even to perform functions, are expected to generate more valuable and magical nanocomposites with enormous application potential. On a higher complexity level, many of these emerging nanocomposites with precise interfacial control and tunable functional properties could revolutionize applications in medical diagnostics, prosthetics, communication, structural engineering, and others.

Further Reading

[1] Dagani R, Putting the nano into composites, *C & EN*, June 7, 1999.

[2] Schulz M J, Kelkar A D and Sundaresan M J, (Eds), *Nanoengineering of structural, functional and smart materials*, CRC Press, Taylor & Francis Group, FL, USA, 2006

[3] Cai D and Song M, Recent Advance in Functionalized Graphene/Polymer Nanocomposites, *J. Mater. Chem.*, 20: 7906, 2010.

[4] Gao J, Zhao B, Itkis M E, Bekyarova E, Hu H and Kranak, Chemical engineering of the single-walled carbon nanotube-nylon 6 interface, *J. Am. Chem. Soc.*, 128: 7492, 2006.

[5] Biercuk M J, Llaguno M C, Radosavljevic M, Hyun J K, Johnson A T Jr and Fischer J E, Carbon nanotube composites for thermal management, *Appl. Phys. Lett.*, 80: 2767, 2002.

[6] José-Yacamán M, Rendón L, Arenas J and Puche MCS. Maya blue paint: An ancient nanostructured material, *Science*, 273: 223, 1996.

[7] Chung D D L, *Composite Materials: Science and applications: Functional Materials for Modern Technologies*, Springer-Verlag London Ltd, UK, 2003.

[8] Sreenivasan C, Do Damascus swords reveal India's mastery of nanotechnology? *Current Science*, 92: 279, 2007.

[9] Kakade B, Mehta R, Durge A, Kulkarni S and Pillai V K, Electric field induced superhydrophobic to superhydrophilic switching in multiwalled carbon nanotube papers, *Nano Lett.*, 8: 2693, 2008.

[10] Kannan R, Kakade B A and Pillai V K, Polymer electrolyte fuel cells using Nafion-based composite membranes with functionalized carbon nanotubes, *Angew. Chem. Int. Ed.*, 47: 2653, 2008.

[11] Kannan R, Parthasarathy M, Maraveedu S U, Kurungot S and Pillai V K, Domain size manipulation of perfluorinated polymer electrolytes by sulfonic-acid functionalized MWCNTs to enhance fuel cell performance, *Langmuir*, 25: 8299, 2009.

[12] Gordon J E, *The New Science of Strong Materials Why You Don't Fall Through the Floor*, Princeton University Press, 2006.

[13] Yoneyama H, Writing with light on polyaniline films, *Adv. Mater.*, 5: 394–96, 1993.

EXERCISES

1. How do naturally occurring composites such as wood and bone help in the design of nanocomposites?
2. If carbon nanotubes are dispersed in a polymer matrix to form a nanocomposite, what are the main advantages?
3. Mention some of the special features of the polymer–graphene nanocomposite? What are its main advantages for applications in nanoelectronics?
4. Discuss various strategies available for making metal–ceramic nanocomposites.
5. Using multi-walled carbon nanotubes–polycarbonate nanocomposite as an example, illustrate how unusual viscosity and modulus variations originate in this class of nanocomposites.
6. Explain the common features in preparing nanocomposites using both polymeric and ceramic matrices with tunable properties.
7. Why are functionalized carbon nanotubes better for preparing polymer–carbon nanotube nanocomposites for specific applications?
8. Explain the lessons material scientists can learn by analyzing the sea cucumber and shark skin for designing polymer–clay nanocomposites.
9. If you are to make composites of single-walled and multiwalled carbon nanotubes with polystyrene, how would you theoretically estimate the compatibility of the nanotubes with the polymer matrix using the Flory–Huggins theory?

9

Going Beyond Functional Materials—Future Directions

This, the last chapter of the book, provides some insight into the overall challenges and major societal considerations of functional materials, in the light of the United Nations Millennium Development Goals and individual road maps of developing countries. The major societal impact of developing next generation materials is explained, focussing on their promise for solving global challenges with respect to resource limitations, sustainable energy generation from renewables and storage, environmental impact and recyclability. Several realistic predictions related to next generation materials are attempted with the help of extrapolations from recent advances in the respective research areas.

LEARNING OBJECTIVES

- To appreciate the importance of the United Nations Millennium Development Goals
- To list the impact of developing functional materials on society and human beings
- To have a broad idea of the environmental problems and recyclability issues in making more and more functional materials
- To realize the challenges in developing next generation of functional materials and devise strategies in accomplishing this
- To indicate the key limitations of functional materials
- To speculate on the nature and type of materials expected in the next few decades, extrapolated from the recent advances in functional materials across the world

9.1 INTRODUCTION

The discussions thus far have, undoubtedly established the importance and promise that functional materials hold for our future demands of energy, health, communications and security. Application of nanotechnology has definitely made materials stronger, lighter, stiffer and smarter, as illustrated by innumerable examples discussed in earlier chapters. Innovation of new materials with improved attributes like intelligence and multiple functionalities assures us of wealth creation as well as commercial success [1–2]. For instance, composite materials are modern examples of materials in which multi-functionality can be easily realized. This is possible because of the synergy in properties between the materials combined to form the composite. One of the outstanding examples for multi-functionality is provided by the type of materials used for aircrafts, in which a given material is tailored to perform differently in different parts (materials with functional gradients), as discussed in *Chapter 8*. A particularly revealing illustration is the multi-functional composite currently used in rocket nozzles with a unique combination of tungsten, silver, carbon, ceramic and steel, each satisfying several conflicting requirements of critical dimensional, mechanical, corrosion and thermal tolerance, and this could be contrasted with silk fibres, often synthesized by bioinspired synthetic strategies, combining the natural strength and elasticity of biopolymers with magnetic, electrical, thermal or elastic properties of inorganic nanowires.

Creating these specialized materials requires networking of different kinds of expertise from scientists and engineers, including the magical synthetic skills of chemists, atom-by-atom precise characterization ability of physicists, and outstanding design sense and application acumen of various engineers. Directed collaborative efforts like joint graduate studies between various science and engineering departments, more incentives for joint interdisciplinary projects (example, between computer science and biology units) and ear-marked projects for networking teams are practiced in many cutting edge R&D organizations to foster these innovations [3–4]. The previous chapters have attempted to provide an overall understanding of the multi-disciplinary field of functional materials. The operational aspects of different types of functional materials—self-assembly, bioinspired synthesis smartness, energy conversion, electronic property and composite—have been expounded using fundamental principles of chemistry, physics, biology and materials engineering. With the help of illustrations from nature and day-to-day life, the commercial potential and scope of different types of functional materials has been emphasized. The objective of this chapter is to summarize our views and to analyze the present status of the field of functional materials as a whole, which is a difficult task.

9.2 LIMITATIONS OF FUNCTIONAL MATERIALS

Many common limitations of functional materials result from their esoteric capabilities being imparted by a sequence of complex operations involving accurate composition tuning by appropriate materials chemistry, atom-by-atom control of the surface and different levels of functionalization, etc. Some of the major limitations are listed below:

- ***Cost*** Many functional materials are very expensive, either due to the presence of noble metal clusters like Au, Pt and Rh in nanostructured form or because of the involvement of highly sophisticated preparation and post-preparation processes, often using unique techniques of atom manipulation.
- ***Durability*** Many molecules and polymers used in nanoelectronics and energy technology have inadequate durability, causing a huge premium on their repeatable use.
- ***Weight and size*** Many smart systems such as smart shoes and e-cloths are not at a stage suitable for individual use and more development is needed to make them lighter and inexpensive for practical ability. Similarly, EV batteries and fuel cells are too bulky for the designed applications.
- ***Biocompatibility*** Many nanocomposites and hybrid materials developed for implantable devices require surface functionalization to make them ready for in vivo applications.
- ***Poor response time*** Some materials—for example, electro rneological fluids and smart polymeric gels—show slow response time and the dynamic timescale requires several orders of magnitude improvements for tangible applications.
- ***Manufacturability*** Many multi-functional materials have a major problem while scaling from lab to industry and enormous repeatability and manufacturing issues need to be resolved for commercial viability.
- ***Limited selectivity*** For practical applications, the selectivity available is limited (e.g. biosensors) and the performance requires improvement.

However, many of these limitations critically depend on the composition and processing variables, and the advent of nanotechnology through atom-by-atom design has offered promising solutions involving unique shape- and size-dependant properties, core–shell designs, organo–inorganic hybrids and dimensionality controlled nanocomposites [3–4]. None of this could have been possible without a strong background in chemistry.

9.3 MAJOR CHALLENGES IN DEVELOPING NEXT GENERATION MATERIALS

The limitations listed above are very general and there are several specific challenges in realizing the successful commercialization of functional materials. Although an exhaustive list is outside the scope of this book, some of the major challenges for realising different types of recyclable functional materials and systems are listed below [4]:

Self-assembled materials

- increased stability at high temperatures, pressures and aggressive environments

Bioinspired materials

- increased cycle life, stability, biocompatibility and response time

Smart materials

- reduced response time
- increased reproducibility and cycle life with improved levels of intelligence

Materials for energy applications

- reduced cost of solar energy and noble metal–free fuel cells
- increased impurity tolerance, fuel flexibility
- to develop current collectors with improved stability, micro-fuel cells, micro-batteries and ultra-capacitors on a chip with robust features
- increased micro-engineering of the gas/electrode/electrolyte interface

Polymer electronics

- to enable lithography
- to develop more rugged passive substrate materials, efficient doping procedures, improve stability under electric field
- no electro-migration and durability issues

Multiferroics

- to synthesize stable semiconductor heterostructures with ferromagnetic properties at room temperature
- to increase tenability and sensitivity cross-communication issues in spintronic devices
- to develop energy efficient fabrication processes and fundamental understanding of existing materials

Functional nanocomposites and e-textiles

- to overcome phase-segregation problems, improve alignment of fillers in the matrix
- to understand the different modes of failure of the composite material and rectify the designs

Magnetic materials for data storage

- to develop materials capable of retaining their magnetic properties close to the Curie point
- to improve oxidative stability, especially at high temperatures
- to develop magnetic nanocomposites of hard and soft materials

Terahertz technology

- improved terahertz sources and detectors, develop imaging techniques

Hopefully, nanotechnology has solutions for many of these issues and control of material processes at the level of electrons, molecules and atoms using perfect atom- and energy-efficient synthesis. Revolutionary new forms of matter with tailored properties are thus expected to solve at least some of the above concerns. However, since many remarkable properties of matter emerge from complex correlations of the atomic or electronic constituents, theory and computational modelling can help enormously to control these properties, especially if we want to master energy and information on the nanoscale to create new technologies with capabilities rivalling those of living things. Equally important would be our ability to characterize and control metastable phases generated under extreme experimental conditions to see its behaviour, as matter often prepared under non-equilibrium conditions show unusual behaviour.

9.4 SOCIAL IMPACT OF FUNCTIONAL MATERIALS

The demands for high-throughput materials for more efficient and cleaner technologies has become more acute with increasing population and anthropogenic environmental threats. Many of these problems can be solved by using functional materials. However, there are many other social and philosophical issues.

An important aspect of any newly-developed material is its environmental impact, especially since plastics pose serious problems to all of us. Most of us are aware of the great Pacific garbage patch, a huge pile of garbage at the bottom of the Pacific ocean. Of the 30 million tones of plastic manufactured each year, about 10% eventually reach the oceans and concerns about their fate are increasingly felt by all. Recyclability and biodegradability are important and we need to ensure that by making more functional materials, we are not compounding the already existing environmental problems.

There are also profound social issues associated with the human tendancy to manipulate nature for short-term benefits. For example, the ethical issues of designing a hybrid material, somewhere between biological and synthetic, are serious problems, due to the rapid strides taken in genetic development and stem cell development. Since the extraordinary pace of development in genome sequencing is a double-edged weapon, with risky long-term environmental impact, we need to adopt a cautionary approach for developing materials for tomorrow's needs.

9.5 FUNCTIONAL MATERIALS AND THE UN MILLENNIUM DEVELOPMENT GOALS

Figure 9.1 shows a projection of world population by the year 2050. For the population projections, the United Nations has put forth a list of Millennium Development Goals to be reached by 2015 in order to solve key issues, as given below:

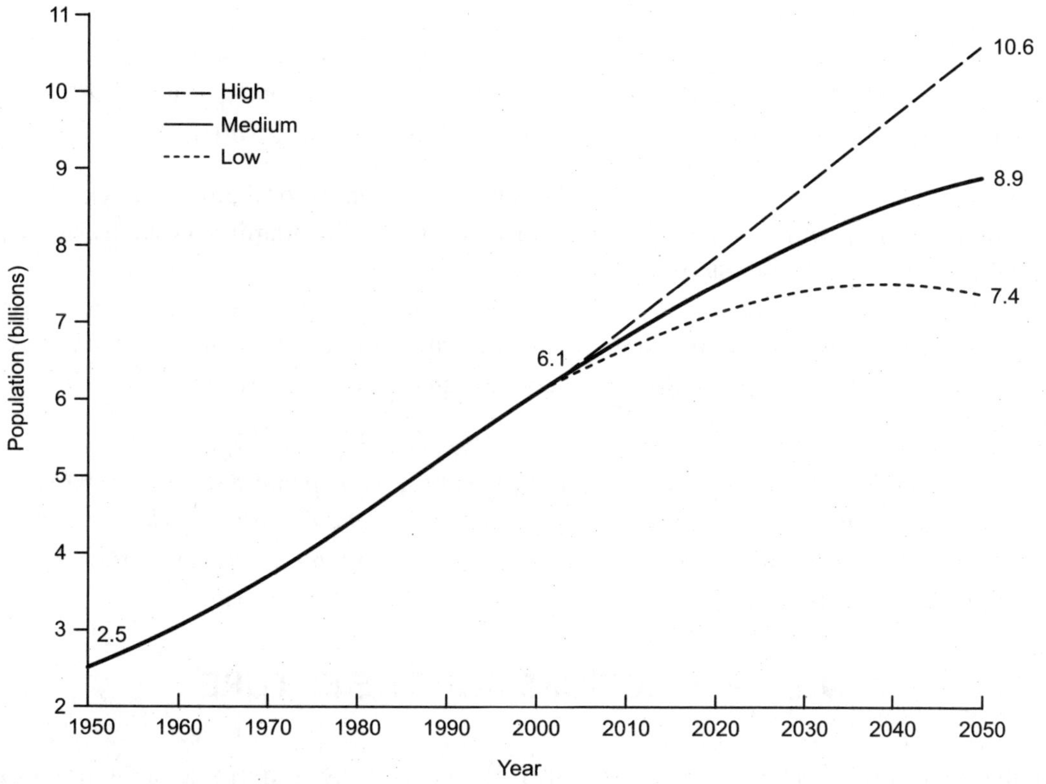

Fig. 9.1 World population projection up to 2050 as estimated by the United Nations Department of Economic and Social Affairs/Population Division [Reproduced from http://www.un.org/esa/population/publications/longrange2/WorldPop230final.pdf]

- Eradicate extreme poverty and hunger
- Achieve universal primary education
- Promote gender equality and empower women
- Reduce child mortality
- Improve maternal health
- Combat HIV/AIDS, malaria and other diseases
- Ensure environmental sustainability
- Develop a global partnership for development

Functional materials can help in achieving several of the above challenges. Development of novel, cost-effective functional materials can have a tremendous effects, especially on the targets identified under 'Ensure environmental sustainability'—to reduce global population to half by 2015, provide access to safe drinking water, basic sanitation or sequester carbon dioxide. As per the UN report,

"Since 1990, 1.6 billion people have gained access to safe water. At this rate, the world is expected to meet the drinking water target, which would require that 89 percent of the population of developing regions use improved sources of drinking water by 2015. Still, nearly one billion people today lack safe sources of drinking water."

Distribution of pure water in rural areas can be ensured by designing a stack of novel functional materials which can effectively remove heavy metal contaminants, bacteria, fungus and other microorganisms, colour and odour.

Functional materials can also be of tremendous importance in achieving other targets such as ensuring environmental sustainability, including immediate action to contain rising greenhouse gas emissions, limiting ozone-depleting substances to mitigate climate change, as per the report:

"Severing the link between energy use and greenhouse gas emissions will require more efficient technologies for the supply and use of energy and a transition to cleaner and renewable energy sources. In response to the growing demand for energy worldwide, large investments in energy projects are expected over the coming years"

9.6 PREDICTIONS FOR THE FUTURE

Predicting future developments in any S&T theme is risky and the area of functional materials is not an exception. An unprecedented variety of functional materials is expected to radically reshape human lifestyle, much beyond what was predicted by Alvin Tofler in his book, *Future Shock* in 1970. However, even realistic predictions are clouded by a plethora of science fiction movies, books and popular articles, confusing even the intelligent reader. There are, of course, optimistic predictions like environment-friendly transportation, synthetic inexpensive petrol (perhaps green petrol!), energy sticks (just like the memory sticks we use, but with an important difference—it would be in mega/giga watts instead of MB/GB) and hydrogen storage sticks for all, but at cost. Similarly, bolder predictions of mini- or micro-suns based on taming nuclear fusion, floating windmills and solar factories in air to rapidly change the energy generation and storage, are possible. Other possibilities include artificial nervous system for robots, DNA computing, solar cloths, designer babies, emotional control through biochips, synthetic celebrities, artificial organs (like liver, kidneys, heart and even brain), insect-like robots, thought recognition, and cheaper voice-driven appliances. Some will focus on internet wars between cyber groups, economic catastrophes, self-destructing nanobots ('grey goos' as envisaged by Micheal Crichton in his book, *Prey*, in 2006), reservation of roads, space colonization, etc.

Many of these predictions like solar cloths and voice-driven furniture are available (in conceptual form) even now, although they will become inexpensive and usable in the short term (5–10 years), while others like web-based transportation, colony in Mars or teleportation might require a longer time period (of about 20–50 years) to come into regular use. Similarly, many of the miracle cures and drugs promised by human genome projects have not been realized, although there is great hope for new functional materials arising from the confluence of nano, bio and information technologies. Both proponents and opponents of all these predictions are, however, unanimous in their opinion that functional materials are going to be central in realizing rapid advancement.

9.7 EPILOGUE

The discussions carried out throughout this book have established the importance and promise that functional materials hold for our future. Application of nanotechnology has definitely made materials stronger, lighter, stiffer and smarter. Innovation of new materials with improved attributes and multiple functionalities assures us of wealth creation as well as commercial success. As new forms of functional materials evolve, demonstrating our present capability of precise manipulation of atoms and molecules, structure, properties and functions of materials will undergo dramatic variations. These types of materials will undoubtedly make our lives simpler, more efficient and comfortable, at least for a small segment of the population. We hope the ideas explained here will urge students to embark on a fascinating journey to explore the world of functional materials, experiencing the awe and inspiration caused by these new materials, and acquire a strong understanding of the fundamental aspects of materials chemistry.

The demand for functional materials is exponentially increasing with every day and is expected to continue, at least for the next few decades [4]. Future milestones in the development of functional materials can be broadly listed as theoretical/mathematical modelling, design-for-manufacture protocols with structural control at the atomic, molecular and mesoscopic levels, and assembly and integration of functions. Simultaneously, improved characterization techniques are required to understand newly emerging functional materials. On the other hand, implementation of new materials in modern instrumentation requires the parallel development of supporting technologies, such as computational coding, preparation of ultrapure materials, measurement of non-equilibrium states, in *situ* probes to monitor fatigue under operating conditions. Realistic economic assessment and planning is needed for the successful commercialization of technologies arising from an overwhelming array of functional materials recently developed.

Further Reading

[1] Mel Schwartz (Ed.), *Smart Materials*, CRC Press, 2006.

[2] Schodek D L and Addington M, *Smart Materials and Technologiesin Architecture*, Architectural *Press, 2004.*

[3] Chianelli R R, Materials Science 2100, MRS Bulletin, September 2000.
[4] *Greatest Engineering Achievements of the Twentieth Century,* National Academy of Engineering, Washington, DC; available at http://www.greatachievements.org.

Exercises

1. Discuss how future developments in functional materials coupled with advances in theory and modelling help to create computer systems that can simulate and emulate the brain's abilities for sensation, perception, action, interaction and cognition, while rivalling its low power consumption and compact size?
2. Mention some of the major limitations of functional materials? How can we overcome them in the long run?
3. Visit a popular futurology website (e.g., http://www.wfs.org/) and speculate on 10 multi-functional materials that will reshape our lifestyle.
4. List the major global challenges faced by human beings and explain how the availability of new materials can solve them to a large extent.
5. According to some groups, the human genome project has not generated miracle materials as cures or drugs for many of our medical problems as promised. Discuss the pros and cons of this with respect to unsolved medical problems.
6. The convergence of nanotechnology, biotechnology and information technology is expected to revolutionize life. Do you agree? Discuss the moral and ethical implications of developing materials with human-like intelligence.

Index